Penny Woolcock started writing a memoir about growing up in the British Community in Argentina, one few people have heard of. She anticipated describing a stifling childhood where girls were trained for marriage and gossiping at tea parties, but discovered that behind this genteel façade lay a dark story of genocide and amnesia.

Woolcock's great-grandparents emigrated from the United Kingdom and settled in Argentina in the middle of the 19th century, along with seven million other Europeans. She spoke English at home, attended British schools where she learned all about the Tudors and the Stuarts, shopped at the only Harrods outside Knightsbridge, played hockey, and remained oblivious to the outside world.

She imagined that the genocide of Indigenous peoples had been carried out hundreds of years earlier, so it was a shock to discover that the so-called Conquest of the Desert–the desert being the fertile Pampas and Patagonia–had taken place fifteen years after her great-grandparents arrived. The genocide was largely funded by British investors. Anglican missionaries in Tierra del Fuego spread deadly diseases with their Christianity, and Scottish and English "Indian hunters" were paid a pound a head to kill Selknam and Yamana people when they defended their lands. The small but influential British community established the banking system, the railways, the meat packing plants, and the tanneries, and British Enlightenment thinkers were crucial in shaping the explicitly white supremacist Argentine constitution.

Woolcock weaves childhood memories and a tumultuous adolescence, falling into radical theatre and in love with the most unsuitable man she could find, with the legacy of violence that followed the initial genocide, six coups including the murderous Junta of the 1970's and early 80's, right up to the current madness of President Milei whose key advisor is his dead mastiff, Conan.

The Man Who Gave Me A Biscuit

The Man Who Gave Me A Biscuit

Love and Death in Argentina

Penny Woolcock

O/R

OR Books

New York • London

Published by OR Books, New York and London

Visit our website at www.orbooks.com

All rights information: rights@orbooks.com

First printing 2025

The manufacturer's authorised representative in the EU for product safety is Authorised Rep Compliance Ltd, 71 Lower Baggot Street, Dublin D02 P593 Ireland (www.arccompliance.com)

Typeset by Lapiz Digital. Printed by BookMobile, USA, and CPI, UK.

paperback ISBN 978-1-68219-667-0 • ebook ISBN 978-1-68219-668-7

To all those we displaced.
And those who are still fighting for justice.

Our ignorance is not innocent: we choose not to know.
–Doris Salcedo

And then one fine day the bourgeoisie is awakened by a terrific boomerang effect: the gestapos are busy, the prisons fill up, the torturers standing around the racks invent, refine, discuss . . .
–Aimé Césaire

The coalition emerges out of your recognition that it's fucked up for you, in the same way that we've already recognized that it's fucked up for us. I don't need your help. I just need you to recognize that this shit is killing you too, however much more softly, you stupid motherfucker, you know?
–Fred Moten

Foreword

This is a story about a nation of settlers.

A settler travels to other places in order to stay there. A settler doesn't care whether anybody else is already living there. A settler doesn't want to share. A settler wants all the land. The people who live there are in the way. The settler wants them out.

I am a settler from a family of settlers. The world I grew up in was so bland, it ought to have been a clue that something monstrous was festering in between the cracks. We lived in a bright Ladybird book world sustained by a death cult.

***

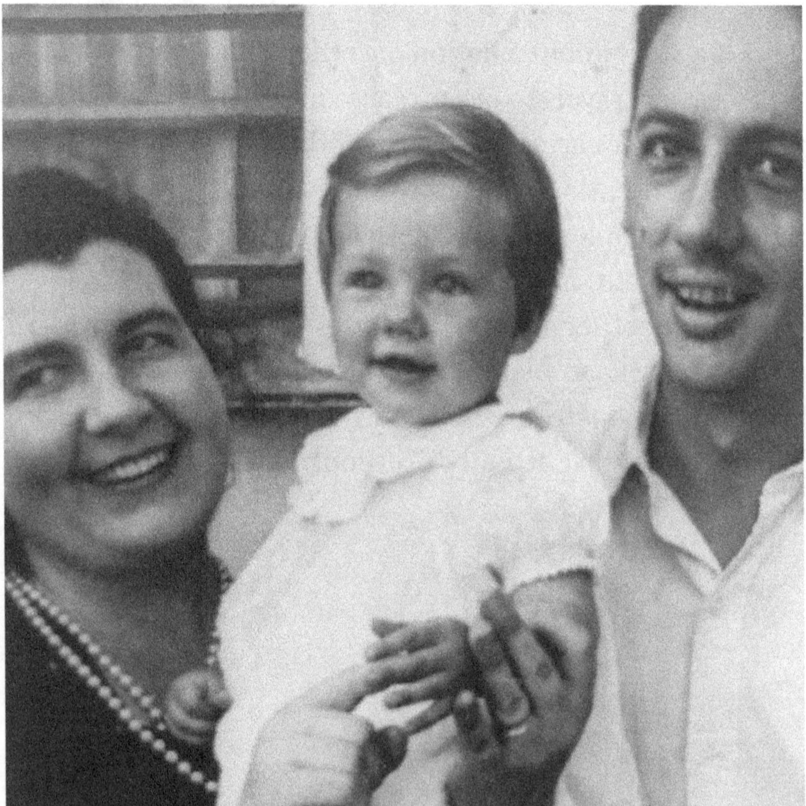

On August 13 1979, I flew from Oxford, England, to visit my parents in Buenos Aires with my ten-year-old son, Dylan.

Mum had made Dylan's favourite milanesas for supper. She tenderised thin strips of lean beef with a small wooden mallet, dipped the strips in beaten egg, coated them in breadcrumbs she bought from the bakery in a little plastic bag and fried them crisp. Dylan and I ate five each with sweet Savora mustard and slices of fresh lemon, mashed potatoes, and salad while I argued with Mum and Dad. In England I had heard about the torture and murders taking place at the ESMA, *Escuela de Mechánica de la Armada*, the naval school on Calle Libertador, where prisoners were taken through the main entrance, had hoods placed over their heads, and marched down to the basement and along a corridor called La Avenida de Felicidad, the Avenue of Happiness. They were stripped naked, tied to a bed, and tortured with electric cattle prods; most of the female prisoners were raped, and almost all of the prisoners vanished. They disappeared.

'That's all lies.' Dad cleared his throat, the way he always did when he was nervous. 'Jimmy Carter and his bloody human rights organisations make these things up.'

Mum agreed. 'The Americans are always trying to make us look bad.'

'No!' I started losing my temper. 'They torture people and drop them naked into the River Plate from little army aeroplanes.'

'Nonsense. If that was going on, we'd know about it.'

'Well, I am telling you now.'

'What do you know? You don't live here anymore.'

'Penny, you don't know what it was like before the military got in.' Mum always said this. 'The kidnappings, the constant fear. Daddy had to go to work in an armoured car with his boss because the guerrillas were kidnapping everyone. It was terrible, terrible! Something had to be done.'

'Are you saying they have to torture and kill people?'

'No, Penny, no'.

Dylan sat quietly, munching through another two milanesas, while we went on and on and on, nobody budging. He quietly took himself off to the little spare bedroom he and I were sharing and fell asleep immediately, tummy full, tired after a long flight.

The argument continued, around in circles while I helped clear the table. Then Dad offered to wash up, an elaborate performance as he slipped on rubber gloves, arms stretched out like a surgeon and instructed Mum and me on the correct way to do it.

I brushed my teeth, put on my pyjamas, and slipped into the other single bed.

There was a little knock on the bedroom door.

Mum was there, holding out two folded thick, brown, furry blankets with stitched cream satin edges.

'Are you cold, Penelope? Do you need another blanket?'

I got up, and we spoke through the half-open door.

'No, thank you. We're fine.'

'Why don't you take them? You might get cold later.'

'No, thank you. It's hot in here.'

'Please. I think you might need them.'

'No, thank you. Really, we don't need more blankets.'

'Take them, just in case.'

I was exasperated. 'Mum, listen to me! We don't need any more blankets.'

I tried to close the door, but Mum blocked me.

'Listen, Penny,' she whispered. 'You mustn't say any of those things in front of our friends. It's like Nazi Germany here.'

We looked at each other for a while, silence thick between us.

'Why were you both saying nothing was going on all the way through supper?'

'Nothing is going on,' she said quickly. 'But you mustn't say a word in front of any of our friends.'

'But why . . .'

'You're my daughter and I don't want anything to happen to you.'

Mum shut the door in my face.

***

When terrible things are done in our name, we know and we don't know at the same time. We don't want to know what we know.

***

Violence, bad faith and lies were there from the start.

The first European visitor to the Americas, Leif Erikson, established a settlement in Newfoundland around 970. According to Icelandic sagas, these early settlers retreated after a decade of hostile skirmishes with Indigenous people, and the Americas were left undisturbed for five hundred years.

The next explorers were not brushed off so easily.

In 1516, twenty-four years after Columbus touched down in the Caribbean, the buccaneer Juan Díaz de Solís was the first European to sail up what became known as the Río de La Plata, the silver river, muddy on the side that became Argentina and sandy on the Uruguayan side. He had heard wonderful tales about a giant silver mountain and was looking forward to helping himself.

Solís sailed up to the mouth of the estuary where it meets the Paraná River and disembarked on the sandy side with two officers and seven men. The official story is that the horrified crew left onboard the ship watched as Charrúa Indians killed Solís, his two officers, and six of the men, and then ate them.

The Charrúa never practised cannibalism.

In 1840, 324 years after Solís sailed down the River Plate, the Charrúa people were declared extinct. Some died from European diseases, others were killed when they resisted their lands being stolen. They were further ravaged by Jesuits who established a mission in 1624 with the open aim of snuffing out Indigenous "godless culture."

In Uruguay, this two-pronged strategy of conversion and murder culminated on April 11, 1831, with the massacre known as '*Salsipuedes*', *Getoutifyoucan.* Uruguayan President Fructuoso Rivera decided it was high time to resolve the 'Indian problem'. He invited forty friendly tribal leaders to his barracks, plied them with food and alcohol, and when they were stupefied, ordered his soldiers to slit their throats and spill their guts on the floor.

An enterprising Frenchman, François de Curel, picked out four of the surviving Charrúa – the shaman Senacua Sénaqué, the warrior Vaimaca-Pirú Sira, and a young couple, Laureano Tacuavé Martínez and his pregnant lover María Micaela Guyunusa – and shipped them off to France. They were exhibited in a freak show in Paris, where they all died, including María's new baby. Three hundred of the remaining Charrúa were sold off as slaves to affluent families in Montevideo.

Selk'nam group with Maurice Maitre at the Universal Exposition in Paris, (Ethnografiska Museet Stockholm), 1889.

The Charrúa were decimated but la 'Garra Charrúa', the Charrúa claw, is the mascot of the Uruguay football team.

In a FIFA video, players from the Uruguayan national team struggle to define 'Garra Charrúa'. 'It's something we have that nobody else has . . . It's another way of saying Uruguayan balls . . . It's leaving your skin on every ball . . . It's playing on when you're badly injured . . . It's being a tiny country with a great big heart . . .' It's many, many things.

Nobody mentions the genocide of the Charrúa.

***

When I refer to my South American upbringing in Argentina and Uruguay, new friends get very excited: 'Wow!' They imagine an exotic childhood with jaguars and jungles, the Day of the Dead, sugar skulls, Indigenous women with bowler hats or iguanas on their heads and dashing caballeros, with handlebar moustaches, sweeping women off their feet. But Buenos Aires is more like Madrid or Paris than La Paz or Quito, and long before I was born, most of the Indigenous people of Argentina and Uruguay – among them the Mapuche, Tehuelche, Atacama, Avá Gurararaní, Tupí Guaraní, Charrúa, Selk'nam, Alcaluf, Haush, and Yamana – had been decimated. I had a vague notion that a smattering of immiserated survivors scratched out a living in the deserts of the far north and the frozen wastes of the south, a long way from Buenos Aires. The train from the suburbs where we lived to the Retiro Terminal passed through a *villa miseria,* a derogatory name for a shanty town, and we called the people who lived there *cabecitas negras* because of their jet-black hair, shiny black eyes and milk chocolate skin. Mummy always pointed out the clusters of television aerials growing out of makeshift dwellings, piled higgledy-piggledy on top of each other, tangled wires spilling out everywhere like cooked spaghetti. 'Look Penny! These people have enough money to buy televisions but not to feed their children.'

We didn't have a television, and we spent our money on sensible things.

Anyway, there they were, the fly in the ointment, a reminder of something we had forgotten before we ever knew it. The ghosts of those who had lived here before we arrived haunted the outer edges of our dreams and traces of them appeared in handcrafted objects: little wooden carvings perched on shelves among the leather belts and wallets in expensive tourist shops.

I have a beautiful little carved wooden duck, but its head has fallen off. I keep meaning to stick it back on.

At the British School we learnt all about the Tudors and the Stuarts, absolutely nothing about the criollo national heroes memorialised in military statues all over town and less than nothing about our violent colonial past. Our education was crafted to prepare boys to work for British companies and us girls to marry them.

I loved Miss Sandiford, my form teacher at what we called 'the British', she was an inspired storyteller with bright-blue button eyes and a wavy blond bob. She taught us that British maritime adventurers were much more fun than the cowardly Spanish. Feisty, saucy Queen Elizabeth with her powdered white face and curly red wig, had a bath once a month whether she needed it or not and dished out licences to the daring sea dogs, Sir Francis Drake, Sir Martin Frobisher, Sir Walter Raleigh, and Sir John Hawkins, authorising them to loot across the high seas. These naughty English pirates were a bit of a giggle unlike the nasty foreign ones. I was entranced by her tales of Sir Walter Raleigh gallantly throwing his cloak over a puddle to prevent his Queen from getting her pretty shoes wet, and Sir John Hawkins defeating the cowardly Spanish Armada by shouting from the bridge: 'Serve God every day! Love one another! Save your provisions! Watch out for fire! Keep good company!'

In 1492 Columbus sailed the ocean blue
What a brave thing that was to do!

Sweet Miss Sandiford skipped over the part where English colonial invaders infected Indigenous people in the Caribbean with diseases to which they had no immunity and forced survivors into slave labour on sugar and coffee plantations. When Indigenous people kept dying or running away, Irish indentured workers were shipped in, but they couldn't physically tolerate tropical conditions so the *final solution* was the transport of tens of millions of enslaved Africans. A third died on the voyage out of Africa, another third within a year of arrival, and the rest were forced into generational enslavement – a novel British innovation – where not only the captured person but their children and their children's children and their children's children's children and their children's children's children's children for twelve or more generations were classified as property, humans who could be tortured or killed with no legal consequences. Dashing Sir John Hawkins and his handsome young cousin Francis Drake personally transported over a thousand Sierra Leonians into slavery and murdered three times as many. Hawkins was the proud architect of the triangular trade, every leg of which was the silver mountain Solís dreamed of. Good Queen Bess, with the body of a weak and feeble woman but the heart and stomach of a king, expressed her concern about the souls of enslaved people, until she realised how profitable slavery could be. Enslaved humans were shipped from Africa and sold in the Caribbean; sugar, tobacco, cotton and coffee were transported to Britain, where they were sold to buy guns, textiles and booze to sell in Africa to buy more enslaved people, and so on and on and on and on and on and on and on and on and on and on and on and on in a catastrophic cycle. I understand that people are sick and tired of hearing about slavery but the statue of James II, formerly the Duke of York and governor of the Royal African Company which transported 187,000 enslaved people to English colonies, many of whom were branded with his initials, still stands resplendent outside the National Gallery on Trafalgar Square.

The politics of forgetting. Remembering is just so exhausting. And it was so long ago.

In Africa and the Far East, a small European managerial class backed up by military force forced native populations to extract whatever they had that we wanted: rubber, teak, palm oil, gold, salt, ivory, copper, diamonds, tea, jute and platinum – they didn't know about coltan yet. The colonial class eventually left those places and people damaged and traumatised, but mostly alive.

In North America and the Southern Cone, Argentina, Chile, and Uruguay, winters are too cold for plantation crops, but these countries have vast grassy plains, perfect for rearing cattle and sheep and growing grain – commodities that require empty land, not intensive labour. European settlers moved in and farmed the land, making the so-called 'Indians', people who had lived there for thousands of years, ten thousand miles away from India, surplus to requirements.

They were in the way.

The rest was history. Except it wasn't. We were settlers with no history, living ahistorical lives. There was a void where history should have been, and we filled it with gossip.

***

I lived in a small world.

I was born in Buenos Aires but most of my childhood was spent in Montevideo, Uruguay. Our little rented house was a white box in a respectable lower-middle-class neighbourhood, next to a small shop that had vegetables piled outside in wooden boxes under a green tarpaulin. The shop was dark inside and sold tins of peaches and bags of flour and yummy chocolates that I yearned after but never had any money to buy. I longed to be a grown-up so I could do whatever I wanted and eat as much chocolate as I liked.

We were the only English-speaking family on that corner, but June and Eddie Ellis lived on the other side of the block with their three boys: Kim, Glen and Chris. They had a real film projector and would invite us over to watch the coronation of Queen Elizabeth and the changing of the guards. London! I longed to go there. As a special treat, Eddie would run the films backwards and all of us, adults and children, would fall about laughing and beg him to do it again.

We had a square sitting room with an armchair, two sofas, and a dining table with six chairs. On the wall was the framed portrait of Jesus that everyone had, with his long, light brown hair and straight nose, hanging next to a faded print of a bunch of chrysanthemums. I hated that picture; the stuffy flowers looked as if they were just about to get stinky and die. There was a small bookcase with Longfellow's *Prose Works*, *The Plays of J. M. Barrie*, and Dad's beloved poetry collections: James Elroy Flecker, Keats, and Tennyson. The only reference to the continent we lived on was *Green Mansions* by the Anglo-Argentine Henry Hudson, who referred to savages who had 'a low cunning.'

Mummy and her sisters, Betty, Anita, Edith and Ethel, attended the Quilmes High School where they sang the school anthem at assembly every morning.

In the morning of our lives,
When the world is young and gay
And we haven't got a trouble or a frown,
Quilmes High School is our home.
We will work and we will play,
And we'll make our school the best in every town.

Mummy welled up whenever she spoke about The Quilmes High School. It was ruled with an iron rod by Miss Ross and Miss Ballantine. As a little girl Mummy lived in mortal terror, particularly of the vicious Miss Ross who taunted her for being fat and stupid. One morning when the whole school was lined up for morning prayers, Miss Ross accidentally tucked her dress into her knickers, exposing her great big bottom stuffed into her great big knickers for all the girls to see. She knelt down with her back to them. *'You could have heard a pin drop,'* Mummy would say tearfully. *'We were all too scared to laugh.'*

***

I was four and Santa Claus had given me a blue rubber ring. It was a boiling hot day on the beach at Pocitos, a block from where we lived. Mummy was distracted, sitting under her canvas umbrella because she didn't know how to swim, so I stepped into my ring and headed into the sea by myself. I floated, paddled peacefully for a few minutes and convinced myself I could swim. I pulled the ring over my head and grabbed it quickly. I threw it a little farther. I lunged and snatched it again. I could definitely swim. I flung it as far away as I could. I did not know how to swim.

I sank. I was drowning and I knew it. The water was clear with sunshine rippling on the surface. It was beautiful.

I hit the bottom and sprang up. My mouth just cleared the surface of the water, and I took a breath and sank again.

I am dying. I am not afraid.

I hit the bottom and sprung up again. I thought I would try and scream for help but there was no time to do anything but breathe. I sank again.

The next time I reached the surface, I tried waving. A child with a bucket looked at me. I sank.

I jumped. *I am still not afraid.*

Jump. Breathe. Jump. Breathe. Jump Breathe.

I heard a whistle.

Next thing, a large man with red hair on his chest dived into the water, swam towards me with a powerful crawl and picked me up like a baby. *I am not a baby.* I tried to fight him off, but he was too strong and carried me in his arms to the shore. I was humiliated. He deposited me at Mummy's feet. She stood up with her big wobbly body squashed into a black, ruched swimming costume. She was really upset. 'Penelope! I can't take my eyes off you for a single second!'

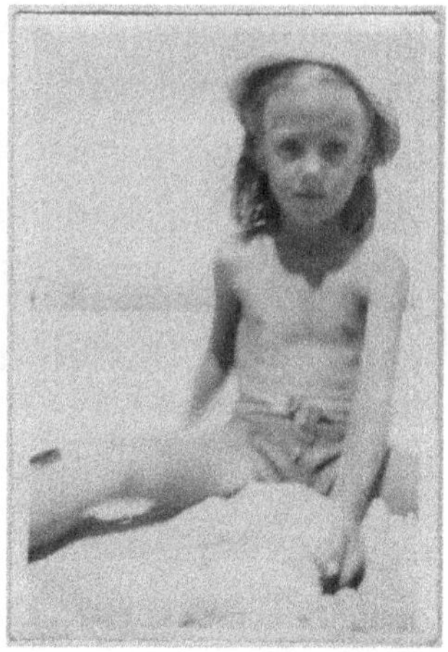

Penny on the Pocitos Beach Montevideo, (Family album), 1953.

I looked out at the bay. My blue rubber ring was floating far, far away, beyond all the swimmers at the edge of the bay. I wanted it back. I pointed. 'My ring. I want my ring!'

My ring was gone.

***

We English felt stranded on the wrong side of the Atlantic. Unlike millions of enslaved Africans, we had not been shipped across the ocean against our will, but we did not belong here. Or anywhere.

In the fifteenth century, Europe was a poor backwater that had nothing anybody else wanted. Europeans were obliged to make arduous journeys overland, paying taxes to Arab middlemen, to bring back spices, silks, silver and gold from India, China and Japan. This changed after the Portuguese copied the design of North African fishing boats and built new light caravels, able to sail into the wind and cross vast oceans without running out of food or water. Now they could avoid taxation by sailing East around Africa.

The Portuguese were joined by disreputable English, Spanish and Italian opportunists, licenced to attack and plunder any ship as long as they paid a cut to whatever monarch funded their expedition.

There is no capitalism without the sea.

Every navigator since antiquity knew the world was round – the dimmest sailor could observe a ship disappearing bottom first as it sailed over the horizon; so the thug we call Christopher Columbus, also known as Cristoforo Colombo or Cristobal Colón, persuaded Queen Isabella of Spain and her husband King Ferdinand, to fund a voyage West, searching for a route to India that didn't involve navigating around Africa.

Columbus was a gifted navigator, but he made two mistakes: He underestimated the length of the journey, believing it was only three thousand miles to India instead of twelve and a half because he'd followed the calculations of the brilliant Arab astronomer Al-Farghani, failing to recognise that Arab nautical miles were longer than Italian miles.

And he didn't know there was another massive continent in the way.

In 1492, when Columbus stumbled across the Americas with his three ships, the *Pinta*, the *Niña* and the *Santa*

María, he assumed he'd arrived in India, so naturally he referred to the people who lived there as 'Indians'.

The name stuck.

***

A few days after Mum had offered me a blanket and begged me to keep my opinions to myself, Dad, Mum, Dylan and I were invited to Ian and Patsy Dover's for the traditional Argentine barbecue. We perched on deck chairs on their freshly mowed lawn, eating our *pancitos,* little chunks of crusty fresh bread, stuffed with big juicy chorizos. Apart from Mum, who never touched alcohol, and Dylan, who was mucking about with the dog, the rest of us knocked back whopping tumblers of neat whiskey on ice and were now guzzling Trapiche vino while we waited for the big cuts of red meat, ribs, flank, and skirt to roast over the firepit. 'You know who I'd like to kick up the arse?'

Ian Dover was over six feet tall, a very rich, solid man with a flat head, a round doughy face, innocent baby blue eyes and a booming voice.

'The Mothers of Plaza de Mayo! I'd like to kick those bitches up their fat culos from here to kingdom come.'

I stiffened. Mum looked over at me, eyes pleading, pursing her lips tight the way she did when she was angry or upset. But this was different. This was fear. She moved her head infinitesimally from side to side.

Shut up. Shut up. Shut up. Please, Penny, shut up.

A year after the March 1976 coup, a group of women with white headscarves knotted under their chins began walking silently, once a week, in a wide circle in front of the pink presidential palace, La Casa Rosada. When young left-wing activists began vanishing, their desperate mothers did the rounds of police stations and hospitals searching for them. Gradually they met other desperate women, and they joined forces. Each mother walked with the name of her child embroidered on her headscarf. Open protests were illegal, so despite their silence, this was very dangerous. Six of the Mothers of the Plaza de Mayo were snatched and joined the ranks of the disappeared. In a televised press conference, President General Jorge Videla said simply: 'They have disappeared. They have no identity. They are not here. They are neither dead nor alive. They have disappeared. They are the disappeared.'

Ian carried on ranting about *las locas, crazy bitches.* I looked down at the grass, concentrating hard on an ant scurrying along the baked earth with a small leaf on its back, and said nothing. Dylan and I would be leaving for the UK in three weeks, and anything I said would have painful repercussions for Mum and Dad.

So, I held my tongue.

***

In 1500, the population of the world was about four hundred million, and between sixty and eighty million of those people inhabited the Americas, roughly the same as the population of Europe. In his logbooks, Columbus records coming across many islands with large populations. Fifty years later, only ten million survived. By 1650, it had gone down to six million. More than seventy million people were wiped out. During that period, the population of Europe increased by up to 500 percent.

A burnt offering.
A mass slaughter.
A genocide.
A holocaust.

***

I was curled up inside Mum's great soft body for nine months. After we parted company on the 1st of January 1950, we were never as close again.

I was born in the British Hospital on Calle Pedriel in Buenos Aires. In those days, doctors drugged women senseless with scopolamine when they went into labour so they were fully in control. The drug prevented memory formation but not pain and Dad described seeing Mum unconscious, strapped flat on her back, thrashing about with her legs open wide and feet up high in stirrups, unable to push. Like most babies of that era, it took me a long time to fight my way out. The story of my birth was often brought out at the lunch table with Mum complaining that when the nurse presented me to her, she had rejected me because the drugs had made her so sleepy. 'Ayyy no!' She always acted out the way she shoved me away, and I secretly felt sorry for myself too. Daddy always added that when they placed me into his hands, he was wide awake and promised to love me whatever I did.

As it turned out he would have quite a lot to forgive me for.

Mummy and Daddy frequently reminded me that I had screamed all night, every single night, for two whole years. Daddy, who was usually a kind father, had been instructed by his own mother that they would be *making a rod for their backs* if they picked me up. So we were all awake and unhappy, and it was all my fault.

Two weeks later, my birth was registered at the British Consulate in Buenos Aires, giving me the right to a British passport, although both my parents, all my aunts and uncles, and two of my grandparents had been born in Argentina. We would never be *Argentine*, however long we stayed there. Not really. We spoke English at home and to each other, but we were relatively bilingual, picking up Spanish from our surroundings and from maids at home, although something was always a bit off; our consonants were too hard, and we sounded like *gringos*. The same was true of the way we spoke English, using Spanish words when we couldn't think of the English one and the hybrids we made up by adding English endings to Spanish words, as in 'I'm going to planchate my clothes' – *planchar* being the verb for ironing in Spanish. We called it Spanglish.

The British community didn't live in gated communities or compounds; we were scattered across suburbs, starting off in Quilmes in the south, then migrating to the middle-class northern suburbs – San Isidro, Martinez, Acassuso, Vicente López and Belgrano – in detached bungalows with bright green manicured lawns, garages and swimming pools. Richer family friends like the Dovers and the Lauries also owned estancias with big houses on the Pampas, which we referred to as 'the camp.'

My parents had not inherited land or money, so we lived in a series of tiny rented houses or apartments. Dad was an accountant on a salary and 'getting to the end of the month' was always a challenge. He was terrified of debt, so it wasn't until the 1970s that he saved up enough to buy a small apartment outright, on the tenth floor of a modern high-rise in Martinez. He refused to tell Mum how much he earned, *none of her business*, apparently, so when he died in 1998, my brother Colin and I had to teach Mum how to write a check and get money out of a cash machine.

After they moved to Martinez, Mum would set off around the block with her shopping basket, turning left onto Eduardo Costa Street, greeting the newspaper-kiosk man in Spanish –'*Hola Señora, como le va*,' – past the Jockey Club Café and the English bookshop, left into Avenida Alvear where she popped into the Italian fruit-and-vegetable shop for a few things before crossing the road to the Panadería El Sol with its array of bread and sweet *facturas,* invariably bumping into four or five British community people she had known all her life. The conversations went like this:

'Hello, Eileen.'
'How are you, Peggy?'
'I'm very well. How's John?'
'John's very well, thank you, how's your John?'
'John's very well too.'
'Send him my love.'
'I will.'
'Lovely to see you, Peggy.'

'You too. Bye-bye, Eileen.'

'Bye-bye.'

Nobody we knew ever talked about politics, apart from the occasional outbursts about Perón and his dead wife, that bloody cow Evita. Praising Pinochet, who had kicked out '*that dreadful fellow Allende,*' was tolerated, but otherwise it was *not done.* Politics was what the *locals* got up to, and all their politicians were *scoundrels with their sticky fingers in the till* and *this would be a lovely country if it wasn't for them, but what can you do?*

It certainly had nothing to do with us. There was a great deal of interest in the activities of Queen Elizabeth and Princess Margaret Rose and occasional sneering at the stupid English National Health Service for pandering to hypochondriacs, but most of the time we gossiped about each other and complained about lazy maids.

***

Wherever Columbus set foot, he rammed a flagpole into the ground, unfurled the Royal Standard and claimed the territory for the Spanish Crown. His logbook makes his intentions clear, 'Generally, it was my wish to pass no island without taking possession of it.' Columbus and the explorers and missionaries and settlers who followed him, meticulously documented their travels. The voices of the Indigenous people they encountered, sophisticated people with no written language, hide in between the lines, wriggling under a mass of contradictions echoing in the silences of the dominant narrative.

In his first logbook, Columbus records that local 'Indians' were very helpful when the Santa María ran aground, so he invited their cacique to join him on board: 'The chief and his counsellors were extremely sorry that they could not understand me nor I them. Nevertheless, I understood him to say that if there was anything I wanted, the whole island was at my disposal.'

In a letter to Ferdinand and Isabella, Columbus described the 'Indians' he encountered in glowing terms: 'They are so affectionate and have so little greed and are in all ways so amenable that I assure your Highness that there is in my opinion no better people and no better land in the world. They love their neighbours as themselves and their way of speaking is the sweetest in the world, always gentle and smiling. Both men and women go naked as their mothers bore them; but your Highnesses must believe me when I say that their behaviour to one another is very good.'

Columbus realised that since the 'Indians' had no metal and were very unskilled in arms it would be easy to subjugate and enslave them. But as a Christian, he had to transmogrify the murder and oppression of these 'gentle smiling people' into a virtuous act. Columbus designed a perfect portal into which a fetid mixture of self-serving lies could be poured and emerge transformed into sacred wine.

Anthropophagy: the eating of human flesh.

Cannibalism. Along with incest, it is forbidden in every culture.

On Sunday, the 13th of January, 'fierce looking' Kalinago 'Indians' greeted Columbus and his crew and when they refused to exchange more than two bows and arrows for useless baubles, Columbus concluded that they were cannibals and ordered his men to attack them with crossbows and swords. The Kalinago word for themselves, *Karibna*, turned into *caníbal* in Spanish, *cannibal* in English, *cannibale* in Italian, and *canibal* in Portuguese: a *man-eating* person.

The conquistadores called all friendly groups 'Arawak' and those they considered hostile cannibals 'Caribs'. They referred to themselves as 'Christians'.

In 1503, Queen Isabella issued the first of several decrees legalising slave raids on Caribs because of their cannibalism. Columbus was given seventeen ships and twelve hundred men for his second journey–fully authorised to loot, kill men and enslave women and children.

***

Columbus sent one of his captains and a group of sailors ashore. News had spread about these pale-faced criminals, so local people fled as soon as they saw the ship. In *Cannibalism and the Colonial World*, Peter Hulme reports that the landing party entered an abandoned hut, where they found two large parrots, a pile of cotton, some food and four or five clean human bones, all of which they took back onboard. Doctor Diego Álvarez Chanca, the ship's medical doctor, who had not gone ashore, immediately concluded that the inhabitants of the hut were Caribs who ate human flesh. These clean bones were clearly connected to domestic funerary rites commonplace in the Caribbean at that time. Thirty years later, in 1587, Doctor Chanca's account was embellished by Peter Martyr d'Anghiera, an

Italian scholar based in Andalusía who had never set foot in the New World. He invented human flesh barbecuing on a spit and the horrifying, blood-soaked, decapitated head of a young boy hanging from a beam.

The story reappeared in 1892 in a publication celebrating the four hundredth anniversary of Columbus's landing in the New World, by this time almost unrecognisable: 'Spaniards entered apartments which were veritable butcher shops. Heads and limbs of men and women were hung up on the walls or suspended from the rafters, in some instances dripping with blood, and, as if to add, if that were possible, to the horror of the scene, dead parrots, geese, dogs and iguanas were hung up without discrimination or preference with the fragments of human bodies. In a pot, some pieces of human limbs were boiling.'

Columbus ruled that every 'Indian' in the goldfields over the age of fourteen had to pay a tribute of a belly full of gold dust or twenty-five pounds of cotton. A compulsory special disc was placed around the neck after the tribute was paid, and any person found without this disc had their hands chopped off. Tens of thousands of people were enslaved, some shipped to Europe, most dying on the journey, and girls as young as nine or ten were forced into sexual slavery. Columbus wrote in his logbook that he was given 'two magnificently attired girls, the elder of whom could not have been more than eleven and the other seven. Both were so shameless that they might have been whores.'

Seven and eleven.

Columbus presented one of his lieutenants, Michele de Cuneo, with a beautiful Carib woman. She resisted and scratched him. Cuneo writes: 'To cut a long story short – I then took a piece of rope and whipped her soundly, and she let forth such incredible screams that you would not have believed your ears. Eventually we came to such terms, I assure you, that you would have thought she had been brought up in a school for whores.'

Where are the voices we can't hear, the *incredible screams* no one responded to? If you listen carefully, you can discern whispers of resistance, of misdirection, from those who did not leave written accounts. Columbus complained bitterly that as soon as he arrived, demanding gold, local 'Indians' – the Taíno, the Kalinago and the Tupinambá – informed him that there was plenty of gold on the other side of that hill, upriver, downriver, on a different island, anywhere but here. They sent him off on wild-goose chases as far away as possible.

***

In March 2022, I speak to my friend Chloe. She's isolating with Covid and is bored and fed up. She asks about my writing. I tell her about the genocide of Indigenous people and how there were none left by the time I was growing up.

'Didn't you have Brown maids?' asks Chloe.

I am a fool.

Our first live-in maid in Uruguay was Sara, she had black eyes and straight jet-black hair and a wide, flat 'Indian' face. She slept in a room with her own small bathroom at the back of the house. Sara was free on Wednesday afternoons and all of Sunday, and she sat on her bed staring into space because she was illiterate.

She didn't know anybody, and like us, she didn't have a television or a radio. It never occurred to me to wonder where she came from.

She and my little brother Colin loved each other; she could make him eat his *papita* by pretending every spoonful was an aeroplane landing in his mouth, and I felt a bit left out. Eventually, Sara found a boyfriend and they got married in a big church where a queue of brides marched up the aisle, one after the other, every few minutes. We arrived early and found ourselves attending several weddings before she arrived.

Mummy, Colin and I visited Sara only once, after she had her own baby. She lived in a bare, windowless apartment with very high ceilings. We sat around the table and had nothing to say to each other. The visit was not a success.

After Sara, we had Mabel who was young, plump and cheerful. She had wavy black hair and eyes, and a bright smile. I often spent the night with my friend Jenny Hyland and her four siblings in their large house. I idolised Jenny's older sister Elizabeth, who had developed pert round breasts and was very daring, swallow-diving off the headboards of her parents' bed, telling us dirty jokes that I laughed at heartily, although I didn't have a clue why they were funny, and encouraging us to smoke disgusting cigarettes in the mimosa tree. The Hyland's maid, Esmeralda, was very pally with Elizabeth, and they played a game in which Elizabeth ordered Esmeralda to 'stand up' and 'sit down', 'stand up' and 'sit down', 'stand up' and 'sit down', and Esmeralda obediently jumped up and down as instructed. She didn't seem to mind, and they both laughed their heads off. Jenny and I laughed along, although I couldn't help noticing that it was never Esmeralda's turn to do it to Elizabeth.

When I went home, I thought I would try it with Mabel.

'*Sentáte.*' Sit. Mabel sat on my bed, smiling tentatively.
'*Paráte.*' Stand. Mabel stood up, her smile wary now.
'*Sentáte.*' She sat. Neither of us was laughing. I didn't understand why this wasn't fun.
I ordered her to stand up again and she did. It was horrible. I was horrible.
I shrugged and muttered, '*Está bien.*'
I avoided Mabel after that, and she kept well out of my way.

After we moved back to Argentina, Teresa became our daily maid for over thirty years. She was from Entre Ríos, so she may have been Qom, Wichí, Lule, Tomocoté, Mocoví, Pilagá or Vilela – we never asked. Maids all came from a vague place we called 'up north'. At seven Teresa had been sent to Buenos Aires because her parents could not afford to feed her. Mum tutted, 'Why do these people have so many children when they can't afford to feed them?' Teresa was a young woman with two small children, Albertito and Graciela. She had straight black hair and round dark eyes and a flattish, pockmarked face like Sara. She had never been to school, but she was clever and very good with numbers. She called Mummy 'Señora' and Mummy called her 'Teresa', but they were each other's closest confidantes. Teresa told Mummy about her husband Alberto bashing her when he was drunk, and

Mummy told Teresa about Daddy's infidelities after I went off the rails and had a baby without being married. Mummy never said a single word about her marital troubles to the British community ladies because she didn't trust any of them an inch. When Dad was out or at work, Teresa and Mum ate lunch together in the dining room, but if he was home, Teresa ate by herself in the kitchen. That was their secret.

I never wondered where Teresa went after work until I was fifteen. Dad, Mum and I had locked ourselves out and had to pick up Teresa's keys all the way out in San Fernando. Colin was at St George College, so the three of us drove through the middle-class suburbs, streetlights getting dimmer until they disappeared completely. We bumped over deep potholes and along unpaved roads lined with one-story breeze block houses, some half-built. Dad was a nervous driver and became increasingly exasperated with the potholes and our incompetent directions, and we were strung out by the time we arrived. Teresa was startled to see us but politely invited us in. She and her husband lived behind a tiny shop where they sold cigarettes, maize, sweets and soft drinks. We walked through a thin chain curtain into a single room at the back, where they ate and slept with their two children. There were four spindly chairs, a small table with a plastic cloth patterned with pink roses, and two mattresses neatly stacked against a green shiny wall. A rough plaster shelf held the only ornaments, a tiny glass giraffe with three legs and a glass horse with no tail and one leg missing at the knee. I felt sick: I collected little glass animals and had chucked these two into the bin after accidentally knocking them over. Teresa caught me staring and apologised profusely.

'Penny, I'm sorry. I found them in the bin, I thought you . . . forgive me.'

'Está bien.' I said, my heart shrivelling. I threw away those things because I am a spoilt brat, and now they are precious to you.

By the 1980s, Teresa's little shop was prospering and she no longer needed to work as a maid. Her husband wanted her in the shop full-time, but Mum explained the two of them kept the cleaning job going because it was the only way they could see each other.

I laughed. '*Mum.* Teresa is your friend! Why can't she just visit without working for you?'

Mum was horrified. 'She's not my friend! How could you say a thing like that?'

'But you tell each other everything.'

Mum was dubious, 'I suppose so.'

Teresa was as appalled as Mum. 'Penny, I could never be at the level of the señora! She's up there and I am down here!' Teresa's gesture suggested that Mum was floating around somewhere near the ceiling.

I persevered. 'Why don't you get a new maid, let Teresa work full time in her own shop and invite her to tea sometimes?'

It worked for a while. Mum would get out her silver teapot and her best china tea set, and they would chat and eat little sandwiches with the crusts cut off, *cañoncitos de dulce de leche, vigilantes con membrillo, alfajores de maicena,* and *libritos* - delicious little book facsimiles crafted out of tissue-thin pastry.

Eventually Mum decided Teresa talked too much and the tea parties petered out. They were both lonely and they both talked too much. Albertito became a bad boy, in and out of trouble, but studious Graciela became a medical doctor.

I insisted that maids always call me by my first name, but I never asked Sara, Mabel or Teresa a single thing about themselves, even after I became a left-wing revolutionary.

***

Europeans fought each other over North America and the Caribbean.

The Spanish invaded Florida and New Mexico and seized Cuba, Puerto Rico, Honduras, Jamaica, Trinidad and the Cayman Islands until they were snatched by the British. They lost Santo Domingo to France and got it back again. The Dutch grabbed Aruba, Curaçao and Sint Maarten. The French stole all the land along the Mississippi and invaded Haiti, Guadeloupe and Martinique after being kicked off Saint Kitts and Nevis by the British and occupied Canada until the British seized that from them too. The British did well, claiming the East Coast of North America and twenty or thirty Caribbean islands, including Jamaica and British Guiana on the mainland.

But in the Southern Cone, Argentina, Uruguay and Chile, there were three hundred years during which Spanish criollo settlements gradually expanded into lands belonging to Indigenous people with no competition from other European countries. In 1806, there were two British military invasions up the River Plate, but they were ignominiously defeated by Spanish troops and resistance from local criollos and enslaved Africans, who did not want to exchange one oppressor for another. The British smartly switched tactics and backed the criollo independence movement, ingratiating themselves with a new bunch of rulers they could do business with.

The criollos were locally born Spanish heritage men plus a few Irish immigrants who assimilated into the fabric of criollo life: Francis Burdett O'Connor, Bernardo O'Higgins and William Brown, who arrived in 1809 and founded the Argentine Navy. There are over a thousand streets and squares named after Brown, but it never occurred to me that he was *one of us* because we always pronounced his name with a Spanish accent.

The criollos bitterly resented the privileged *peninsulares*, Spanish-born administrators who were forbidden from marrying criollo women, and eventually rose up across Latin America, inspired by the 1789 French Revolution and Thomas Jefferson's Declaration of Independence in 1776: 'We hold these truths to be self-evident, that all men are created equal, that they are endowed by their Creator with certain unalienable Rights, that among these are Life, Liberty and the pursuit of Happiness.'

'All men' excluded all poor white men, all women, all enslaved Africans and all Indigenous people.

On May 18, 1816, a group of rebellious criollo conspirators took themselves off to watch *Rome Saved!* a play about resisting tyranny. Juan José Paso - the street in Martinez where Mum and Dad lived was named after him - was so inspired by a speech in the play that he sprang up in the auditorium and cried out for the freedom of Buenos Aires. A small fight broke out, triggering the revolution.

Argentina declared independence from Spain on May 25, 1816. The new Junta, composed entirely of a small group of men of Spanish heritage, saw no contradiction in celebrating their new freedom while denying it to everybody else - African slavery was not abolished until 1861, women could not vote until 1947, and Indigenous people had no official status at all.

At this time the 'Indian Frontier' was only a hundred miles from the capital. Indigenous tribes still occupied about half the country; the semi-nomadic Mapuche, the Requel, Tehuelche, Huilliche, Yaghan and the Selk'nam were defending lands from Córdoba in the North all the way down through the Pampas to Patagonia and Tierra del Fuego. For three hundred years there had been periods of co-existence and bloody skirmishes as 'Indians' drove settlers and cattle off their lands with lances, bows and arrows, and bolas -stone balls attached to long leather thongs.

Being Argentine was not for everyone.

It was nearly time for my people to make a move.

***

The new criollo government immediately confiscated all private property owned by the peninsulares, designated Indigenous lands as terra nullius, and flung open the doors of Argentina to millions of European immigrants for their nation-building project.

From the mid-nineteenth century to the early twentieth century, seven million Europeans, including my great-grandfathers and their families, sailed across the ocean to seek their fortunes in Argentina. The saying went like this: *Mexicans descend from Aztecs, Peruvians descend from Incas and Argentines descend from ships.*

In 1844, President Domingo Sarmiento opened the doors of Argentina to European immigration, extending a special invitation to Northern Europeans to settle in a country that was 'clamouring for industry and civilisation'. He claimed that the original 'miserable inhabitants', the 'Indians', 'have hearts that do not beat for pleasure or hope, they are capable only of feeling fear and live their lives in a state of numb stupidity.'

Argentina was second only to the United States as the land of opportunity for Europeans looking for a better life.

By 1913, three-quarters of adult men in Argentina were foreign-born. Over two million impoverished Spanish peasants, many from Galicia, swiftly became the butt of dumb jokes, like the Irish in Britain, Poles in the United States and Belgians in France. 'The girl at the box office exclaims, "Sir! This is the fifth ticket you have bought for this performance!" The Gallego replies, 'That's because that bastard at the door keeps tearing them up!'

They were joined by three million destitute Italians, who were also prepared to work for very little. Afro-Argentine freelance street porters, washerwomen, and street vendors complained bitterly that these new immigrants were taking their jobs.

Southern European peasants were followed by tens of thousands of Yiddish-speaking Ashkenazi Jews escaping pogroms in Russia. Buenos Aires still has a substantial Jewish community; the cleverest girls at Northlands School for Girls were Jews, and they stuck together just like we did.

The Spanish, the Italians and the Ashkenazi Jews were joined by hundreds of thousands of Eastern Europeans, Germans, Poles and Russians fleeing revolutionary upheavals, educated political refugees who set up what remains a powerful trade union movement. All these immigrants sent their children to local schools, and within a generation they spoke Spanish and regarded themselves as Argentine.

We did not.

From the mid-nineteenth century, about sixty thousand emigrants from all corners of the British Isles travelled to Argentina. We were not escaping hunger or political persecution, we just wanted to make money. At its height, the British community was only around a hundred thousand strong, but we made our presence felt.

Locally, the English were mocked as drunks, *el borracho inglés* was a cartoon figure, but Juan Bautista Alberdi, chief architect of the Constitution, believed the English to be:

> The most perfect of men . . . Put the bum, the gaucho, the peasant, the basic element of our population, through all the transformations of the best systems of education; in one hundred years you won't make of him an English worker, who works, consumes, and lives in dignity and comfort.

We agreed. We believed we were doing the others a favour by being there.

The wealthiest British immigrants, those with capital and farming expertise, bought huge estancias at knock-down prices in the Pampas, Patagonia and Tierra del Fuego; but the majority were genteel middle and lower middle-class businessmen like my great grandfathers and we congealed into a solidly middle-class business community in Buenos Aires and Montevideo.

Most working-class Brits, *dirty poms*, emigrated to Australia and New Zealand, and Mum often moaned that she wished her grandfather, Peter Archibald Forbes, had sailed to Australia instead of *this place* because Australia was a nice clean white country where people knew how to behave.

'Mum, none of us would exist if he'd gone to Australia.
Not even you.'
And Mum would feel *got at*, purse her lips tight, and
shrug.
'I suppose so.'

Our sticky fingers were all over Argentina. The British founded *La Bolsa,* the Stock Exchange, and the Bank of London and South America; British engineers built and ran a modern railway system that carried beef and grain from the Pampas to the port of Buenos Aires, where the British owned the grain silos, leather tanneries and refrigerated meat-packing plants that enabled the fabulously lucrative export trade to Europe. In return, Argentina imported Welsh coal, British textiles, railway supplies, pipes, galvanised roofing, corrugated iron, bicycles, shoes, haberdashery and furniture, everything from a needle to an automobile. Vladimir Lenin classified Argentina as an informal colony controlled indirectly through trade without the expense of administering it.

Unlike other European settlers, we clung to an unwavering belief in our own superiority, referred to our fellow immigrants, who had arrived at exactly the same time, as 'natives' or 'locals', attended English Schools, read our news in the *Buenos Aires Herald*, shopped at the only Harrods outside Knightsbridge, played cricket and polo at the Hurlingham Club and drank gin and tonics while reading week-old copies of *The Daily Telegraph* in the English Club.

One red-letter day, British community children were invited to the British Embassy to celebrate Queen Elizabeth's birthday. We were presented with real English food, slabs of greasy Wall's ice-cream squashed between thin wafers and a Kit-Kat, which I thought was the most delicious thing I had ever tasted. I longed to live in England where I could eat Marmite and Kit-Kats!

Nobody, or nobody I ever met, showed a scintilla of curiosity about other cultures. The British community extruded a surfeit of businessmen, accountants and lawyers but no artists or atheists, no philosophers or poets, no scientists or dreamers. Our cultural contribution consisted entirely of sporting activities. English and Scottish immigrants introduced football in 1903, and their original team names survive to this day: Newell's Old Boys, after Isaac Newell; Racing, which started as the British Railways club; Boca Juniors; and the most successful club of all,

River Plate, pronounced *Reever.* In the early days, only the English were allowed to play, but before long, football became a national passion.

Los Pumas, founded in 1910, still play rugby at an international level. The first cricket club was founded by James Brittain, who also established the first bank, and visiting Royals like Prince Harry followed in the footsteps of his grandfather Prince Philip by playing polo with rich boys, like his best friend, Nacho Figueras. And Oh, what larks! Susan Barrantes, mother of Sarah Ferguson, the Duchess of York, eloped with an Argentine polo player.

***

A few years ago, I accepted an invitation to speak about the British in Argentina at the Argentine Embassy in London. A week later, I was disinvited. It turned out that Google revealed that my attitude towards the British community was 'too negative' for an event that was meant to help mend strained relations over the Malvinas.

After all, we had always been the right kind of immigrants. In *The Forgotten Colony,* journalist Andrew Graham-Yool concludes, 'Argentina is a far better country for the British drive that pushed through it.' That doesn't make any sense, but it toes the right line.

The Avenida 9 de Julio is the widest street in the world, commemorating the day Argentina declared independence from Spain. One hundred and fifty years later, I stood under the obelisk at one end of it, my drenched clothes sticking to my skinny body after a downpour, the usual crazy careening traffic swerving across lanes, horns beeping. The wet road reflected pools of red-and-yellow lights and joy whooshed up from the soles of my feet and poured out of my shiny, wet eyes. It was 1966, I was sixteen and about to jump into my real life. I hadn't enjoyed being little and I knew I didn't want to become like Mum or the other ladies, I didn't know what might be waiting for me, but I was ready for anything. Wet concrete opened at my feet, and I was swallowed up again.

***

A year later, on the last day of school, while all the other girls were weeping about those being the best years of their lives, I leapt into the swimming pool in my uniform and stormed off shouting: 'These weren't the best days of my life and I'm never coming back!' I took the bus home dripping wet. I never did go back.

I had read about artists in books, so I knew they must exist in the real world, even though I had never actually met one. I sauntered into town in one of the many outfits that Chuchi, my mother's dressmaker made to my design, a mini smock worn over bunchy bloomers one day, a patterned silky bell-bottom duo the next, or my favourite black-and-white polka-dot minidress with a see-through plastic collar and a big orange plastic jewel above my flat chest. I was naturally thin with long straight hair when those things were fashionable. My aim was to look like Twiggy in *Honey* magazine, which arrived a month late on a Royal Mail ship from London.

I crossed the wide Avenida Libertador by Retiro and headed up through Plaza San Martín with its massive grey ombú trees twisting out from mounds of mangled roots, past the seductive smells of the sugar-coated peanut seller and the sad photographer in his creased suit, moping hopefully by his tripod, sniffing irritably at the lewd layabouts stretched out on benches with their unbuttoned shirts, 'Ay mamita que linda que estás!' I headed up Reconquista, down San Martín, up Florida, down Maipú and up Esmeralda. I came across a couple of tiny modern art galleries but they were completely empty.

After several days tramping around town and drinking too much coffee, I stumbled across El Bar Moderno.

The perfect name. Mum was always moaning, 'Penny, why do you have to be so modern?'

I peered in. It was a long, dark bar, but I could just make out a table full of what looked to me like artists sitting in clouds of smoke. The men had dishevelled, longish hair and beards, and I was particularly excited to see that one of them had paint splashes on his clothes and a beret like Che Guevara's. There were two serious-looking women, but I wasn't interested in them. I sashayed in casually and although the bar was almost empty, I carefully positioned myself at a small table nearest the group. I ordered a *cafecito* from the middle-aged waiter, pulled out a Jockey Club filtered cigarette from its classic soft red packet with a little drawing of a jockey's cap and crop, and sparked up. I kicked myself for not asking them for a light. Idiot.

I sat trying to look as though I was lost in artistic thoughts and attempted to blow a smoke ring. It was a messy blur and I glanced nervously over at the artist's table to check whether anybody had noticed. They were all talking over each other so it was hard to figure out what they were saying. I made out odd phrases, '*exquisitamente racional*', and I heard the word '*intelectual*' which I took as a good sign because I had read the whole of *The Idiot,* which had really depressed me, and quite a bit of T. S. Eliot.

The waiter brought me a black coffee in a tiny thick white cup with a teeny biscuit wrapped in cellophane on the saucer. I swallowed it in one and immediately regretted not making it last. I didn't want to eat the biscuit so after unwrapping it I had nothing else to do. I lit a second Jockey Club from the first and peeped at the artists, clocking a handsome man holding forth. I smoked the cigarette down to the filter and started on a third but smoking so much was starting to make me feel sick, so I stubbed it out and glanced over again. A plain man with short hair and a kind face, sitting across from the handsome one, caught my eye. He smiled sympathetically, picked up a plate of chocolate biscuits and offered it to me. I yelped loudly and nearly fell off my chair.

'No! No gracias!'

I hadn't meant to squeal.

I knew exactly what he was up to. Mummy had warned me many times about strange men offering girls sweets and biscuits laced with heroin; if you accepted, you'd wake up in Morocco, in the tent of a sex obsessed sheikh, a slave in his personal harem. Years later you'd be spat out, drained by all that *sex* and shipped back to Argentina, spoilt goods, a pariah nobody would speak to, let alone marry, and that would be your life over. I could see the Sheikh clearly, towering over me in red and gold embroidered robes, flashing his teeth and eyes, waving a scimitar glinting in the sun, his *thing*, all red and poking out of his pantaloons.

The kind man read my mind. He smiled, bit into one of the biscuits and offered me the other half. I was too embarrassed to refuse so I popped it in my mouth. He turned back to his friends.

I sat rigid while the biscuit coagulated into a lump of sludge on my tongue. I forced it down.

I didn't dare look at the artist table. Light poured through a half-open door at the back of the dark bar, and I was pretty sure I could hear a getaway car waiting by the dustbins with the engine running. When I keeled over, they'd drag me out and nobody would ever find out what had happened to me. Clearly the waiter was in on it, he probably had a daughter of his own, and I wondered indignantly how he would like it if this happened to her? These people probably sat here every day, pretending to be artists, waiting for gullible girls to drug. The waiter only had to turn a blind eye to get his cut. I was sure an English girl would be worth quite a bit. I was probably the latest in a long line who had disappeared. Rubbed out. I thought how sad Mummy and Daddy would be even though they didn't understand that I was an artist. I would have started crying if I hadn't been so afraid.

I smoked another cigarette.

Nothing happened. Nothing at all. Eventually I called the waiter and asked for the bill. I paid and left, feeling perfectly well and very foolish.

After that I was afraid of nothing. I became reckless.

***

What I didn't know back then was that a white slave trade had operated in Argentina between 1875 and 1936, but it did not involve abducting middle-class Anglo-Argentine girls and sweeping them off to satisfy the sexual proclivities of lusty sheikhs in the Middle East.

You have to flip these bogey stories to get the truth.

During the era of mass immigration to Argentina, there was a surplus of lonely European gentlemen, two or three men to every woman. Like single immigrant men everywhere, they were saving up to bring over fiancées they had left behind. One version has it that impoverished Eastern European women were tricked into coming to Argentina by the Zwi Migdal, an Ashkenazi network that lured young women to the New World with fake marriage contracts and put them in brothels when they arrived. A disproportionate number of Buenos Aires prostitutes were Jews but that doesn't prove they were hoodwinked into coming. There was also a French organisation, Le Milieu, trafficking women from Marseille. *Trafficking* is a loaded word and although some women may have been tricked into crossing the ocean and forced into sex work, then as now it might be a rational choice for an impecunious young woman to choose sex work over domestic labour. Both are dictated by poverty, but it does give agency to sex workers, subverting the narrative of relentless victimisation.

I was never in danger of being enslaved, and my ancestors may well have availed themselves of the services of these women.

What is true is that thousands of women were abducted and vanished during the Dirty War from 1976 to1983 and most of them were left-wing, middle-class young women like me.

But the original erasure remained unspoken.

***

After independence, the land wasn't empty. Not yet.

I had a vague idea that something bad had happened to the 'Indians' a long, long time ago, in the distant past, a faded watercolour painting that certainly had nothing to do with me.

Around 1862, Mummy's grandfather, Peter Archibald Forbes, sailed to Argentina from Wick at the northern tip of Scotland with his wife, Elizabeth Gow, and his six daughters, and around the same time, Alfred Lovett, Daddy's grandfather, set off from Richmond in Southwest London.

My maternal great-grandparents, Elizabeth Gow and Peter Archibald Forbes, Buenos Aires, (Family album), c.1870.

My paternal family, the Lovetts in Richmond, London, (Family Album), c. 1890.

It had never, ever, occurred to me that the slaughter of Indigenous people had taken place after the arrival of my family in Argentina. To make space for us.

General Julio Argentino Roca announced a new campaign:

> Our self-respect as a virile people obliges us to put down as soon as possible, by reason or by force, this handful of savages who destroy our wealth and prevent us from definitely occupying, in the name of law, progress and our own security, the richest and most fertile lands of the Republic.

Between 1878 and 1890, Roca led the Conquest of the Desert, a military campaign to drive the Mapuche and Tehuelche out of the Pampas and Patagonia. Roca knew these were vast, fertile, inhabited lands, ideal for rearing cattle and growing wheat and corn, and in recent years, flax, soya and marijuana.

The Pampas was never a desert. There is always a desert in these settler stories.

Indigenous tribes had their own laws and distinct ways of living, but they were not nation states, and they faced a modern army armed with the game-changing, breech-loading Remington Rifle, effective at five hundred metres, out of range of the most skilful archer, capable of picking the enemy off in their thousands without suffering a single casualty. Unlike the old muskets that often misfired and took over a minute to reload from a standing position, the Remington could be loaded lying down so the handler was no longer an easy target. Severe penalties were imposed on dealers who sold Remington rifles to 'Indians' and pitching these rifles against lances, arrows and bolas turned battles into massacres. This was effectively a genocide.

General Alsina addressed Congress in 1878: 'We must give up the old system and seek the Indian in his encampment, to defeat him or drive him out, leaving him trapped not only by a large man-made ditch but by the great and impassable barrier of the Rio Negro.' Alsina prepared the way for General Roca, sweeping his army across the Pampas and down to the south, digging trenches and palisades behind them, building new roads and telegraph lines and bringing in agriculture and cattle breeding. As the Argentine army pushed onwards, Indigenous troops were left to starve behind enemy lines. Those who surrendered were pressed into concentration camps or sent up north as enslaved labour in sugar plantations.

General Roca regarded Alsina as too soft and completed the massacre efficiently. According to official statistics, Argentine soldiers, armed with their new killing machines, wiped out fourteen thousand Mapuche, killing prisoners, enslaving survivors and preventing them from having children. Roca was brutally honest about the nature of his mission: 'Punishing, liberating and colonising - it is necessary to break the spirit of the Indians and keep fear and terror alive among them.'

The Conquest of the Desert was funded by selling government bonds out of the Argentine embassy in London; each bond could be exchanged for five and a half kilometres of land. By 1900, the entire Pampa was owned by private shareholders and almost all traces of the Indigenous peoples who had lived there for thousands of years had been erased. Almost but not all. Place names like Pichi Huinca, Neuquén, Chacharramendi and Quehué are signs of an alternative cartography, maps that tell different stories.

In 1887, bankers in the City of London threw a banquet for President Roca, and he expressed his heartfelt gratitude: 'I have always had a huge affection for England. The Argentine Republic will be a great nation one day and we will never forget that the progressive state we find ourselves in, is owed in great part to English capital.'

Argentina was no longer a terra nullius.

***

Terra nullius is Latin for 'nobody's land'. According to international law, if land belongs to nobody, anybody can claim it. Land is not required to be empty to be terra nullius; it may well be inhabited, but if the people who live there have trod lightly, have not altered it by farming, or if they have altered it by farming but they do not share a common language, history and culture, or if they do share a common language, history and culture but are not deemed to have developed an organised state and if they have no title deeds because they have always lived there, essentially if these people are in the way of other people who are better armed and organised, they can be legally dispossessed without repercussions.

> For a territory to be terra nullius, that is, unpossessed by a recognized state, and therefore appropriable- it must not be inhabited by a political society accepted as an equal in the Family of Nations. Areas which may be considered to constitute terra nullius include uninhabited lands, territories inhabited by individuals not permanently united for political action, and derelict areas that have been abandoned by former possessory states.

North and South America, Africa, Australia and New Zealand fulfilled the infinitely flexible legal criteria that justified Europeans pushing other people out of their homes and moving in themselves.

***

Until the end of her long life, Mum referred querulously to 'these people here', never considering for a single second that she was one of them, although her own father, another Peter Archibald Forbes, was born in Argentina in 1877, and she herself was born in Buenos Aires in 1919 and did not visit England until she was over forty. Mum claimed her grandfather was a wealthy ships chandler who'd been swindled by his business partner, but a distant relative did a bit of digging and discovered that Peter had been a tax collector in Mid Clyth, a shabby town in Northern Scotland.

Mum's mother, Margaret Wilkinson, was born in Sunderland, England, in 1896 and travelled to Argentina with her mother and sisters. I believe her father had been a shipbuilder, and I don't know what happened to him. I have a collection of sepia photographs showing Madge as a lively, pretty, young woman twenty years younger than her unattractive husband, who had a great big tummy that required his trousers to be held up by suspenders. I can only imagine she was running away from some sadness at home. Mum recalled her beloved young mama permanently pregnant and always ill, with a baby at her breast and a book in her hand. They lived in an isolated small holding in Burzaco where she squeezed out eight babies in quick succession, Betty, my mum Peggy, Edith, Georgie, Peter, Anita, Ethel and Johnny. Mum always muttered darkly that her Papa should not have kept *bothering* Mama which explains why she believed that sex was something dirty that men inflicted on women. Georgie and Peter died as little boys, and in 1934, Madge and Peter died within three months of each other. Mum was only fifteen. The newly orphaned Betty, Peggy, Anita, Edith, Ethel and little Johnny were taken in by Peter's elderly unmarried sisters known as the Aunties. Legend goes that their Victorian father had forbidden his daughters from marrying because he wanted them gathered around his deathbed. Two of them disobeyed and were never spoken of again.

Mum and Betty had to leave school and work as secretaries while the Aunties gave private English classes to pay for the young girls to finish their education at the Quilmes High School and Johnnie at St George's College. God forbid they should go to Argentine schools.

I loved visiting Mummy's aunties in their crumbling, rented colonial house with its wild overgrown garden. They were very old, I thought probably hundreds of years old, with scrunched up crinkly faces. I adored Aunt Meg because she didn't have big, fat titties like Mummy's that hung down to her tummy; Aunt Meg had little stringy ones that caved in under her saggy vest, and when I asked her to draw me a mouse her hands shook so much that the mouse's hairs stuck out all over as if he'd had an electric shock. If I remembered to be a very good girl, she would take a tray of chocolates out of her secret drawer, and if I picked the one nearest me, even if it wasn't the one I really wanted, she let me have another one straight away and smiled with her big yellow teeth, wispy bits of white hair in a shiny halo around her head. 'Good girl, Penelope.'

Aunt Meg gave private English lessons to Argentine men so they could try to speak like us even though they never would in a million years, and when they arrived for their lessons, I had to be very quiet and not ask her to draw me a mouse. The boss of the Aunties. Nanina was a thousand years old and she warned me never to trust Argentine men, specially if they had small feet, or eyes too close together. If I saw one like that, I must narrow my eyes and give them a *look* like Nanina showed me, to let them know *they were no better than they should be.* Then there was Aunt Patty, who was nearly as little as me and she could make Mummy giggle when Mummy was cross and Méme, who never smiled at me, even when I was being a good girl.

China was their cousin, and she wore a flowery housecoat and did all the cooking. I disliked her funny voice, too loud and gurgly like clotted cream and things I hated and her funny accent, maybe it was Chinese, she looked Chinese. China stirred great big bubbling pots that had funny smells and was always yelling *lunch* when I wasn't hungry, so I would run away and hide, but 'Penelope, Penelope, where are you, Penelope?' I was always dragged out of my hiding place and made to sit down at that great big table on an enormous chair piled with cushions; and there were always horrible green bits and bobs floating around in the soup in that big, dark room with its nasty brown chenille tablecloth hanging down all the way to the floor because Aunt Meg said men would get excited and not be able to contain themselves if they saw a table leg, because it would remind them of a ladies leg and I never wanted to eat and I tried to put that spoon in my mouth, but, 'I will be sick if I have to eat this. I'm not hungry. Please, can I leave the table? Pleeeease.'

***

The Aunties' house, Los Nisperos, had an inner courtyard with red, green and yellow tiles and thin green pillars rising all the way up to a skylight, and leading off the courtyard were doors to forbidden rooms. I remember a pen-and-ink cartoon of a crooked man with a big hooked nose wearing a frockcoat, 'That's Disraeli with Queen Victoria Penelope, dreadful man and Gladstone not much better', and above it a telephone dangling off a silk rope, 'Don't be naughty,

Penelope, don't touch, Penelope, naughty, don't touch, don't touch' that was for chatting to people who weren't there, 'Don't touch, don't touch, naughty', like the radio that had little people inside who sang to you, tiny ladies in long blue dresses, with golden hair, all smooth and shiny, and lipstick and soft voices but when I peeped in round the back . . . I couldn't see anybody. 'Tell me a story, tell me a story, tell me a story before you go to bed'. I believed people lived inside that telephone. Maybe Daddy was in there and I missed Daddy when Mummy and I visited the Aunties so when the big people went for their siesta, I slid out of bed, carried a heavy chair over, climbed up and carefully took the round black thing off the hook. It screamed at me, 'Número por favor! Numero!' There was an angry lady hiding inside who didn't speak English . . . she wanted a number and I didn't have a number – so I dropped it and she carried on screaching, 'número, número!' and I was terrified and ran away, far away, into a dark room crammed with little tables with lace doilies and big shells from the ocean and porcelain-coloured flowers and a little milk truck with tiny bottles in it and stacks of *Illustrated London News* and *The Wonder Book of Wonders* and hid under the table and wept waiting for the police to bang on the door and take me away, because I was a *bad, bad girl.*

***

Outside the Aunties' front door was a veranda with a swinging chair and a loquat tree with shiny leaves and disgusting little yellow fruit that made your tongue all furry and a water tower with a big metal ladder, 'Don't you dare go up that tower, Penelope; it'll be the death of you, you hear me'. But I wanted to see the whole world, and my cousin David was visiting and I was a big girl because I was four and he was only three and a half so I said to him, I said, 'Come outside, David; let's climb the water tower. 'So David came with me but when he saw how high, how very high the ladder was all the way to a big round yellow tank at the top, David said, 'I don't want to do it'; and I didn't want to do it anymore either, but I couldn't say so because David was a scaredy-cat not me, so I said, 'Come on, David', and he said, 'no, no', so I went up, one step at a time, one two three four, and I was very frightened and looked down and David was squinting up at me all serious with his floppy hair and I said 'go away', but he didn't go away so I carried on up, up, up; I looked down and David was still looking worried and I tried to say 'go away', but nothing came out, just a little squeak, and I went on, up, up, up, and I wet my pants a little bit and I looked down and David could see my knickers and I tried to say 'go away' again but it was a whisper and he couldn't hear me and I wanted to cry and I kept climbing up and up and up and what if Mummy or one of the Aunties came out and caught me they would say I was the 'absolute limit' and kill me and I would be dead and everyone would be sad and I went up and up and up past the loquat tree but my hands were all wet and sticky and slippery and I had to hold on tight and I looked down and David was still there and I wanted to let go so I could quickly be back down on the ground next to David and never be naughty again, baby

Jesus, help, please Jesus, help me, but I kept climbing and climbing until I got to the top and David was still there and I looked round very quickly something inside my mouth was bang, bang, banging in my ears and there was nothing to see nothing but sky and more houses all the same and I climbed down again as fast as I could.

***

My father's grandfather, Alfred Lovett, set off for Argentina from a big house in Richmond around 1870. There is a sepia photograph of him dressed as a gaucho up north next to some *cholas* in bunchy skirts and nobody knows what he did, but whatever it was, he made enough money to send for his German fiancée, Elsa Englebach. Alfred had met Elsa at a party just before he left London and fallen head over heels in love. Elsa's parents seemed to think nothing of sending their daughter all by herself on a ship to marry a virtual stranger on the other side of the world. When Alfred saw her ship approaching the Port of Buenos Aires, he was so desperate to welcome his beloved that he jumped onto the tugboat sent to guide her in, but unfortunately the sea was choppy, and like Dad, like me, like my youngest granddaughter Juliet, Alfred was a terrible sailor. When they drew up to the mother ship, Alfred scrambled up the rope ladder, collapsed in a sodden heap and vomited at her feet. The captain took pity and offered to return Elsa to Europe free of charge, but Elsa was made of strong stuff. She and Alfred had two children, my Granny Jessie, and Dad's Uncle Charlie, a brutish man Dad hated.

My maternal great-grandfather Alfred Lovett, his wife Elsa and my granny Jessie as a baby. Buenos Aires, (Family album), c.1895.

In 1909, Dad's father, Robert Gordon Woolcock, emigrated to Buenos Aires from Redruth in Cornwall, putting an ocean in between himself and the stepfather he loathed. Gordon found himself a job at the Bank of London and South America, now Lloyds Bank, and married Jessie Lovett. Gordon and Jessie had two sons, my dad John, and Uncle Peter. Grandpa Gordon retired to Worthing on the South Coast of England, proud that after forty years in Argentina he had only learnt a few words of Spanish, 'Una cerveza por favour. What? What? What?' Gordon was afraid that too much Spanish would make him 'go native'. Dad was afraid of his father when he was little and despised him as an adult.

Dad married my Mum, Peggy Forbes, and his brother Peter married her sister Ethel. Mum's sister Edith married Ronnie Fell, Betty married Jack Peters, Nita married Bobbie Lumsdaine, and Johnnie married the redhaired Lily Pettigrew. They were all members of the British community, born in Argentina, but they never considered themselves really Argentine or contemplated marrying anybody who was.

It just wasn't done.

***

When I was two years old, Unilever posted Dad from Buenos Aires to Uruguay and we slipped seamlessly into an identical British community in 'Monty', which is what we called Montevideo. It was a sleepy little city with gas guzzling, pastel-coloured Chevrolets and Impalas and ancient Ford T's cruising around little plazas with modest fountains, palm trees and statues of military men. Between the ages of five and thirteen I attended The British Schools, plural from the days when boys and girls were separate, known as 'The British'. On Saturdays we took the bus to the Montevideo Cricket Club where everyone spoke English like we did, played rugby in winter and cricket and swimming in Summer; on Sundays we trotted off to Sunday school or matins at Holy Trinity Anglican Church where the Reverend Isaacs confidently announced that the most important thing about the Church was that services started on time. We sang *All Things Bright and Beautiful*:

The rich man at his castle,
the poor man at his gate,
God made them high, or lowly,
and ordered their estate.

In 1964 Dad was posted back to Argentina where I boarded for a year at St Hilda's School for Girls in Hurlingham and eventually finished off an expensive and rather useless education as a day girl at Northlands School for Girls in Olivos. We were taught Spanish as a foreign language and sat 'O' and 'A' level exams that were mailed to England to be marked by the Cambridge Board. I managed to fail 'O' level art two years in a row.

***

My father, my Uncle Peter, and later my brother Colin boarded at St George's College in Quilmes close to the girls' school Mum and her sisters attended. The College, as it was known, was established in 1898 by Canon Stevenson, 'To give the boys a sound Christian upbringing in a country where the moral standards are so low.' It was run along the lines of an English public school, the Eton of South America, and poor Dad was bullied by other boys and tortured by teachers. I often begged him to regale me with insane stories about teachers thrashing small boys for minor misdemeanours and forcing them to stand on tiptoe, with their arms stretched above their heads holding heavy rifles for hours at a time. If their arms buckled, they were beaten again.

On Sunday nights the boys gathered to write the compulsory letter home. Dad kept one of his.

> *Dear Mummy and Daddy,*
> *It was very hot in chapel. Two people almost fainted it was so hot. It is very hot to go about in a suit and Eton collars. This afternoon we will go for a walk I suppose in this heat.*
>
> *Daddy is quite wrong about saying we have pillow fights in the dorm at nights as we are not allowed to move a toe, the captain is so strict. Mr. George is our gym master. When he gets angry, he shouts, 'Shut your noise, or I'll warm your behind for you.'*
>
> *I remain,*
> *Your affectionate son*
> *John*

For fuck's sake. I remain your affectionate son. When Moten says this shit is not good for us either, he is not joking.

In 1950, Perón outlawed corporal punishment in schools, an act widely seen as a dig at St George's. It was too late for Dad, but when my brother Colin went to St George's at the age of eight, they still had 'fagging', which compelled younger boys to act as personal servants to older prefects, but they were no longer allowed to cane them.

***

Jessie's brother, Daddy's Uncle Charlie, had a very low opinion of his nephew: 'That boy will never amount to anything'. Nobody was impressed when Dad won prizes for every academic subject, English and History, Science and Mathematics, Latin and Geography. Academic cleverness was literally nothing to write home about. John had grown over six foot by the time he was twelve and was too spindly to be good at rugger. He also had a choking stammer. When I say choking, I mean that he didn't simply repeat syllables, a word would get trapped at the back of his throat and make him gag. Dad said he could see the troublesome word ahead, flashing a red light, warning that it was going to trip him up and he would flip through every alternative he could think of in the vain hope that one of them would find its way out. He was deeply conservative in many ways, fond of the old cliché 'anybody under twenty-five who is not a socialist is a knave and anyone who remains one after that age is a fool', versions of which have been attributed to everyone from Edmund Burke to King Oscar of Sweden, but he was socially liberal. In 1936 he was editor of *The Democrat*, a school magazine that split from the official rag, actually called *The Fascist*, and he objected to the vicious antisemitism that was unremarkable at the time, vocally disagreed with apartheid South Africa and declared that being homosexual was like having blue eyes or brown eyes. During the dictatorship he was accused of 'breaking the colour bar' for inviting the Black Bishop of Togo to the English Club for a drink.

On prizegiving days, Mr Cuff, headmaster of St George's, feigned faux exhaustion when John Woolcock won every academic prize, handsome leather-bound books with beautiful, marbled edges and front and end pages. I saved several of them, the title and author stamped in gold on red-leather spines and on the front covers, a winged figure on horseback wielding a sword over the school motto: *Vestigia Nulla Retrorsum: Don't Turn Back*

We certainly never looked back.

John wrote poetry in his adolescence, a time of great unhappiness, during which, Uncle Peter told me, he had contemplated suicide. I found a scrap of flimsy paper in the tiny leather case where he kept his treasures.

I sometimes dream in poetry.
Blinding clear
And scintillating flashes of perfect ver
Crowd in my mind.

I didn't know Dad dreamt in poetry.

Stammerers are not afflicted when they sing or commit a text to memory, so he sang loudly and tunelessly and recited swathes of poetry and lines swim around my brain *silent upon a peak in Darien, the curse is come upon me, cried The Lady of Shalott, by the shore of Gitche Gumee, by the shining Big-Sea-Water, what immortal hand or eye shall frame thy fearful symmetry, I am the gate toward the sea: O sailor men, pass out from me! water water everywhere nor any drop to drink. Yea, I was desolate and bowed my head: I have been faithful to thee, Cynara! in my fashion.* If only I had listened less impatiently! If only you weren't dead, I would listen to you now. Daddy.

Dad was born into a philistine community where artistic pursuits were scorned, so he became an accountant like everybody else. Uncle Charlie warned him that if he didn't 'bloody well stop stammering', he faced a bleak future with the workhouse at the end of it. Jessie and Gordon packed him off to speech therapy clinics where he was forbidden to speak at all for days, then made to repeat 'ma-ma-ma' and 'da-da-da' like a baby until he was permitted to form a full sentence, upon which they pronounced this clever sensitive boy cured, and sent him home.

I found a sheaf of papers, browned with age and covered in Dad's distinctive handwriting. I suppose he was writing it for himself.

I wonder if anyone who has not active experience of it can realise the tortures of the damned that are the everyday lot of the habitual stammerer . . . The telephone rang (and if there was one thing I hated in those days, it was the telephone bell: who knew who was at the other end, and what he would think if I failed to blurt out my replies) and my father told me to answer it. I seized as an excuse the fact that I was on my way to do something, but he would have none of it and in peremptory tones ordered me to answer. What with the jangling of the bell and the barking tones of my father I was in a fine state of nerves when I picked up the receiver, and of course, spluttered out a very poor attempt at lucid speech and turned to face my father's wrath. 'I say now! Enough of that! Take a deep breath

> *man! What are you making faces for? Come, come, snap out of it you can talk properly if you want to! Why have we gone to the trouble of sending you to the clinic? You're a real disgrace, pull yourself together!'*

John finished school with top marks and no prospects, so Uncle Charlie arranged for a post as an office boy at Lever Brothers, rubbing his nose into how lucky he was to be employed when he couldn't even speak properly. When World War II broke out Dad volunteered to enlist in the British army, and it was a source of eternal shame that he had been rejected on medical grounds. Dad worked for Unilever until he retired, never daring to move on for fear of not getting another job. He said his proudest achievement was the day he was promoted over the highest position ever achieved by the now long-dead Uncle Charlie.

A cloud of unfulfilled promise hung over him. I felt guilty. If Daddy hadn't had to fork out school fees so that Colin and I didn't have to attend local schools with *these people here*, he could have been a poet instead of a chartered accountant. He said he would get down to his writing when Colin and I left school but by then it was too late, the dream was long gone, and he couldn't be bothered.

I was determined that would never happen to me.

***

By 1914 Argentina was the seventh richest country in the world, above France, Denmark, Sweden and Germany and only just below Britain and the United States. It had a literate, skilled immigrant population, an organised working class and a fabulously wealthy landowning elite. Families like the Martínez de Hoz, the Anchorenas and the Menéndez Behety called themselves the 'gente bién', the 'people who matter', and they shopped in Paris, London and Milan. Every estancia had a mansion and a huge garden adorned with imported plants, exotic birds and animals, artificial lakes, pools and tennis courts encircled by a protective shell of eucalyptus trees to hold off the gales that howled across the flat Pampas.

'Rich as an Argentine' was an expression at that time.

Argentina has slid to ninety-third in the world rankings.

***

Uncle Johnny's wife Lily Pettigrew, had a younger sister, Sylvia, who I met only once when we were living in Montevideo. Sylvia was nine years younger than Lily with the same red hair and pale-green eyes. I could tell she had been dragged to our boring, little house against her will, and she was sullen in a pair of sky-blue slacks with a zip at the side and a loose pale-pink shirt with a frilly collar and pearl buttons. I had somehow picked up that Sylvia was naughty, and I imagined her with a car-mechanic boyfriend, devilishly handsome with grease stains on his overalls and hands that slid around, touching her, touching me where I didn't want to be touched. I was a gawky ten-year-old, and I was desperate for her to pay me some attention because I suspected that I was going to be naughty too, and I needed someone to tell me it would be all right.

Sylvia completely ignored me.

When we all went in for tea, she remained outside by herself, standing under the willow tree at the bottom of our small patch of grass, legs wide apart, gazing into the distance with her pale eyes. I could tell she despised us. I was a little afraid of her, she was nothing like the other ladies I knew. In fact, she wasn't like a lady at all.

In 1979 a few days after the Dover barbecue when Ian Dover was desperate to kick bereaved women in their backsides and I had kept my trap shut, Mum and I were in the kitchen and she handed me a glass of freshly squeezed orange juice with a queer expression. I couldn't work out what it meant.

'Sylvia's gone.'

I was startled, 'Where's she gone?'

Everything went very bright; the sun poured through the little balcony window. Mum pursed her lips and sighed in that special way that meant she didn't want to talk about it.

'What d'you mean? Gone? Gone where?'

'All I know is that she was making bombs in her kitchen.' Her little boy pleaded with her', Mum was a good mimic and turned herself into a bleating child – 'Mamá, porqué hacemos esto?' Why are we doing this?' And Sylvia replied, 'For the revolution.'

I tried to take this in.

'How do you know this conversation took place? Were you there?'

Mum admitted she was not, nor was anybody else, as far as she knew.

'Was there a court case, witnesses, evidence and a jury that found her guilty?'

'I suppose not.'

'Why do you believe it then?'

Mum shrugged. *Hmm.* I knew that expression, lips pursed and a little head movement, down and to the side.

'Lily's cousin Henry has a contact high up in the navy. He enquired about her and the man said, 'Sylvia está borrada. No pregunte más. Sylvia's been rubbed out. No more questions.'

Sylvia had been making bombs in her kitchen and that was that. Her four small children were taken in by a neighbour.

In 1979 the word *dictatorship* was forbidden but the junta was fully in control. Just as we were taught that Columbus had 'discovered' a continent where eighty million people were already living, the Argentine military junta ordered news outlets and the entire population to refer to it as 'The Process of National Reorganisation' – *El Proceso* for short. El Proceso was reluctantly engaged in a 'Dirty War', to rinse out subversion and corruption and confirm Argentina's place in the Western Christian world.

Around thirty thousand people disappeared with no formal arrests or trials. Even ultra-conservative, law-abiding families like mine were touched by it.

But Sylvia was only an aunt by marriage, and she had been making bombs in her kitchen.

***

I decided to head out of the suburbs and join the Madres de Plaza de Mayo for their silent protest. I was pretty sure they met on Tuesday afternoons, but this was long before the internet and I had nobody to ask.

I told Dylan and Mum I was going shopping and left them playing canasta while I took the General Mitre train from Martinez, rattling through the northern suburbs, La Lucila, Olivos, Vicente Lopez, Rivadavia, Nuñez, Belgrano and Lisandro de La Torre, finally speeding through the Villa 31 slum before the main Retiro Terminal.

I wanted to walk for Sylvia.

By this time my politics had aligned with what I imagined hers had been, and I believed that Sylvia had suffered the fate waiting for me if I had stayed in Argentina.

I walked up to Plaza de Mayo with my heart in my mouth. If I died, Dylan would have to live with my parents and be sent to St George's, and he would be angry with me for the rest of his life for taking risks that left him orphaned.

***

The Casa Rosada, the magnificent pink presidential palace, was on my left, guarded by a couple of *granaderos* in shiny uniforms and one solitary policeman. The Plaza de Mayo was otherwise completely empty. I contemplated asking the policeman if this was the day the Madres came. Idiot. It was December, early summer in Argentina, a lovely, warm day unlike the sweltering, enervating, damp heat of February, when your clothes stick to your bum. I strolled around hesitantly, anxious that the policeman was eyeing me suspiciously. I looked up at the balcony from which President

Juan Perón had addressed crowds in his heyday, standing next to the beautiful Evita, arms wide open, like those waving golden cats with red collars they sell in Chinatown. I felt the policeman's eyes on me and quickly looked down in case it was obvious that I was thinking about Perón and Evita. I feigned an elaborate interest in a pigeon landing on the equestrian statue of Manuel Belgrano waving an Argentine flag next to mop-headed palm trees. A couple of dapper businessmen with gelled hair and handkerchiefs folded in their jacket pockets strolled past jauntily, chatting about some *boludo* who had annoyed them. I decided to retreat down Calle Florida to see if I could find the radical Instituto Di Tella building where I'd had my eyes opened to op art, agit-prop theatre, and left-wing politics. I knew that President Onganía had shut it down in 1970 as part of his campaign against 'immoralism'. As his successor, General Rafael Videla, explained a few years later, 'A terrorist is not just someone with a gun or a bomb, but also someone who spreads ideas that are contrary to Western and Christian civilisation.'

The Instituto Di Tella had completely disappeared but Harrods with its marble staircase and cedar flooring still stood impressive on the corner of Florida and San Martín. I strolled back to Plaza de Mayo very slowly, three times, but there were no signs of any Madres. Eventually I gave up and trudged back to Retiro, across the Plaza San Martín, down the hill to the English Clock modelled on Big Ben, where the English slave market had once been, and took the train back to the suburbs.

Back in England, I learnt that the Madres walked on Thursdays not Tuesdays.

***

Bodies have been recovered from mass graves, dredged out of the sea or washed up on the coast of Uruguay, but most of the disappeared were rubbed out like Sylvia. These days there are thousands of headshots of young people on black and white posters, in artworks, on murals and in the ESMA, the torture centre which has become a museum of memory.

The current vice-president of Argentina, Victoria Villarruel, daughter of one of the junta generals, is calling for the museum to be closed.

***

On the poem's page of my British School autograph book, Martha wrote: *When you get married and have twins don't come to me for safety pins.* Jennifer Jones wrote, *God made the niggers, he made them in the night, he made them in a hurry and forgot to make them white*; and R. A. Fullerton - who wore glasses and had a scarily thin dad we had to tip-toe around because he'd only been given a spoonful of rice a day in a Japanese prisoner of war camp and now had a terrible temper - Robert wrote, *Once there was a cassowary on the plains of Timbuctoo and he ate a missionary skin and bones and hymn book too.*

I thought a cassowary was a Black man.

It is a bird.

I knew nothing about anything.

***

In 1990, a few years after the fall of the dictatorship, I visited my parents again. I was eating lunch in the large communal dining hall at the headquarters of the Trotskyist Movimiento al Socialismo, MAS, sitting opposite a short, cheerful trade union activist from Cordoba. He chuckled, 'I was lucky because I was arrested officially, so my family knew where I was. The worst part was when they made us sweep our cells and eat the sweepings. We had woollen mattresses that shed tufts of wool everywhere and I tell you, the wool and all the little sticks and dust really stuck in your throat.'

He laughed again.

This man had taken part in the Cordobazo, radical uprisings in a northern town two weeks after I left Argentina in May 1968 and then again in 1971. After the 1976 coup, they no longer bothered with formal arrests. *Los chupaban,* they 'sucked them up', secretly, in full view. It was a spectacle of violence that disappeared before the applause started. There were always eyewitnesses, but they didn't see anything. When it's best not to see what you see, then you 'unsee it'. Like Mum, they did not want to know what they knew.

I am slowly understanding that those Mum called 'these people here' were European settlers just like we were. We weren't special. We were immigrants trying to make a buck like everyone else and we had all arrived at around the same time.

There is a process of decentring that makes us see the world in a different way. I hear the Korean artist Do Ho Suh laughing about the phrase, 'The Far East. Far from where?'

***

Mummy sent me to school several months later than everyone else because she'd had my baby brother Colin and couldn't pull herself together to take me. Postnatal depression wasn't a thing in those days. I arrived at school utterly bewildered; friendship groups had already formed and everyone knew what they were supposed to do. Diana Beare and Bruce Coates were the clever clogs, sticking their hands straight up eagerly answering every question while I tossed around on a great grey sea, drowning.

I wept all day. I cried leaving the house before getting on the school bus, on the bus, at playtime and often during lessons. I couldn't help it. I learnt to read quickly but the books were so boring, Jane was always helping Mummy in the kitchen; I didn't want to help Mummy in the kitchen, and I didn't like the way Peter bossed her around either: 'Jump, Jane! Jump!'

One morning, my teacher, Miss Rathbone, who had wavy blond hair and a big fake smile, read us the story of the *Three Little Pigs and the Big Bad Wolf.* I sat quivering on my little yellow wooden chair, feeling the wind howling across the classroom and the rain on my face as the wolf huffed and he puffed and he blew my house down, his teeth, his teeth, sharp and pointed like a witch's tit, his long red tongue licking me, tenderising my flesh so he could gobble me up, biting my head off, ripping off my arm, tearing at my tummy. I heard a howl come out from somewhere deep inside me. A teaching assistant, with jet-black hair scraped into a bun and a thin red lip-sticked mouth, yanked me roughly off my tiny yellow chair and dragged me out of the classroom, hissing: 'You're spoiling it for everybody!'

My greatest fears were reserved for our headmistress, Mrs Nery. She had a bony face, a hooked nose and wore thin crumpled cardigans over sad, pointy breasts. She taught us arithmetic, but I couldn't retain a word she said because I was convinced she was a witch. When she spoke, I froze, petrified, convinced that she was going to throw me alive into the bubbling cauldron boiling away in her disgusting hovel. Mrs. Nery was a cannibal, and I am still innumerate.

***

I came home from school reciting: 'Eeny, meeny, miny, mo / catch a nigger by his toe / if he hollers, let him go / eeny, meeny, miny, mo'. Daddy and Mummy said it wasn't kind and I must say 'tiger' instead. I was indignant. Why did I have to say 'tiger'? I didn't even know what the other word meant.

I didn't think I had ever met a Black person.

***

When I dug out my first British School class photograph to check whether I had correctly remembered Mrs

Rathbone's wavy blond hair and big teeth (I had), to my surprise, there I am, beaming in the middle row, standing right next to a small Black girl. I immediately remembered her name was Maya and that we were friendly, bonded by our fear of Mrs Nery.

The British School, Montevideo, Uruguay. Penny fourth from left in the middle row, (Family album), 1955.

I slip back in time, Maya and I stand together on the edge of the big concrete playground, watching other more confident children dashing about shrieking; we were so very tiny, and the world was so huge and bewildering, two little specks of dust on a great tide of unknowing. Other children understood the rules of a game, we didn't even know the name of the game and we shrank smaller and smaller, drowning in terror and nothingness. Maya left Uruguay at the end of that year, and I never saw her again.

She was the only Black girl in my eleven years at school, and I forgot her.

I remember her now.

***

At the end of that year, during the summer holidays, I decided to stop crying forever. I was six. I made Mummy cut off my pigtails, and I strutted into school with dry eyes. I had a boyfriend, Eddie Suarez, who was skinny with freckles and big ears, and he chased me around the playground trying to kiss me. One day Eddie asked whether I knew what had happened to that girl who cried all the time. I told him she had 'left the school'. And in a way that was true. She turned up in my dreams sometimes, wide-eyed and afraid, but during the day she never came near me.

Our friends were other settler families, the Campbells, the Hylands, the Henmans, the Olivers, the Dees, the Days and the Ellis's. I knew that we were poor because we were poorer than most of my friends but obviously not as poor as the *cabecitas negras*, who some people called 'darkies'. Many of my school friends lived in big houses with large gardens and swimming pools, while I shared a bedroom with my brother, and we only had a threadbare backyard with a wonky willow tree. We lived a block away from Pocitos Beach, where we made sandcastles and swam in the sea, apart from times when the council spewed untreated sewage into the sea and then lumps of poo bobbed about on the waves, and we laughed and screamed and ran back to our beach umbrellas, where Mum always sat because she couldn't swim very well. Sometimes the sea was brown, but at other times the ocean flowed in green and fresh from the Atlantic and schools of silver porpoises swooped and dived and we oohed and aahed until blooms of magical, transparent, big jelly fish and little tiny ones we called semolina stung us all over our legs.

***

Daddy read two newspapers every day, one in Spanish, one English. On January 17, 1961, the headline was 'Lumumba Muerto' under a photograph of a Black man with a neat bow tie, glasses and a centre parting. Perhaps I remember it so vividly because black faces only appeared in print during carnival, dancing down the street in fancy dress, maybe it was his tie, Dad loved a bow tie, I don't know but that photograph blew around the wastelands of my memory along with other things that didn't make any sense.

In Montevideo, Daddy worked for Atkinsons. Before J & E Atkinson was acquired by Lever Brothers in 1920, they sold pots of pomade, made of bears' grease and 'perfumed with otto of roses distilled from fresh petals' out of a shop off Bond Street in London. In 1927 Atkinsons set up a small factory in Montevideo making Lux soap, English lavender water and eau de cologne. At home we were always loyal to the Lever products that paid Daddy's wages, Mummy dabbed English lavender water behind her ears, we washed ourselves with Lux soap, each bar individually wrapped and decorated with a picture of a smiling Sophia Loren next to a blush-pink rose, and we brushed our teeth with Pepsodent. It was decades before I could buy a tube of Colgate, made by arch-rival Palmolive, without a twinge of guilt.

I believed soap was made out of soap.

Palm oil is the main ingredient in Lux soap, 'used by nine out of ten film stars'. Up to 50 percent of supermarket commodities, beauty products and food – contain palm oil, but it is listed as ethyl palmitate, octyl palmitate and glyceryl. There are over two hundred names for palm oil but only 10 percent of them use the word *palm*.

In 1911, two years after the death of King Leopold II of Belgium, Unilever expanded into the Congo under the name Huileries du Congo Belge. The sickening atrocities committed under King Leopold's despotic rule are well documented and photographed. Leopold oversaw a reign of terror in which amputations of hands and feet and lashings with the *chicotte* – a whip fashioned out of hippopotamus hide, trimmed like a corkscrew with razor sharp edges – were routine punishments for men, women and small children who failed to meet unrealistic quotas.

Ten million people, around half the population, were murdered.

A holocaust.

I am sure stories of Congolese resistance exist, if not in libraries, then in songs and dreams and living memory but I haven't found them. Easier to unearth are campaigns by prominent Western writers, including Mark Twain and Arthur Conan Doyle, the Irish nationalist Roger Casement, and George Washington Williams, a resolute Baptist minister, that eventually tarnished Leopold's international reputation.

After Leopold's death, the Belgian State took over administration of the Congo from the Crown, which had run it as a private business and set about polishing a shiny new image. William Lever from Bolton in Lancashire was the perfect choice – an enlightened employer who paid his workers decent wages and built them Port Sunlight, a model village in Merseyside, England.

Unilever, where Dad spent his working life, was offered two million acres of terra nullius in Congo. These were tribal lands, but the people who lived there were not judged to have altered the land in any permanent way, so they had no legal rights. Lever's company forced tens of thousands of Congolese people into compulsory labour as palm cutters and set them quotas with no regard to seasonal cultivation times, and when they failed to achieve their targets or reneged on their legal obligation to work, they were thrashed with the chicotte and jailed. Amputation was no longer used because William Lever couldn't see the logic in maiming his workforce and rendering them permanently incapable of holding a machete. Unlike Leopold, who never set foot in Africa, William Lever visited the Congo many times, sailing up and down the river under a mosquito net, boasting that his social work in the Huileries was second only to Port Sunlight.

Lever Brothers continued these forced labour practices right up to and beyond Congolese independence. In 2009 Unilever sold all its shares to Feronia, a company registered in the Cayman Islands, leaving millions of unpaid wages. Whippings and prison sentences continue to this day.

In 1960, when Congolese independence from Belgium was won, King Baudouin made a speech praising the genius of his great-grandfather Leopold. The new prime minister,

Patrice Lumumba, six years and one day younger than Mum, was galvanised into responding with an impromptu speech:

> 'For this independence of the Congo, although being proclaimed today by agreement with Belgium, an amicable country, with which we are on equal terms, no Congolese worthy of the name will ever be able to forget that it was by fighting that it has been won, a day-to-day fight, an ardent and idealistic fight, a fight in which we were spared neither privation nor suffering, and for which we gave "our strength and our blood. We are proud of this struggle, of tears, of fire, and of blood, to the depths of our being, for it was a noble and just struggle, and indispensable to put an end to the humiliating slavery which was imposed upon us by force.'

Lumumba was denounced by the international press for what they called this 'venomous attack'. Ten weeks later, he was overthrown in a CIA-backed coup and assassinated in the presence of Belgian officials. Belgian officers hacked Lumumba to pieces and dissolved his body in a barrel of sulphuric acid.

One officer kept a single gold-capped tooth as a trophy.

On September 10, 2020, a Belgian judge ruled that Lumumba's remains, this solitary tooth, be returned to his family in the Democratic Republic of Congo. The ceremony took place on June 20, 2022. The current King Philippe, despite professing his regret over past cruelties, gave the ceremony a miss.

***

In Montevideo, during our long summer holidays, for forty days from the end of January, dark-skinned young men burst out of poor neighbourhoods and swarmed around suburban streets playing drums all night in groups we incorrectly called *murgas.* Only poor people 'swarm', invading places where they don't belong. Normal people just go to places. The drumming was loud, sexy and dangerous, disturbing the subdued silences of our quiet streets. Mummy and Daddy, often so different from each other, were as one, complaining about 'this dreadful racket,' gritting their teeth and longing for it to be over. Tacka, tacka, tacka, tacka, *Tack*! Tacka, tacka, tacka, tacka, *Tack*!

I loved carnival. I lay in bed until the drumming stopped in the early hours, wide awake on clean ironed sheets in my crisp, clean, ironed pyjamas, tucked in tight under brown blankets with a satin cream stripe along the edge, topped by an eiderdown with tiny pink flowers. I hated that eiderdown. I was spotless, my teeth, my hair, my fingernails, behind my ears, everything was spotless. The murgas gave me a funny feeling in my lower tummy that I got when Peggy Lee crooned 'Fever' from our pile of 78s.

He gives me fever
With his kisses,
Fever when he holds me tight,
Fever!
I'm his missus,
Daddy, won't you treat him right?

Colin and I ran up and down our street with other neighbourhood kids in fancy dress, squirting water at each other out of little squeezy plastic bottles, getting bolder until we dared chuck whole buckets at furious grown-ups and scarpered laughing our heads off.

Colin had a clown costume and Mummy bought me a pink tulle dress with a tiny wand and glittering wings, which I loathed. I was obsessed with dressing up as a tramp, a *bichicome,* in Daddy's dirty, old boiler suit, splashed with paint and oil, a filthy hat and a stick over my shoulder with a handkerchief tied to the end of it. As I ran off, Mummy stood tearfully at the gate, 'Penny why can't you be a fairy like all the other little girls?' I honestly didn't know why I couldn't be a fairy like all the other little girls, I was the cuckoo in the nest, and for many years I was convinced I'd been adopted.

On the last weekend of carnival, we stood with the crowds on the Ramblas watching the *corsos* with floats and dancers, highly decorated trucks and gigantic plaster heads called *cabezones* that chased us when we taunted them. On the final day, the last truck rolled up carrying the beautiful Queen of Carnival sitting in clouds of chiffon, clutching a gold painted sceptre, wearing red lipstick and a sparkling diamante crown. I was shocked when Daddy snorted, 'She's just a bloody maid from the Cerro'. The Cerro was the hill where the poorest people lived, and we never dared go anywhere near it.

Carnival was my only taste of the wild. It was a crack through which I glimpsed another possible world. The *murgas* hinted at something that was missing where I lived, something I feared and longed for.

***

I never danced with the murgas but Mummy made me attend Scottish Highland dancing lessons once a week. I was a tomboy and hated girly things, so I protested loudly about wearing a kilt, basically another name for a skirt, but I had fun hurtling around dancing the Eightsome Reel, the Dashing White Sergeant, Strip the Willow and the Highland Fling for the Children's Caledonian Ball in October. Our group won a prize and we were presented with little plastic Scottish dolls in clear plastic tubes; I treasured mine for years, gazing at her tiny white face and red lips, her little bagpipes, tiny kilt and furry hat. Mummy often reminded me I was quarter Scottish.

When I finally arrived in London, I was dismayed to see thousands of copies of my precious doll stacked with all the other cheap tat in the tourist traps around Piccadilly Circus.

***

I was keen to join the Brownies because Jenny Hyland, my best friend, worst friend, my *frenemy*, was joining too. Auntie Betty Whitaker was our Brown Owl. We called all our parent's friends Auntie and Uncle even when we weren't related to them, but when we were at Brownies, we called Auntie Betty, Brown Owl. Brown Owl allocated us to packs called Sixes, and I was extremely put out when she made me a Pixie because I wanted to be an Elf like Jenny or a Fairy like Virginia or even a Sprite. Each Six had a special treasure box on a shelf in Brown Owl's dark garage, which we were forbidden to open until we had made our 'Promise'.

Six weeks and many good deeds later, I was ready in my new brown uniform, brown belt and toggled gold bandana. I stood up straight, proudly raised my right hand to my shoulder, put my thumb over my little fingernail and fourth finger, raised my index and middle fingers and repeated the vow I had doggedly memorised, 'I promise that I will do my best to do my duty to God, to serve the Queen and my country, to help other people and do a good deed every day.'

I was deeply confused about 'my country'. Was my country the England I read about in The Secret Seven and Famous Five stories I devoured? I had never been there, but apparently it was a sunny, green place where girls could have proper adventures. Obviously, I wanted to be tomboy George and not boring Ann who had nothing to say for herself. I didn't think my country was Uruguay; we were only living there to show *these people* how to behave even though they didn't want to listen; or even Argentina where Mummy, Daddy and I were born and my great aunts and Mummy's sisters Edith and Nita and my crazy cousin Patsy still lived? I loved the way Buenos Aires smelt of petrol and the way people beeped their horns and yelled at each other the whole time, but I didn't think it was my country.

As soon as I made my Brownie vow, I raced off to investigate the secret Pixie box. It was up there with life's great disappointments. Instead of treasure, all it held were a few manky feathers, some crumpled gold sweet wrappings and a few pebbles. Jenny and the Elves were smirking, gloating over their booty while I skulked by myself. I waited until the land was clear and, heart in mouth, sneaked a peek into the Elf, Fairy and Sprite boxes. There was only bits of rubbish in them too. Jenny was lying!

Jenny's family were Roman Catholic because her father's grandparents had emigrated to Uruguay from Ireland. I was a tomboy, so I didn't mind missing out on wearing a frilly white dress for my First Communion, but I was jealous about confession, anxious that I was missing out on interesting sins. My life was excruciatingly uneventful, and I suspected there might be something really naughty I could be getting up to if only I knew what it was. I pestered Jenny to tell me what she revealed to the priest, but she remained tight-lipped. Finally, during a sleepover, I badgered her until she caved and told me she confessed to telling fibs and pulling her sister's hair.

Another massive let down!

***

At school we called people 'Indian givers' if they gave you something and later demanded it back. Private property was an article of faith. This is mine. That's yours. Mine. Yours. Mainly mine. It was natural. We never imagined there might be other ways of living.

In his logbook, Admiral Columbus records his astonishment at the strange attitude Indigenous people had to private property: 'If one asks for anything they have, they never say no. On the contrary, they offer a share to anyone with demonstrations of heartfelt affection.' He was a bit concerned that trading bells, glass beads, feathers and bits of broken crockery for gold was cheating ignorant savages, but the Taino and other Indigenous peoples were baffled by the Christian obsession with gold. Gold is a useless soft metal, a bauble like feathers and beads and other shiny things. Columbus's son Hernando Colón reports on visiting a village:

> 'On entering these houses, the Indians whom the Admiral brought from Isabela promptly seized anything that pleased them and the owners showed no sign of resentment. They seemed to hold all possessions in common. Similarly, whenever any of the natives went up to a Christian, they took from him whatever they liked in the belief that similar customs obtained among us. But they were quickly undeceived when they saw that this was not the case.'

They realised their mistake.

In his *Four Voyages*, Amerigo Vespucci remarked:

> 'They are quite content with what nature freely offers them. They are by nature so very generous that they never deny anything that is asked of them and do not value gold, nor pearls, nor gems, nor such other things as we consider precious here in Europe.

Thomas More's *Utopia*, published in 1516, takes the form of a conversation between More and a traveller returning from the New World. More had certainly read Vespucci's *Four Voyages* and might have come across Columbus's logbooks, but more significantly, he wrote *Utopia* in the busy Belgian port city of Antwerp, where ideas flowed across the Atlantic on ships sailing back and forth from the New World. In More's *Utopia*, gold is regarded as silly, far less valuable than the 'greatest blessings, like earth, air, and water.' Utopians make gold chamber pots to piss in and punish criminals by making them walk around adorned with gold crowns, rings and necklaces, like great big stupid babies.

The traveller says:

> 'I don't see how you can ever get any real justice or prosperity, so long as there's private property, and everything's judged in terms of money . . . unless you're prepared to call a country prosperous, in which all the wealth is owned by a tiny minority – who aren't entirely happy even so, while everyone else is simply miserable.'

***

I worried about going to hell. I believed that when I died, God, a huge unsmiling grey-haired man in a shiny white robe, would force me to sit on a white cloud next to my sniggering classmates while he played them a film of edited highlights of every embarrassing thing I had ever done. I pooed. I picked my nose. I had once stolen an election brooch from a blazer in the changing room and returned it after a sleepless night. I had bad thoughts about Mummy who I loved less than I loved Daddy, although I always pretended I didn't. I was a monster.

But what real horrors were lurking in the shadows of these trivial misdemeanours?

***

The Spanish Dominican missionary Bartolomé de Las Casas tells the story of Hatuey, a local cacique who fled to Cuba from Haiti to escape from the 'Christians'. He was captured and tied to a stake to be burned alive. A Franciscan friar promised that if he converted to Christianity, he would go straight to Heaven and eternal rest...

> 'If not he would be consigned to Hell, where he would endure everlasting pain and torment. The Lord Hatuey thought for a short while and then asked the friars whether Christians went to heaven. When he discovered this was indeed the case, he chose to go to Hell to ensure that he would never again have to clap eyes on those cruel brutes.'

Initially a slave owner, Las Casas was increasingly horrified by the cruelty of his countrymen and became a staunch defender of Indigenous rights. He witnessed 'Indians' welcoming Christians with food and gifts and then 'without the slightest provocation, butchered before my eyes, some three thousand souls - men women and children - as they sat there in front of us.' He saw hundreds commit suicide, seven thousand children dying of famine while their parents worked in the mines and others hunted down like dogs until the island was transformed into 'one vast, barren wasteland.'

It was 'a different time' is an excuse reliably paraded to justify prejudice, violence, enslavement, rape and racism. But five hundred years ago, there were those like Las Casas, who kept their humanity and saw what was going on in front of their eyes. When Las Casas woke up, he released the Indigenous people he had enslaved but kept the Africans until he understood how utterly immoral this was and released them, too. After that he was relentless.

***

By 1503, the Spanish had established the encomienda, a system by which each conquistador was presented with a parcel of land and ownership of the 'Indians' living there who were forced to pay the new owner a tribute and work for nothing.

Seven years later, the Council of Castile wrote *the Requerimiento,* to be read out loud in Latin by the conquistadors as they galloped up to ravage a village. *The Requerimiento* was a Latin ultimatum, a language not even the conquistadores understood, demanding that the 'Indians' accept Spanish rule and convert to Christianity, warning that if they did not, they and their families would be enslaved and everything taken from them and they would be killed.

Then they destroyed the village.

Over several decades, theologians in Europe earnestly debated whether 'Indians' were social beings with rights, capable of self-governance, and whether Christians invading villages shouting incomprehensible ultimatums were justified in enslaving and killing those who disobeyed.

Bartolomé de Las Casas never abandoned his principles; he refused confession and absolution to slave owners on their deathbeds if they refused to release those they enslaved. In 1537, he persuaded Pope Paul III to accept the full humanity of the 'Indians to enjoy their freedom and the possession of their own things and not be enslaved.'

Enslavement and genocide continued anyway.

***

In 1550, the Holy Roman Emperor King Charles V organised the Valladolid debate to settle the question of whether the invasion of the Americas was a 'just' war. Spanish philosopher and theologian Juan Ginés de Sepulveda was the apologist for the conquest. He acknowledged that the usual causes for a just war had not been met. The war was not reparation for an injustice because the 'Indians' had not attacked first; recovery of stolen treasure and property was not a defence because the 'Indians' had stolen nothing. Sepulveda rested his case on Aristotle's notion of *natural slavery,* arguing that some people exist in a condition of natural servitude and their inferiority justifies their subjugation. Although Sepulveda had never visited the Americas, he determined that 'Indians' were barbarians who committed sins against nature, including cannibalism, idolatry and sodomy. 'They adore the belly and the most abhorrent parts of the body as God and have as religion or virtue the pleasures of the body, as if they had admired the sky, always on the ground, prone to the habits of pigs.' The worship of idols was the greatest sin, and the innocent needed to be protected from barbarism, therefore 'Indians' must be subjugated to make them docile enough to accept the gospel.

The Spanish Dominican Francisco de Vitoria also supported the conquest, although he disagreed with both the legality of the Requerimiento and the Aristotelian concept of natural slavery. He argued that the Pope had no jurisdiction over barbarians and accepted that 'every country is full of sinners' and that many Christians committed the same sins as the 'Indians'. Vitoria defended the conquest as a just war based on the principle of free trade and travel, upholding the right of the Spanish to exploit and trade natural resources wherever they found them.

Bartolomé de Las Casas did not concur, and he did not do so briefly. His speech lasted five whole days in which he claimed that Spanish invaders were the real barbarians and because of their cruel actions, 'the native peoples of all parts of the Indies where we entered, have the acquired right to lead an extremely just war against us and to remove us from the face of the earth, and this right will last until the Day of Judgement!'

They have a right to remove us from the face of the earth.

***

When I attended the Adelaide Film Festival several years ago, I was struck by a curious ritual before every cultural event. We would chat, sipping glasses of chilled Chardonnay until a tinkling ordered a hush and there'd be an awkward pause for a few words honouring the people on whose stolen land we were standing. Sometimes an Aboriginal person was there to remind us of ... something. We refrained from drinking for a minute or two, guilty as charged, the uninvited guests, the gate crashers, the burglars, suddenly too big, too white, too fat, too present, feeling a brief unease, a moment of expiation, *mea culpa, mea culpa, mea culpa.*

Then we'd recover and carry on chatting and drinking.

***

A former steelworker told me a joke:

> A man goes for a walk. The landowner accosts him and tells him to get off his land. The man asks, 'How did you get the land?'
>
> 'My father left it to me.'
>
> 'And how did he get it?'
>
> 'His father left it to him.'
>
> 'And how did he get it?'
>
> 'His father left it to him.'
>
> 'And how did he get it?'
>
> 'His father left it to him.'
>
> 'And how did he get it?'
>
> 'Why, he fought for it!'
>
> The man takes off his coat, 'I'll fight you for it now, you bastard!'

***

In Grenada in 1651, the entire Kalinago population, men, women and children, followed their Chief Karouane and threw themselves off a cliff at the end of the island, choosing death over living as slaves. It's one of the 'things to do', recommended by the Grenadian Tourist Board. Tourists flock to Leaper's Hill or Carib's Leap to commemorate the event, and artist Steve McQueen made an art film about it.

But it turns out that only forty warriors leapt to their deaths in Grenada, not the entire population. Rubbing things out makes things simpler. On the left, we shed tears, and on the right, they say it was a long time ago and these people were on the way out anyway.

There was slaughter and rape and torture on a catastrophic scale, but it was not a total erasure. People resisted, some of them survived, and their descendants demand justice. There is still a case to be answered.

That's what nobody wants to deal with.

***

At the British School in Montevideo, we had soft exercise books to practice our writing. I have a vivid memory of a tiny line drawing at the bottom right of every page, a bare-chested 'Indian', his head bowed, squatting on one knee with an arrow in his back. His name was Tabaré. But when I posted on the British School Facebook page to see whether anybody else remembered, I drew a blank. Then Marcela Dutra, sitting on the far left of the bottom row in our class photograph, with an endearing little plaster on her knee, did a more efficient search and posted a picture of our exercise books showing a cover colour plate of Tabaré, sprawled across a riverbank clutching his heart, head flung back, his magnificent feather headdress fanned out on the grass.

Tabaré is the eponymous tragic hero of a fictional epic poem written in 1878, the year of the Conquest of the Desert in Argentina. Tabaré, mestizo son of a Charrúa chief and a white woman, falls in love with the beautiful Blanca, sister of the conquistador Don Gonzalo de Orgaz. When Blanca is kidnapped by another Charrúa chief, Tabaré risks his life to return her to Don Gonzalo, who blames him for the kidnapping and kills him.

Blanca means 'white'.

***

By the time I was eight, school had become more bearable, but I was still petrified of the dreaded Mrs Nery. One morning, dear Miss Sandiford picked me to debate with Alan Cordery. Alan and I faced each other at the front of the class on a raised dais on opposite sides of the teacher's table while Miss Sandiford sat in my chair. I was bursting for a wee, but to my horror, Mrs Nery slipped in to observe the class, and I didn't dare ask to be excused. Alan Cordery launched into his speech. I can see him now with his square head and straight blond hair, spick and span in his blazer with the British School badge that his mum had sewn on the top pocket. Alan had once slipped me a folded note hidden inside a little trapdoor he had ingeniously carved into a rubber. It read I LOVE YOU. I promptly wrote back I HATE YOU. I barely heard a word of Alan's argument because I was concentrating too hard on holding in my pee. When it was my turn, I launched into a tirade about taxing peasants, but as I was saying, 'But the farmers need the milk' - Oh, those lines are still crystal clear sixty-six years later, warm wee gushed out and down through my knickers, flooding the bloomers we wore over them, pouring down my thighs, soaking my knee-length socks and splashing into and around my shoes. In a way it was a relief. I continued orating without missing a beat.

When I ran out of steam, Mrs Nery left the classroom without looking back. I returned to my seat and spent the rest of the lesson gazing at my puddle of wee.

***

Peedelee is what we called Punta Del Este. To this day, it remains a resort for global jetsetters near the mouth of the estuary where the River Plate pours into the Atlantic and the water is always fresh and green. Rich Argentines and affluent British community families holidayed in Punta, while salaried families like mine, rented summer houses in the more modest Parque del Plata, where we roamed around the pine forests and sand dunes and taught ourselves to dive into the waves to avoid being dragged down by the undercurrent and scraped along the sand.

The Ellis's and the Campbells rented houses near ours. One time I went for a walk with Daddy and Auntie Heather and she pointed to a row of little houses farther down the beach and remarked chattily, 'They're all dirty Jews down there.' Daddy harumphed. 'Well, well, well, no, no, no, well, I say!' I always wished he would keep quiet and not stick up for these people. It was embarrassing. In the 1950s nobody ever mentioned the European

Holocaust, we talked about 'The War', admired the Queen Mother for looking the East End in the eye and watched films about plucky British soldiers and dastardly Jerries. Grandpa was fond of saying that the 'only good German is a dead German.'

Heather ignored Daddy's harumphing, 'They call themselves Rose! Ha! Rosenbaum, more like! Have you seen their noses?' Auntie Heather was statuesque and had red hair and freckles and told us wonderful made-up stories about two boys called Jack and Bill. Daddy found Heather very attractive, which drove Mummy mad, but Heather's long-suffering husband, Lesley, didn't seem to mind at all. That wasn't surprising because years later it emerged that Lesley himself was having a longstanding affair with someone described as 'that woman'!

In 1998, after Dad's funeral service at St Saviour's in Martinez, Heather, who had flown over specially from Uruguay, patiently stumped through the crowd in the courtyard. I spotted her tap, tap, tapping with her walking stick, making a beeline for me. She came right up, fixed me with a beady eye and announced, 'John was a very, very, naughty boy.' Here she paused for dramatic effect. 'And I knew him in *every* way!' Having got that off her chest, she headed off. Mum was standing right next to me, but I don't think she heard. I hope not anyway.

I was ten. It was hot and I was wearing only a pair of small blue shorts racing around with the Campbell children while the grownups sat around the barbecue pit. I never understood how adults could bear to sit on their bums *yakking* for so many hours, the men drinking whiskey and telling off-colour jokes, while the ladies prepared salads and talked about lady things. I ran into a tiny outdoor toilet for a quick pee and caught my reflection in a small piece of mirrored glass. That girl was me. Me. Greeny blue-grey eyes, hair-streaked blond and skin tinted brown by the sun. There was a me-ness about this me, looking back at me. I could hear the others outside and they sounded a very long way away. It was very simple.

When I emerged, nobody noticed that I knew who I was. They carried on drinking and talking and I ran back into the woods.

When I was 70, a local artist asked whether she could paint my portrait. It was a lovely spring day, and I walked across Highbury Fields in North London, near where I now live, up to her beautiful little mews house. I sat very still for a couple of hours while she looked at me and I slipped back to that little bathroom in Parque del Plata, to that me with a flat, little belly and skinny legs, tight nut-brown, no crepey skin around my thighs or crumpled arms, peering at myself in a piece of broken mirror hanging on a rusty nail, and there she still is, that little girl.

***

In 1958, Richard Nixon visited Monty on his tour around Latin America and I saw newspaper pictures of angry demonstrators attacking his car and shouting, 'Yankee go home!' I felt very sorry for him, but to my surprise, Daddy called him Tricky Dicky and didn't seem that bothered.

Daddy had other things to worry about and so did I, because that was the year Mummy converted to Christian Science. *Science*, as she and her fellow Scientists always called it, was founded in 1866 by Mary Baker Eddy, around the same time as my family and tens of millions of other Europeans were flooding across the Atlantic Ocean to settle in Argentina and the United States and across the Pacific to Australia and New Zealand.

Mummy was ripe for the plucking. I always felt she was missing a layer of skin; she was soft and bruised easily like a crab without a shell and she protected herself with fat. She loved sweet things and struggled with her weight her entire life, *I'm fat, I've always been fat.* Daddy's roving eye didn't help. They often went to parties with other British community couples, Mummy always wailing, 'I haven't a thing to wear!' The following morning, Mum would tearfully tell me about Daddy smooching Heather Campbell or June Ellis, 'With tongues and everything, leaving me on the sofa by myself like a great big lump'. I was only eight, so I didn't really know how to advise her. I once tried to intercede by suggesting to Daddy that he should dance with Mummy instead of other ladies, and Daddy, who was always nice to me, told me sharply to mind my own business. When Mummy hosted a tea party, I'd hide under the tablecloth or lurk within earshot as the tea party ladies gossiped about how lazy and dishonest their maids were and then picked each other's bones clean. I learnt that women were each other's enemies and would push each other down any time they could.

The 1950s were a brutal time for women.

Life went on the same until a mannish, stocky woman with short grey hair began popping in to see Mum and they sat facing each other for hours on single sofas by the front window, muttering nonstop. I was a professional eavesdropper when there was trouble in the air, but I couldn't make head or tail of any of it: 'science' and 'knowing the truth' and 'infinite mind' and its 'infinite manifestation'. At night I lay in bed listening to Mummy and Daddy arguing with raised voices and I worried they'd get divorced; Daddy would leave home, and Colin and I would have to live on our own with Mummy and go to what we called a 'screamy school' and wear white overalls with blue bows over our normal clothes. Eventually, the strange woman stopped visiting, but her job was done. From then on, if anything unpleasant happened, however small, like a headache or a lost wallet, or however large, terminal illness, war or famine, Mummy immediately denied the reality of it and *knew the truth*. And the truth was simple. Nothing negative existed because God had not created it! If you couldn't do this prayerful work for yourself, you could ring a practitioner and pay them to know the truth for you. Two or three years later, Mummy and her best friend, Margaret Blencowe, attended a special class in Boston, and Mum became a practitioner herself. Her name was on a list at the end of the Christian Science Sentinel and the phone rang constantly with people telling her their problems and begging her to know the truth, which was that their problems didn't exist! In the Christian Science world, Mummy was powerful and respected, outside it, she was John Woolcock's dumpy wife who had 'let herself go'. Dad forked out for her training and the hefty contribution she insisted on making to the church, and although he thought it was utter nonsense, voices were no longer raised. *Anything for peace.* Divorce was unheard of, and anyway, they couldn't afford it.

Christian Science has no priests, just lay readers, very often women, who read the weekly lesson out loud at the Wednesday testimony meeting and again on Sunday. The weekly lesson is comprised of Bible passages with corresponding selections from *Science and Health with Key to the Scriptures* by Mary Baker Eddy. Church members dutifully marked up the new lesson every Sunday with soft-blue chalk and metal markers and read it every single day. Mum read hers after breakfast, and we knew not to interrupt her. Nothing ever got in the way of Mummy reading her lesson.

Colin was only three, so he accepted the new order, but Dad and I thought Christian Science was gibberish and resented it bitterly. Science made me stoical, and I would go to school uncomplaining, with a high temperature or a bad tummy ache, hiding any pains or worries because anything was better than listening to Mum repeating the scientific statement of being:

> *There is no life, substance or intelligence in matter, all is infinite mind and its infinite manifestation. For God is All-in All. Spirit is immortal Truth; matter is mortal error. Spirit is the real and eternal; matter is the unreal and temporal. Spirit is God, and man is His image and likeness. Therefore ...* and this was the triumphant bit Mummy recited with relish ... *man is not material; he is spiritual!*

When Mummy was focused on 'knowing the truth', she became impenetrable, her eyes fixed glassily on a point in the far distance. If there was an unpleasant item on the news, a mention of a person being ill, or someone letting slip that something was wrong, Mummy clammed up and fervently denied the reality of whatever it was and attempted to convert them: friends, complete strangers, waiters in a restaurant or people in a bus queue, everyone was fair game. I found it mortifying. Sometimes Mum would be forcing Christian Science on a stranger while Dad was having a choking, stammering fit and then I just wanted the earth to swallow me up.

Although Christian Science insisted everything was spiritual, there was a great emphasis on the harmful effects of *animal magnetism* and *mortal mind*, also known as *error* which had to be strongly denied by prayerful work. Mary Baker Eddy believed her third husband, Asa Gilbert Eddy, had been killed by *mental assassination.*

Mummy swiftly rose in the ranks; she played the piano at services and was soon elected Second Reader and then First Reader, positions that went to whoever the congregation felt was most spiritually advanced. The *Manual of the Mother Church* written by Mrs Eddy requires the Reader to 'keep themselves unspotted from the world - uncontaminated with evil'. The *Manual* also includes a bizarre Golden Rule, forbidding members from strolling past Mrs Eddy's house or setting up summer resorts nearby. Christian Scientists are not encouraged to read widely and to my knowledge, the only book my mother read apart from the Bible and Science and Health with key to the Scriptures was *My Story*, the autobiography of Sarah Ferguson, former wife of the disgraced Prince Andrew. Mum subscribed to the *Christian Science Monitor*, a serious newspaper that she claimed only printed 'nice news', but copies stacked up unopened until they went into the bin.

Mary Baker Eddy had encountered sacred Indian texts, and up to the 33rd edition of *Science and Health with Key to the Scriptures*, she quoted from the Bhagavad Gita about a powerful force that creates the cosmic illusion that the phenomenal world is real. These references vanished in further editions, and she pretended she had made it all up herself. I was surprised to discover that Mark Twain, who was no fool, claimed that Mary Baker Eddy was 'the most interesting woman I ever met'.

Every Wednesday evening, Mummy dragged Colin and me to the dreaded testimony meeting in an old cinema. Mummy tinkled at the piano for a bit, and after a short reading from the lesson, the First Reader would invite the congregation to share their healings. After a long painful pause, a brave soul would raise a tentative hand. I remember a skinny woman who looked like a whipped dog coming up with this one:

> On Monday I couldn't find my wallet. This was terrible because all my money was in there, and I had to buy food for my children and pay the electricity bill, and my husband doesn't get paid until the end of the month, and he would be angry. I was crying, but I rang Peggy, and she reminded me that nothing

> is lost in God because God doesn't lose anything. I put the phone down and something made me lift up a cushion on the sofa and there it was!

A ripple of approval washed across the small congregation. Mummy would beam at her special mention, and the First Reader would move her head very slightly to one side in a gesture of appreciation and prepare herself for the next long wait.

One fateful Wednesday, the First Reader invited a professional opera singer, a podgy woman with dyed-black hair, purple lipstick and thick mascara that made her look as if she had squashed dead flies on her eyelids. She raised her eyes to the ceiling and began warbling in an unsteady vibrato, a plump hand bouncing on her capacious bosom. I started giggling, and however much I bit the inside of my mouth and tried to think of sad things, I couldn't control myself. I was shaking and that set off Jenny Blencowe, daughter of Mummy's best friend, and we snorted like piggies, shoulders heaving. Mummy glared, which only made it worse. The more she glared, the more I spluttered.

That night, Mummy rebuked me sternly. I had embarrassed her, made a spectacle of myself, and what's more I was a bad influence on Jenny who was a proper little Scientist in the making. In future, I would have to stay at home alone while she went to testimony meetings with Colin.

Victory.

A small, framed portrait of Mary Baker Eddy was hung opposite the one of Jesus with his faraway stare, right next to the horrible chrysanthemum print in the sitting room.

Mary Baker Eddy was tightly buttoned into an embroidered blue top with a diamond-studded cross fixed to her lace collar, she had marcelled silver hair, pink powdered cheeks and deep-set blue eyes gazing into the distance. They made a fine pair.

***

Mum needed to deny reality.

She was married to a clever man who wasn't in love with her, and she lived with unresolved grief over the death of her parents. Emotions were not encouraged in the British community and Mum found Christian Science very comforting, so I shouldn't still hate it so much.

Mary Baker Eddy, Boston, United States, (Photographer unknown), c.1890.

I feel guilty about saying she was in a loveless marriage. What do I know about marriage? I've never been married! Those two put me off. I still think Dad would have enjoyed being with someone who liked sex and ideas, and Mum would have preferred somebody who didn't make her feel fat and stupid. But they stayed together for over sixty years, and that counts for a lot.

***

When I was ten, I got a very high mark for a project about the American Civil War. I still have it, laced into a stiff cover with a pattern that looks like cat's fur. I was very proud of it. I severely castigated the anti-slave activist John Brown for his egoistic actions although I loftily accepted that he had noble motives. I extolled the virtues of 'the glorious King Cotton, the golden days of the South. Slave labour was an essential and without actually wrecking the economic stability of the whole South, the slaves could not be freed.'

Slavery was rarely mentioned; we believed that although it had been endemic in Brazil, it had never been practised in Argentina or Uruguay and our carnival emerged from enslaved people who had fled to lovely democratic Uruguay.

Between the sixteenth and the nineteenth centuries, over two hundred thousand enslaved Africans landed in the ports of Montevideo and Buenos Aires. Large numbers of people were shipped up to barbaric sugar plantations in Brazil and those that remained were forced into domestic service in Buenos Aires or sent up north to the sugar plantations in Tucumán. The British had their own slave market near the Retiro Terminal and used this license to smuggle in cloth to smarten up slaves for sale and sell more cloth on the side. Afro-Argentines were forbidden from wearing silk, lace, or pearls, walking around after nightfall, holding civil office, or going to the same schools as whites. Their contribution to cultural life has been virtually erased but the tango, one of the trio of the sexiest symbols of Argentina, along with Maradona and Evita, was born in the *candombe* dances held by Afro-Argentines in the *quilombos*.

In 1778, Africans made up 37 percent of the population in Argentina but by 1887 this had plummeted to 2 percent and by the census of 2010, the percentage of Africans had fallen to only 1 percent. I never recall seeing a single black person. One theory is that yellow fever and cholera epidemics disproportionately killed poor people, and the Black population was disproportionately poor. Another is that troops of Black soldiers were used as cannon fodder in the War of the Triple Alliance fought by Argentina, Uruguay and Brazil against Paraguay between 1864 and 1870, propelling African women to have their children with white men, leading to *mestizaje* or *blanqueamiento,* literally 'whitening'. In Britain and the United States, a person is identified as Black however light-skinned they are 'a touch of the tar brush' makes a person 'mixed-race', 'half-caste', 'dual heritage'– *not white* – but in Central and Latin America, race is more fluid, and whiteness is a much broader category.

In 1905, the journalist Juan José de Soiza Reilly wrote:

> Little by little, this race is becoming extinct . . . The race is losing its primitive colour in the mixture. It becomes grey. It dissolves. It lightens. The African tree is producing white Caucasian flowers.

After lockdown, I had supper with two retired academics. Leslie Bethell lives in Rio de Janeiro and related that he'd been approached by a PhD student seeking advice about gated communities. Leslie told her that unfortunately he knew nothing at all about gated communities.

Then it dawned on him that he lived in one.

Leslie asks about my work, and I explain that I am trying to figure out the disappearance of the African Argentine community. Leslie's scornful. Oh, come on Penny! I live in Brazil where 50 percent of the population are Black, and I never see a single black person. Not in the restaurants I eat in or the shopping malls I go to.

Are they hiding in plain sight?

***

On April 17, 1961, my classmates huddled together in the science lab after the bell instead of rushing out to the playground. We knew that Nikita Khrushchev had sent a telegram to the divine Jack Kennedy threatening to drop a nuclear bomb on America, and we were all going to die. There were two American girls in our class, Cindy Albertal and Penny Moulton. Penny, who was very tall with strawberry blond hair, was reassuring, 'Don't worry guys. You took care of World War II and we're gonna take care of this one!'

We were a bit offended that being British implied we could no longer take care of things.

Mr Griffiths asked us to write an essay about who we thought was the most evil man in the world. I knew exactly who he was. Nikita Khrushchev had no manners and banged his shoe on the table and yelled rude things like, 'If you've seen one skyscraper, you've seen them all!' Kennedy built Disneyland and brought peace and bubble gum to the world, plus he was cute and had an adorable wife who wore pillbox hats and Chanel suits. Mr Griffiths scribbled 'better the devil you know' in the margin, which I found astonishing. Surely there was no devil worse than that terrible man? But that remark stuck in my throat like a little fish bone and made me feel a bit naive.

In 1958, Fidel Castro, along with his brother Raúl and Ernesto Che Guevara, led the Cuban revolution against the dictator Fulgencio Batista. Cuba has sugar and tobacco but no oil or coal, so Castro flew off to Washington looking for a deal, but President Eisenhower refused to meet him. Nikita Khrushchev spotted his chance to secure a foothold in America's backyard and offered to sell Castro heavily subsidised oil and buy Cuban sugar and tobacco at high prices. When US oil companies refused to refine Soviet crude oil, Castro decided he was a Socialist and nationalised every single business, from the big tobacco companies to street peanut sellers.

The cute Kennedy brothers, John and Robert, were obsessed with assassinating Castro, and the CIA cooked up increasingly surreal plots to kill the heavy-smoking, scuba-diving Castro. They designed a diving suit infected with tuberculosis, planned to place a booby-trapped conch shell painted with exotic colours on the sea floor, a box of cigars spiked with a botulinum toxin, and concocted a scheme to spray his broadcasting studio with a hallucinatory drug. In August 1960, the CIA tried to make a deal with gangsters from the Chicago mafia to put a hit on Fidel, Raúl, and Che Guevara in exchange for a monopoly on gaming, prostitution and drugs.

When these bizarre plots came to nothing, the CIA trained anti-communist troops to overthrow the revolutionary government and replace it with wealthy landlords, businessmen, plantation and factory owners, playboys and soldiers loyal to Batista. They were convinced that the local population and the Cuban army would welcome them with open arms, but unmarked American planes flown in to support the invasion were shot down by Castro's troops, and many of the invaders they called *gusanos*, 'worms', were killed or captured. Eventually, seventeen hundred prisoners were exchanged for fifty-three million dollars' worth of baby food.

Che Guevara wrote to President Kennedy, thanking him for the invasion because it had consolidated the revolution.

***

1961, the year Lumumba was assassinated, Barbie got Ken, Yuri Gagarin orbited Earth, and the United Kingdom sent troops into Iraq for the first time.

I distinguished myself that year with many random acts of cruelty, mainly directed at Diana Beare, a gentle girl who couldn't defend herself. Diana had been top dog when we were five but by eleven, she had plummeted down the pecking order.

On March 9, 1962, I returned to school after the long summer holiday, quietly confident that I could reestablish my reasonably high position in my friendship group. As usual I had spent most of the summer holidays without seeing my school friends. Martita, my neighbourhood, working-class friend was the daughter of an electrician, she didn't speak English and attended the local school. We spent happy hours on her roof terrace throwing a large pink ball at each other and playing endless games of canasta. I didn't mix her with my school friends after one unsuccessful attempt with Jenny Hyland, but Martita was relaxing company, and we were always happy to see each other.

School was what Mum called a 'different kettle of fish'. Jenny was notoriously unreliable, her home life was stressful with lots of brothers and sisters and a hot-tempered mother, and she sadistically ruled the roost at school to compensate. I turned up on the first morning armed with a lump of plastic poo, a plastic fly you could float in a glass of water, and a kaleidoscope that gave the viewer a black eye, hoping that these tricks would smooth my reentry into the group after the long break. I attempted to show them off as soon as we gathered in our new classroom for the register before assembly, but Jenny gave her second-in-command, Christine Fox, a sly sideways glance and sneered. The rest of the group, Jennifer Jones, Susan Lake and Diana Beare, tittered, relieved that I had been picked on. My fate was sealed, and I knew it.

We stood in a row at assembly. On an invisible signal, the rest of the group stepped forward, leaving me alone. I panicked and stepped forward to join them. The invisible signal triggered another move back, leaving me by myself. I tried to scuttle forward again. Virginia Campbell turned and signalled that I could join her group, but I refused. At break, Jenny, Christine, Jennifer, Susan and Diana ran away from me, and I humiliated myself, chasing after them.

When I got home, Mummy asked, 'How was school?'

'Fine.'

I never shared my troubles at home because being forced to listen to Mum reciting the 'scientific statement of being' just made things worse. I didn't want to upset Daddy and anyway his grim advice, 'In a hundred years we'll all be dust', didn't help either. I had to be happy Penny, thin Penny, popular Penny, because she was the daughter they needed.

The following day I turned up at school expecting to be tormented, but much to my relief, Jenny had selected a new victim. It was Susan Lake's turn, and I was so relieved that I joined in energetically, thrilled to be off the hook myself. The rest of that year I continued flip-flopping between torturer and victim. I settled at number three, under our leader, Jenny, and Christine Fox, pretty as a little doll with her button blue eyes and curly blond hair who never got picked on. I had to take my turn but poor Diana was always at the bottom of the pile. Even when Jenny and Christine were not there to initiate the torture, I'd launch unprovoked attacks on Diana with jibes about her runny egg sandwiches and her rabbity teeth until I made her cry. I once slipped an anonymous note into her desk that said, 'you are a pig'.

I was ashamed, and shame made me crueller. I marched around punching other girls in the arm with my knuckles and one awful Saturday I viciously set upon a younger girl, Jean Billet, in the Montevideo Cricket Club and convinced her that we would drive off without her and she would be alone all weekend, day and night, with no food, and her family wouldn't even notice her absence. I was relentless and eventually Jean collapsed in a ditch, sobbing in the foetal position while I hissed threats at her. The sun was setting, black clouds were pressing down on us and I hated myself, but I couldn't stop myself. I wanted to squash her like a fly while I grew gigantic and monstrous, pure evil with nasty wings sprouting out of my skinny back.

'What's going on?' Mummy had come looking for us, coat on, ready to go home.

'Nothing,' I said. 'Jean tripped.'

Jean scrambled to her feet, weeping, and we left. Her sister, Frances, who I really liked, told her mother, Joyce, to tell my mother that she didn't want to be friends with me anymore.

I was devastated.

That Monday as soon as I got off the school bus, it was immediately obvious that it was my turn to be abused. I just couldn't face it. I took myself off to the school nurse and insisted that I had a blinding headache. She made me lie on a hard hospital bed, which was agony because I was feeling perfectly well, and insisted that I was in too much pain to return to the classroom, which was true. Eventually a taxi was called to take me home, a taxi my parents could not afford. Mummy was cross and tucked me up between freshly ironed sheets and rang Margaret Blencowe to help her 'work for me'. Margaret was a big, soft giggly woman with a goofy smile and a terrible husband who mucked about with other women. They stood at the foot of my bed droning on and on about how the headache I did not have, did not exist because God had not created it. I glared at them balefully until they left me alone.

I was angry all the time. A prefect I disliked sat in the front seat of the school bus, and every morning I deliberately stamped on his foot with an evil cackle. My punishment was to write 'I must not stamp on people's feet' and stand outside the headmaster's office all the way through break and lunch, and it is only writing this now that I understand that I had found a way of avoiding life in the playground.

1961 was also the year of my first school dance. I chose a new brown-corduroy pleated skirt and a pair of kitten heels, pushed my hair back with a plastic headband and set off feeling like a proper teenager even though I was only eleven. They played 'Let's Twist Again' by Chubby Checker and I got lost in the music, twisting and twisting, my skirt whirling around and around and all the boys gathered in a circle watching and cheering. When the lights came up at the end of the evening, I went to the bathroom to admire myself and saw my face was all red and sweaty and my headband had slipped forward and screwed up my hair like a scarecrow. I consoled myself with the thought that at least I was a fantastic dancer. When I got home, I repeated my dance in front of the big wardrobe mirror in Mummy and Daddy's room, my wide brown skirt flew up revealing my knickers and the garters holding up my nylons. I wanted to die.

Then Sarah Fell got her period, *the curse,* and I was the only girl who didn't know what it was, and everyone laughed at me.

That horrible year finally ended.

I spent the summer holiday back on Martita's roof terrace, and we were nice to each. It was a huge relief. I was sick to death of being horrible.

It began to occur to me that I had a choice about what kind of person I wanted to be.

***

I walked back into school after the long break.

Jenny rushed up and I smiled, said 'hi' and walked on. In that instant, all the power I had given her drained away. She was just an ordinary girl.

It was over.

Diana never returned to the British School because she had begged her mother to remove her, and I didn't see her for a long time.

Twenty years later I visited Uruguay with my parents and Dylan. Virginia and I were sitting on a row of deck chairs in the evening sun, drinking gin and tonics with Mum, Dad, Uncle Lesley, Auntie Heather and Auntie Betty. I knew Diana was expected and I was ready for her.

Diana flew in the gate, a magnificent avenging angel in a red dress, stretched out her right arm and pointed. 'Penny Woolcock, Jenny Hyland and Christine Fox, you made my life hell!'

Mum was horrified, 'No, no! She didn't.''

I stood up. 'You're right, and I am so, so sorry.

Diana and I scurried off and I continued apologising, explaining how much bullying her had haunted me, until Diana started comforting me and saying it was 'all right'. It wasn't all right. The damage had been done and nothing I could say or do would ever put it right.

***

By 1979, the year Mum tried to give me a blanket, I had lost touch with everyone from school.

One day while my parents were taking their daily siesta and Dylan was watching a movie on cable television, I walked the ten blocks down to the river from their flat. It was August, chilly with a thin winter sun when a dark-green car began cruising slowly beside me. I assumed it was a kerb crawler and turned angrily. The driver and his companion were wearing mirrored sunglasses, the car drove ahead very, very slowly to let me see that it had no number plate, then slowed down again. My heart started beating faster, my mouth dried and I stumbled straight ahead. The car slowed down; I hurried up and it kept pace with me. I looked again, the driver stared back and I fell into the black holes where his eyes should have been. He grinned and sped off. He had enjoyed frightening me. It was cold but I was sweating.

That night I asked Dad about it. 'Yes, er, Ford Falcons, Ford Falcons, something called the Triple A, set up by that Lopez Rega chap. He's er this bloody fool who, er . . . hangs around with that dreadful woman.' This time he meant Peron's second wife, Isabelita, not Evita.

'Oh, Penny!' exclaimed Mum. 'Don't go wandering about by yourself like that. It's not safe.'

These cars, Ford Falcons with blank plates, did their rounds across the city and the suburbs all day and night, and I learnt how to notice them like everyone else, without turning my head, seeing them without seeing them. They were everywhere and they were nowhere.

The seizing of suspected terrorists, enemies of the state, could happen at any time, even in broad daylight. It was always a spectacle, up to five Ford Falcons would screech up, if it was at night, a bright light was splashed on the house of the suspect, armed men in civilian clothes would spring out, bash down the door, charge inside and drag someone out with a coat over their head. Neighbours twitched their curtains to see what they were meant to see and not see. It was a theatre of violence where spectators were forced to pretend they were not watching the performances they were compelled to attend.

***

In 2006, I visited Dachau with my then lover, a fat, bald, little liar leading a double life, a man with no number plates, although I did not know that then. We walked through the massive wrought-iron gates crowned by the motto Arbeit Macht Frei, work makes you free, the lie hiding in plain sight. I was overwhelmed by a weird heaviness. I was wearing a huge brown camel hair Max Mara coat that had cost me £900 during a period when I was getting plenty of well-paid film work. My big coat grew denser and more leaden until it weighed a ton and I sank to the kerb. The liar waddled on cheerfully with the other tourists, taking pictures of them posing with their tiny children in front of the gas oven. *Smile!*

It took us only twenty minutes to walk back to the centre of Dachau. When the camp was functioning, emaciated camp prisoners were frog-marched into town every morning to provide slave labour for local factories; gaunt strangers stumbling down the streets, some townspeople would surreptitiously slip them food, but nobody saw them. Not really.

***

I made a film on Century Road in Cobham, a small town on the east coast of England to mark the second millennium. Behind every unprepossessing front door lived old working-class people who had seldom stepped away from where they were born. Charlie Rose had been a ladies' man. Now in his eighties, he lived in a smelly house with a cat that pooped in an overfilled litter dish, his grey, soiled old man's underpants draped over the radiators. Charlie still had a twinkle in his eye and was very disapproving of Dick who lived up the road for being a 'miserable old bugger'. Dick had what beauticians call 'marionette lines' etched deep from his nose to his chin. He wept in a tidy sitting room with his wife, Joyce holding his hand and looking at him anxiously, sniffing as he told us about being with the troops that liberated Belsen. He muttered that they had smelt rotting, burning flesh miles away.

Everyone knew.

I booked a slot at the Imperial War Museum where, before digitisation, they stored tins of thirty-five-millimetre film cans with handwritten labels stating filmed by young men with names like Sergeant Ginger, men who had been high street photographers or worked in the film industry and were now in charge of recording death. I threaded reels on an old Steinbeck and watched what Dick had described, British teenage soldiers with handkerchiefs tied over their noses driving diggers scooping up piles of skeletal bodies falling apart like spillikins as they were shovelled up and dumped in mass graves. British officers eventually commandeered Belsen townspeople to come and clear up the mess they had not seen or smelt. Joyce said Dick still had nightmares, grinding his teeth.

Dick's son Nigel had felt the heavy weight of his father's unhappiness throughout his childhood and didn't understand where it came from until he saw the film.

***

Argentina is built on the bloodshed of the fifteenth, sixteenth, seventeenth, eighteenth and nineteenth centuries, and the violence rolled on and on. There was a joke that did the rounds in Argentina until 1976, when it became no laughing matter. *There are more deaths at a Mexican wedding than an Argentine coup.*

A coup takes place when a small number of military officers, with the support of at least part of the army and the police, violently overthrow a government and seize power themselves. Violence is a habit that is hard to break.

There were six coups in Argentina in the twentieth century.

***

The first was on September 6, 1930, when General Uriburu overthrew the democratically elected President Hipólito Yrigoyen. Yrigoyen was a rich, liberal landowner who paid his workers properly, supported workers' rights, and believed Argentina should control its natural resources. The rest of the landowning establishment and the business community supported the coup, and General Uriburu set a precedent by using torture against his political opponents, particularly anarchists and communists and this model was faithfully adhered to by every subsequent coup.

***

The second coup was on June 4, 1943. President Ramon Castillo, a corrupt conservative, was overthrown by military factions allied to the Catholic Church. Three military dictators followed in quick succession over the next three years. General Arturo Rawson managed to cling on to power for three days. General Pedro Ramirez hung on for eight months. Ramirez was a Fascist and the great uncle of Raúl Martinez, my first lover and my son Dylan's father. Raúl's mother, Carmen Ramirez, had been disowned by her upper-class family for marrying a Peronist factory worker and had six children with him. He battered her and Raúl, his eldest son, until, at fourteen, Raúl knocked his father down. Maybe that explains why he had no idea how to be a father himself and disappeared for forty years when Dylan was one year old. Many years later we learnt that Dylan had a half-sister, Ana, who had also been abandoned by Raúl and had a tough time in foster care. Violence spills through people's veins for generations until somebody stops it.

General Edelmiro Farrell toppled Ramirez to become the third of this unsavoury trio of dictators.

During the Rawson, Ramirez, and Farrell dictatorships, trade unions, Socialists and Communists, formed an alliance with a group of ambitious young army officers led by Colonel Juan Perón. Juán Perón was the minister of labour under both General Rawson and General Ramirez and made himself very popular by organising a relief effort for victims of a devastating earthquake in the province of San Juán. Perón was a widower who had been very fond of his first wife until she died of cancer. He called her 'Potota', which Dad mocked because it was 'common'. Perón quickly hooked up with a glamorous matinée star twenty-four years his junior, Eva Duarte – always known as Evita – played by Madonna in a 90s film directed by Alan Parker.

In her autobiography, *The Reason for my Life,* Evita called the day she met Perón at a fundraising gala 'my marvellous day.'

Perón continued climbing the greasy poll, backing General Farrell when he toppled General Ramirez and was rewarded with the vice presidency. With the beautiful Evita at his side, he was ready for greatness.

***

In 1946, Perón, 'Mi General', to his supporters, easily won a democratic election. Five years later, Evita persuaded him to push through universal suffrage, and Perón won another landslide election. According to Mum and Dad, people didn't understand what they were voting for.

Towards the end of 1952, when I was two, six months after Evita died, Mummy, Daddy and I moved from Argentina to Uruguay, missing the last three years of Perón's presidency. They talked about him frequently:

> 'You don't know what it was like, Penny, it was a dictatorship! Everyone had to contribute two days' wages to Evita Perón's charity whether they wanted to or not, can you imagine! Dad was forced to chip in just like everybody else.'

Dad would relive feelings of enormous injustice every time he told this story. He didn't see why he should contribute to that *bloody woman's* charity, he'd bloody well decide what charities he wanted to support! Mum and Dad, Auntie Edie and the rest of the family talked about living in fear during that terrible time. They never spoke about the Dirty War dictatorship with anything like the same venom. According to them, nothing was ever as dreadful as that early democratic Peronist period.

***

Perón and Evita spooked wealthy Argentinians and the British community, but they had phenomenal popular support until Evita's death. Perón was a slippery customer, swerving between the Right and the Left until, towards the end of 1954, he alienated the Catholic Church by proposing the legalisation of divorce and prostitution. He was swiftly excommunicated and within three months overthrown by the combined forces of the army, navy and air force.

The British community celebrated at the English club. That *dreadful fellow* had gone.

Perón escaped up the Paraná River on a gunboat provided by the Paraguayan dictator Alfredo Stroessner. Stroessner had a fondness for having sex with thirteen-year-old girls and marrying them off to military colleagues when they got pregnant. He was a sadist who relished eating his dinner while listening on his telephone to the screams of the secretary of the Communist Party as he was dismembered with a chainsaw. His Department of Investigations interviewed suspects in baths of human vomit and faeces and rammed electric cattle rods up their rectums. Stroessner placed Paraguay under a state of siege during his entire thirty-five years in office, welcomed Nazi war criminals and won seven elections, in which all other candidates were banned. Land was cleared for US and European corporations, including Unilever, Coca-Cola, Deloitte and Nestlé, under the leadership of the psychopathic Manuel de Jesús Pereira, who killed, raped and sold Indigenous Aché men, women and children over several decades.

None of this prevented the British from building Stroessner an arsenal, a railway system and shipyards. Business is business.

Stroessner was Perón's *buén amigo*.

There were decades when you couldn't go into a bar or a shopping mall without Elaine Paige, Julie Covington or

Madonna screeching 'Don't cry for me Argentina' from the musical *Evita*. For years, people would sing it at me, imagining they were being original, but it means nothing to young people. Evita, like Che Guevara, died young and beautiful and left a hell of a myth behind her.

Eva Duarte Perón in a Christian Dior frock, Buenos Aires, (Photographer unknown), c.1949.

Evita was detested by the British community, they called her *la Gran Puta,* the Great Whore. The writer Jorge Luís Borges claimed that her mother had run a brothel in Junín and that Evita was already a 'common prostitute' at fifteen when she left for Buenos Aires and had whored her way into Perón's bed. They claimed that the Eva Perón Foundation, which Dad had resented paying into, had swindled vast sums of money and that Evita was a jumped-up hussy, handing out fistfuls of money that didn't belong to her to street urchins and the undeserving poor. They said she was spiteful and had spilled cartloads of rotten fish under the windows of the aristocratic Jockey Club to literally get up their noses, which is hilarious if it is true.

Unlike the middle-class Perón, Evita had lived experience of poverty, she was born out of wedlock, and when her father died, his official wife and family turned Evita and her siblings away from viewing the casket, fuelling her hatred for what she always called the 'oligarchy'. She pursued a modestly successful career as a radio actress and a minor movie star until she met Perón, and had her huge moment in the sun before dying of cancer at thirty-three. The Eva Perón Foundation replaced a beneficent society run by eighty-seven society women who compelled the destitute children in their care to shave their heads and go out begging at Christmas. Evita despised these women. Her beauty and extravagant gestures endeared her to the poor, who loved seeing her looking fabulous, dripping with jewels, draped in Christian Dior frocks and glorious furs. Her foundation employed fourteen thousand workers, distributed half a million pairs of shoes, cooking pots and sewing machines, built hundreds of new houses, schools, hospitals, and orphanages and a model town, Ciudad Evita. The writer Tomás Eloy Martinez refutes the allegation that she stole from her charity to buy glamorous clothes, and no private Swiss bank accounts were found after her death.

After Evita died in July 1952, Perón's popularity plummeted, she was Princess Diana to his Prince Charles.

***

It's odd that in all my years of listening to vitriol about Perón, nobody ever mentioned Nelly Rivas. After Evita's death, fifty-nine-year-old Perón had a relationship with a thirteen-year-old child, Nélida Rivas. When challenged, he snorted, 'well I'm not superstitious.' There are stomach-churning photographs of this tall, stout, elderly man stuffed into his uniform, standing proprietorially next to a beaming little girl.

Juán Perón with Nelly Rivas, Buenos Aires, (Photographer unknown), c. 1954.

Nelly's mother was the janitor of an apartment building and her father was a low-wage chocolate-factory worker, and Nelly relayed that the three of them worshipped Perón like a God in their one-room apartment. Nelly was one of many teenage delegates from the Union of Secondary School Students who were invited to be hosted by Perón at the presidential estate in the Olivos suburb, just up the road from Northlands School for Girls.

Perón dished out five-hundred-peso bills to lucky girls and picked a select few to eat lunch with him. Nelly was, 'Speechless. I felt a chill run through my body. I began trembling like a leaf . . . I had been stunned by his simplicity and charm. I hadn't expected him to be so handsome either.'

Perón offered Nelly private motorbike lessons on Sunday mornings before the other girls arrived. In her memoir, Nelly complains that Armando Méndez San Martín, the minister of education, worried about his boss's reputation, and had warned Nelly to back off. Nelly went running to Perón who ordered Méndez San Martín to mind his own business. Nelly was flattered, 'I don't know why he chose me. There were many girls with pretty faces and magnificent figures, I was small and looked like a child.'

At an intimate party for his favourite girls on Christmas Eve, Perón gave Nelly a gold ring and confessed that he was lonely. She felt very sorry for him, and they began meeting alone for little lunches, and in the afternoons while he was busy with presidential business, she watched films with his pet poodles in his private cinema. When one of the poodles got sick, Nelly decided it would be a good idea for her to move to the presidential palace. She reminded her parents that they had each other for company, while the poor president, the man who had done so much for workers like her father, was all alone. Perón bought Nelly's parents a house and she moved in with him.

Nelly was thrilled to be offered the bedroom Eva herself had slept in! She took a bubble bath, just like the ones she'd seen in movies and sprayed herself liberally with cologne and talcum powder. She descended the stairs like a princess. Perón sniffed the air and joked that Atkinsons - Dad's company – had moved in and gently told her off for wearing lipstick. 'That is for grown-up women.' 'Yes, Daddy,' she replied. She called him 'Papi' or 'Papito' and he called her 'Nena' or 'Nenita,' girlie.

Little Nelly worked hard at polishing her diction and tried hard to refrain from waving her hands around in the Neapolitan way, realising it was unsuitable for polite society. She writes that they had behaved like father and daughter for a few days after she moved in, but 'All of a sudden, the mutual attraction that had been creeping up on us, took us by surprise and defeated us.' *Nos venció.*

Nelly prided herself on being a proper helpmate, unlike Evita who had been too busy to fetch her husband's cigarettes and slippers, and despite the new turn their relationship had taken, she carried on being his little girl, the daughter he'd always longed for. Nelly loved the movies: 'Daddy, your little girl wants to go to the Mar del Plata Film Festival.' Perón arranged a festival pass for her and there's a photograph of a delighted Nelly, looking just like a child at a fancy-dress party, draped in a mink stole, a fancy frock, ruby earrings, an aquamarine brooch, and a diamond necklace borrowed from Evita's wardrobe.

On September 16, 1955, the day of the coup, Perón kissed Nelly goodbye and sent her back to her parents with 400,000 pesos. She never saw him again.

Police ransacked the family home, impounded the jewels and clothes Perón had given her, arrested Nelly's parents and packed her off to a correctional institute for minors. In an interview that poor little Nelly gave to an Argentine newspaper, she complained that the sheets were dirty and that all the other girls were *obsessed with sex.* She never blamed Perón for dumping her and looked back fondly at the two years they spent together, teenyweeny Cinderella and her Prince.

Nelly had spirit and there is something admirable about her determination to live out her dreams and not cast herself as a victim.

***

The top of the wardrobe was a land of forbidden delights; it was where Dad kept a little leather suitcase that held his secret Freemason gear, an embroidered apron and two or three tiny booklets. Dad was a Freemason like most of his friends, and after he died, men in dark suits visited Mum's flat and collected his secret stuff. When we were little, I'd persuade a reluctant Colin to keep watch while I inspected the contents of the little case on our parents' bed. I read about 'the stone the builder rejected which became the cornerstone'. I didn't think that was much of a secret, but looking at forbidden stuff was a thrill. Dad rarely got angry with me and he never hit us, but I didn't know what he would do if he caught me fiddling with his masonic gear and I didn't want to find out.

Most of the settler leaders of independence movements in the Americas were Freemasons. George Washington and Benjamin Franklin in the United States, and in Latin America, Francisco de Miranda and José de San Martín - both of whom spent time in London - Simón Bolivar, Bernardo O'Higgins and Manuel Belgrano. More recently, many of those on the extreme right were Freemasons, including López Rega and Admiral Emilio Eduardo Massera, but so was the left-wing Salvador Allende, who was overthrown by the fascist General Pinochet, himself a Freemason.

Dad was a devoted Freemason in Montevideo, active in two British community masonic lodges, Acacia and Silver River, one for the managerial class and another for the lower middle-class. I can't remember which was which. Conspiracy theorists love to blame Freemasons, Jewish Bankers and shape-shifting lizards for all the ills of the world, but Mum and I thought Masons were a bit of a joke. We believed that Dad loved dressing up in the little aprons and going to meetings because he was brilliant at memorising hours of ritual. It was also a good cover for him to get out of the house and do whatever else he wanted to do. After I left home, the 'naughty boy' Heather had referred to at Dad's funeral really came into his own, and he rarely came home before one or two in the morning. On social occasions, Mum might mention a lodge meeting that week, and other lodge members would reveal there had been no such meeting. Mum both knew and did not want to know that Dad was having affairs and visiting waitress bars. She blamed me for leaving home and making home a less entertaining place. I blamed myself too.

Next to the masonic briefcase sat a gold-embossed, unexpurgated copy of *Grimm's Fairy Tales*, which had been presented to my Uncle Bobby Lumsdaine by St George's College in 1914. Uncle Bobby was a cadaverous old man, married to saintly Auntie Nita and they had a daughter, our crazy cousin Patsy who was obsessed with cats, hi-fi speakers and the popstar Palito Ortega. There was something wrong with Bobby's leg and when he drove us up to their house in Cordoba, his foot cramped and jammed down on the accelerator, making these journeys truly terrifying, careering through sleepy little towns at one hundred and fifty kilometres an hour, swerving around traffic with Nita sucking breath through her teeth and Bobby snapping,' Stop making that noise!' Daddy loathed Uncle Bobby because he only wanted to talk about car engines and whenever his name came up Dad spluttered, 'What the hell is a baffle on the manifold!'

Mummy disapproved of the extreme violence and bloodshed in Grimm's gruesome tales and banned it. I got a guilty kick out of *The Three Little Men in the Wood*, which ended with a wicked old woman shoved into a cask that had nails knocked into it and rolled down a hill; other wicked old women were torn to pieces by wild animals or burnt to death and I hate to admit, even now, that I always imagined it was Mum in the casket being pierced by nails. Mum was never cruel so I can't account for my sadism. I knew that rage and violence existed because I felt them myself, but I shoved them deep down inside me, where they blossomed into strange, ghoulish bloodstained creatures.

***

In May 1830, Captain Robert Fitzroy conducted an experiment to see whether 'savages' from Tierra del Fuego could be civilised. He invited Orundellico, a curious Yamana boy, to leave his uncle's canoe, climb onto his ship, the *Beagle*, flung a shining mother-of-pearl button at the boy's uncle, and sailed off. He renamed the boy Jemmy Button and observed that the boy 'seemed to be pleased at his change,' content to leave his family and community. Later it emerged that the boy's mother, grief-stricken at the disappearance of her child, had spent months walking up and down the coast searching for him.

Fitzroy kidnapped two other young men and a girl from the Alcaluf tribe and gave them all amusing names, Elleparu became York Minster, the girl, Yokcushlu, was Fuegia Basket, and another tall young man whose own name was not recorded was dubbed Boat Memory. Fitzroy took them to England, buttoned them up, taught them to use knives and forks, converted them to Christianity and sent them to Walthamstow Primary School in North London which the adult Elleparu did not appreciate. They became minor celebrities in London where they were introduced to King William IV and Queen Adelaide, who gave Fuegia Basket a little bonnet and a ring.

Boat Memory died in England. A year later the *Beagle* returned to Tierra del Fuego with a cargo of seeds, tools, clothes, cut-glass decanters, chamber pots and silk handkerchiefs, the three survivors plus the Reverend Richard Matthews and a young scientist Charles Darwin, recruited to help keep 'the blue evils' at bay from the depressive Captain Fitzroy.

When Yamana people paddled out in their canoes to greet the *Beagle*, people held their arms out in a pleading gesture, crying out 'yammerschooner! yammerschooner!' Darwin and other Europeans found these cries very irritating and assumed they were begging.

Darwin was shocked.

'Viewing such men, one can hardly make oneself believe they are fellow creatures, and inhabitants of

> the same world. At night, five or six human beings, naked and scarcely protected from the wind and rain of this tempestuous climate, sleep on the wet ground coiled up like animals.'

Darwin didn't understand their language so he concluded that they communicated through grunts and announced that they ate their old women when they were hungry. This empty lie was picked up by eugenicists like Herbert Spencer to justify their white supremacist episteme.

Captain Fitzroy ordered his sailors to build shelters and plant a garden and sailed off, leaving Orundellico, Yokcushlu and Elleparu onshore with Reverend Matthews, tasked with establishing a civilising Christian mission.

When the *Beagle* returned, fifteen days later, they found Matthews completely naked, his garden trampled and his possessions plundered, being chased around by laughing Natives who had cheerfully returned to their own ways. A devout Christian, Captain Fitzroy became an embittered opponent of his old friend Charles Darwin's theory of evolution, and the 'blue evils' caught up with him. He slit his throat with a razor.

Natural selection simply replaced Christianity as a way of establishing that Europeans were at the top of the evolutionary tree. Survival of the fittest meant that we had risen to the top, like cream. Or scum.

***

From 1871, the missionary Reverend Thomas Bridges lived alongside the Yamana and the Selk'nam, learnt their languages and taught them to his children. Bridges compiled a comprehensive dictionary of 32,000 words, now held in the British Library. The Yamana language is subtle, complex and sophisticated, with more inflections than Greek and more words to describe family relationships, friendships and the natural world, than English.

Thomas and Mary Bridges' third son, Lucas, took a special interest in Indigenous culture, appreciating the richness and nuances of their language, where among many words for the verb *to bite* was one that meant 'coming unexpectedly on a hard substance while eating something soft'. Lucas Bridges hunted with young Selk'nam men on expeditions that lasted for several days, sleeping out around a fire in the freezing cold and taking part in wrestling competitions. He observed that 'these so-called savages were more gentlemanly in their respect for the rules of the game than many white sportsmen.'

During an extreme famine in Patagonia, Thomas Bridges reports that the Yamana ate their rawhide thongs but never contemplated eating human flesh. In 1880 Lucas read out loud a report about Fuegian cannibalism in the *Liverpool Weekly News* to a group of Yamana. Initially they roared with laughter, then the face of one of them, Halupaianjiz, became grave. 'Why do these people tell lies about us? We do not say bad things about them.'

When I first came across Lucas Bridges, I felt I could breathe again.

I was wrong.

***

When Daddy got paid at the end of the month, it was a very special day. Mummy always took me to the one English bookshop in Montevideo and waited patiently as I spent hours choosing a book.

On one of these excursions, I was three years old, Mummy and I were walking up a steep town street, hand in hand. She was a big shape against the sky and I felt very small, alone and afraid.

We arrived at the crest of the hill, and Mummy hesitated. *Now, which way is it?* The city spread out on all sides, rows and rows of little houses stretched out to infinity and I realised that people lived in them, people I didn't know, who didn't know me and would never know me and the world was vast, bigger than I ever imagined and Mummy and I were lost and we would never find Daddy again.

I howled.

You might reasonably assume that suburban life might be boring but at least it's safe, safe as houses, a place where nothing really bad ever happens. You might think that since we absolutely knew we were better than all the others, that would make us safe, safe as houses. You might think that since we spoke English and we were here but not from here because we were better than from here, you might think that would make us feel safe, safe as houses. You might imagine that because we had a Mummy and a Daddy and a nice, clean bed and a roof over our heads that we were safe as houses. You might think that since we had no sadists like Manuel de Jesús Pereira drowning our Dads in baths of shit, raping us girls and our Mums, you might think that since there were no dangerous snakes or scorpions, no poisonous spiders, no tigers or lions, you might well think that since our names were not on any secret police list, you might think that because we had God on our side, you might well think that all these things would made us feel safe, safe as houses. But we were frightened all the time, and we didn't know why.

At eighteen, I read Frantz Fanon's *The Wretched of the Earth* and recognised myself with a jolt.

> The settlers' town is a strongly built town; the streets are covered in asphalt, and the garbage cans swallow all the leavings, unseen, unknown and hardly thought about. The settler's feet are never visible, except perhaps in the sea; but there you're never close enough to see them. His feet are protected by strong shoes although the streets of his town are clean and even, with no holes or stones. The settler's town is a well-fed town, an easy-going town; its belly is always full of good things. The settler's town is a town of white people, of foreigners.

***

Mummy could whip cakes up by eye without weighing ingredients, her cakes never flopped, as everyone said, 'Peggy's cakes melt in your mouth.' She was an artist. My friends loved gobbling them up, but I shrugged. *Another cake. Another week, another cake.* Poor Mummy, a daughter who didn't even have a sweet tooth.

Mummy was especially famous for her magic Angel Food cake made with no butter, or egg yolks.

> *One and three-quarters cups of granulated sugar pulsed fine. One cup and two tablespoons of cake flour. Quarter of a teaspoon of salt. Twelve large egg whites at room temperature. One and half teaspoons of cream of tartar, One and a half teaspoons vanilla extract. Whip the egg whites until they form soft peaks and add the vanilla and sift the flour mixture into the egg white and fold it in very slowly with a rubber spatula. Pour the mixture into an ungreased pan and bake for forty to forty-five minutes and run a thin knife around the edges and gently tap the pan on the counter until the cake releases.*

Mummy piled hers with cream and strawberries, and even though I wasn't a cake lover, I knew I was in the presence of greatness. It was a cake as light as air. Barely there.

One day, Mum mysteriously stopped making cakes and that was the end of that.

***

The fourth coup was on March 29, 1962. Arturo Frondizi, the democratically elected Radical Party president, was escorted out of the presidential palace by Eduardo Lockhart, military captain of the house, and flown to the Island of Marín García, where he was briefly incarcerated. It is rare to come across a British name like Lockhart in the military or political sphere. We stuck to business and talking about the weather and, as it happens, Lockhart recalls that on the flight he and Frondizi spoke only about the weather.

Frondizi was a centrist who backed import substitution, local car manufacture and heavy industry while simultaneously inviting multinationals to invest in Argentina. He managed to piss off the establishment by allowing a Peronist front, the Popular Union Party, to stand in provincial elections while Perón was still exiled in Madrid. Ten of the fourteen provinces, including Buenos Aires, were won by Peronists, and although Frondizi tried to roll back on these results, his number was up.

The coup was a non-event. Its military leader, General Raúl Poggi, entered the Pink House fully expecting to be made president, only to discover that a civilian, José María Guido, had been sworn in behind his back. He stormed around the corridors snarling, 'I don't want to speak to anybody', so red in the face that his assistants got concerned about his blood pressure and made him take two aspirins to calm himself down.

The army was split between a blue faction that respected the Constitution and supported the swearing in of Guido and a red faction insisting that civilian governments should always remain under the authority of the military and removed whenever they disobeyed.

The red faction lost this round, and Poggi was forced to retire, but hard-liners just waited in the wings biding their time.

They didn't have long to wait.

***

I was twelve when Frondizi was deposed. We were still living in Uruguay, a democracy in which the Colorado Party, the Reds, took turns with the Blanco Party, the Whites. There was great excitement among us girls when two new American boys, Jack and Tom, appeared at the British School. We always had a few Americans at The British, their parents worked for Chiclets chewing gum or Philip Morris cigarettes, and they had more money than the rest of us. The game was already well and truly up for the British in South America, but we still hadn't woken up to it. The United States had a very similar immigrant population, and their manufacturers understood that people wanted transistor radios, vacuum cleaners and air conditioners, not old-fashioned bone china tea sets, Sheffield stainless steel, and cut glass with the royal seal of approval.

Tom had red hair and was clever and interesting. Jack was exactly like Barbie's Ken, a miniature little man, new out of the box, with a straight little nose, blue eyes, and dark hair gelled and combed into a perfect slick. Jack rarely spoke, he didn't have to, every girl had a massive crush on him anyway. But it was Tom who put the first crack in my insular world. He was an *atheist*. I had never even heard of such a thing. I had never questioned God, Jesus, Joseph and his coat of many colours, Daniel in the lion's den or the parting of the Red Sea. I would have liked a few more miracles like in the old days and I wished Mummy was an Anglican like everybody else, but I lived in an ideological fortress, things were the way they were, there was right and there was wrong, and we knew exactly what they were, and that, my dear, was that.

As soon as I heard about Tom's atheism, I confronted him indignantly. 'You don't believe in God?'

'No, I don't,' Tom replied calmly.

'That's impossible! If there is no God who made the world?'

'If that's impossible, who made God?'

A bomb detonated in my brain. A thread had been pulled, the cloth had started unravelling and it was never the same again.

***

By the time I was twelve, I had shed my old skin like a snake.

Both Mum and Dad had fathers who frightened and belittled them. Many of my close women friends have experienced that too. I was never afraid of Dad. He sometimes joked that he regretted not enforcing blind obedience because it meant he couldn't stop me running off with *that blighter*, but he didn't mean it. I knew he admired what he called my 'chutzpah', bravery that borders on recklessness.

Dad loved Dorothy Parker's 'The Whistling Girl' because it reminded him of me:

Back of my back, they wag their chins,
Whinny and bleat and sigh;
But better a heart a-bloom with sins
Than hearts gone yellow and dry!

But I was only twelve and not ready for lovers, not yet. Neither a bully nor a victim, for the first time in my life I was free to live as I pleased.

I made new friends. One was Amalia Conde, daughter of the Spanish ambassador who lived in a replica of a Disney palace. One day Daddy dropped me off to spend the day with her and while he and I hovered in a marble hallway he suggested that he shout, 'Down with Franco!'

'No! Daddy! No!'

'He's a dictator.'

'Don't, Daddy, don't, please don't! Pleeeease.'

Mrs Conde, Amalia's exquisitely beautiful mother, appeared at the top of the stairs and waved. I gave Daddy a final pleading glance and fled.

Mrs Conde ordered Amalia's older brother, Jesús María, to teach us how to waltz because, 'a girl who can't dance will never find the right husband.' She sat by the record player spinning Strauss's *The Blue Danube* on repeat, issuing instructions in her dulcet tones:

> 'Girls, follow the boy. Follow the boy. Surrender, let go; let the boy take you where he wants to go. He steps forward with his left foot and you step back with your right foot, move your whole body back with your right foot, keep your distance girls, no body pressing, surrender to the dance but don't let him get the wrong impression, feel the firmness of that hand in the small of your back, surrender

> but keep that distance, move your left foot sideways, close your right foot to the left foot, forwards with the left foot, take a step back and to the right with your right foot and close your left foot to the right foot.'

Jesús María was ancient, at least fifteen, practically an old man, so we couldn't wait for the class to end. When Amalia's mother finally disappeared to dress for dinner, Amalia and I blocked Jesús María from leaving the room.

> 'Where do you put your nose?'
> 'Move. What are you talking about?'
> 'When you kiss a girl, stupid, where do you put your nose?'

Amalia and I had practised kissing each other, rubbing each other's noses in what we called 'eskimo style'. Jesús María sighed, 'It's obvious.'

'Do you want me to be an old maid for the rest of my life? Every time you look around, I'll be there.'

I hadn't really thought about sex; I didn't even have my period and I was dreading blood coming out of my *you know what* and having to put disgusting bits of scrunched up cotton wool soaked in blood in the bathroom wastebin like Mummy. But I also didn't want to be the only girl who didn't bleed. I didn't even have a name for my *you know what,* Mummy simply referred to it as *down there.*

I got funny feelings *down there* sometimes that startled me, and I wondered whether other people noticed I was having them.

Like the Antarctic, *down there* was far, far away, a place I had never investigated, a frozen wasteland inhabited by strange men.

***

As Jesús María was teaching us where to put our noses with his chaste kisses, our lips snapped shut, our tongues safely padlocked in sweaty little pink caves, the Uruguayan economy was tanking. Glamorous synthetic fibres, nylon and rayon were replacing wool, and the gorgeous gas-guzzling, pastel-coloured Chevrolet Impalas were looking as tired as the old Ford T's chugging down the broad avenues. Years later, collectors descended on Montevideo and snapped up all the vintage cars, but at that time we craved brand new things and dismissed these beautiful cars as *cachilas,* old bangers. The economy was in meltdown, inflation had soared to 49 percent and was spiralling out of control, banks closed their doors and there were daily strikes, demonstrations, and riots.

There wasn't even the echo of a whiff about any of this in my world. In our little British bubble we regarded our fellow European settlers as 'Natives', and Indigenous people didn't feature at all. My one-time lodger Catalina tells me her friend's Uruguayan husband doesn't regard himself as Latino. He's European.

'No Somos Latinos', is a song by Uruguayan rock band, El Cuarteto de Nos. It goes like this:

We're not Latinos
Yankies and Europeans think we're a banana republic,

hot with palm trees
don't fuck with me, we're not Latinos,
I was brought up in the Switzerland of the South
I'd rather chat to a Swedish philosopher than a
Bolivian peasant.

Uruguay is proud of its progressive history. As early as 1914, the Colorado President, José Batlle y Ordóñez, introduced a generous welfare system with unemployment benefits, universal suffrage, free school and university education for women and men, health care, and an eight-hour working day, decades before Britain had considered any of it. Uruguayan settlers love to distinguish themselves from the bumptious Argentine *Porteños* who talk too loudly and throw their weight around. Only the notoriously dirty Uruguayan football players offer a clue to the violence that lies under the surface.

When I was six or seven, Daddy's office friend gave him two tickets for a football match between arch-rivals, Nacional and Peñarol and he took me with him because Mummy wasn't interested.

We were standing behind the Nacional team goal and the atmosphere was electric. Grown-ups were shouting and swearing! There was a cry from the crowd above us and Daddy's friend explained that a Peñarol fan had peed into an upside-down umbrella and poured urine on the heads of the fans below. I was most impressed. The players ran around chasing the ball until a scuffle on the pitch broke into a full-on brawl and the game had to be abandoned. Daddy held my hand tight, and we scuttled away as smoke bombs exploded and police on horseback charged around on a far more exciting planet than I had ever lived on. When we got home, Mummy was cross and said that Daddy should never have taken me and we must never go again.

I have loved football ever since.

***

There is a saying, 'When Argentina sneezes, Uruguay gets a cold'.

Uruguay and Argentina had been running expensive welfare states paid for by exports of grain and beef. During and after World War II, British people like to call this war 'the war' as if we were not in a perpetual state of war, Argentina and Uruguay were the bread, meat and wool baskets of the world. In the post-war period, European countries were relatively impoverished so Latin America faced stiff competition from Australia and New Zealand, driving down wool, grain and meat prices.

In every crisis poor people get poorer.

And when poor people get poorer, they resist.

***

These were volatile material conditions in which new things could happen.

In 1962, Raúl Sendic, a charismatic Marxist lawyer, brilliant son of a peasant labourer, founded the Tupamaros a clandestine guerrilla group named after Túpac Amaru II, an Inca cacique who had led a daring armed rebellion against Spanish rule in 1780. Túpac's uprising swept through Perú

Ernesto 'Che' Guevara. Havana, Cuba, (Photographer Alberto Korda), 1960.

and Argentina until it was viciously crushed by the Spanish authorities, who forced him to watch his two sons having their tongues cut out before they were executed. His wife, Micaela Bastides, an even more gifted military leader, suffered the same fate. Then in a grotesque spectacle of violence, Túpac's own tongue was sliced out, his arms and legs tied to four horses galloping off in different directions that only managed to dislocate rather than rip out his limbs, which had to be hacked off before his torso was finally beheaded on the garrotte.

Inca clothing, language and culture were banned.

Sendic was also inspired by his contemporary, the charismatic middle-class Argentinian doctor, Ernesto 'Che' Guevara. In those days, Che wasn't just a handsome face on a T-shirt. In Uruguay and Argentina, we call each other 'che', something like 'mate' or 'Yo'. 'Che', Penny, do you want to come for supper?' 'Che, why do you look so glum?' 'Dale, 'che', hurry up'. It's gender neutral and ubiquitous and that's how Che Guevara got his nickname.

Raúl Sendic organised low-paid sugar cane and beet workers when he was a law student and led four hundred of them on a peaceful march to Montevideo. When the march was violently suppressed, Sendic became convinced that armed insurrection was the only option. French academic Régis Debray, a close friend of Che Guevara's, had developed the Foco theory based on the success of the Cuban revolution. It goes something like this: A small vanguardist group carries out a series of armed interventions against an oppressive regime, provoking the state into ripping off its democratic façade, revealing its true bloodthirsty nature with such disproportionate violence that it fuels popular discontent and jump-starts the revolution. It worked in Cuba because a small group could slip down the mountain, launch an impactful attack against a more powerful enemy and disappear back into the jungle. But unlike Cuba or Colombia, Uruguay is a flat country with nowhere to hide. So Sendic developed the idea of the *urban foco,* with anonymous safe houses in towns and cities instead of forested mountains.

The Tupamaros had a cellular structure; each cell had up to six members who always referred to each other by their aliases. Raúl Sendic was *El Bebé,* Baby. When comrades were arrested, they had been trained to resist torture for twenty-four hours, giving their comrades time to reorganise. After that they could sing like birds.

***

Years later, one of the Monty ladies told me and Mum how impressed she had been by a group of middle-class young men doing innocent early-morning callisthenics on the Carrasco beach. Much later she realised they'd been training for the guerrilla.

***

Guerrillas need arms and money.

In 1963, the Tupamaros attacked the Swiss Gun Club and liberated their stock of weapons. Over the next five years they robbed gun shops, banks and private businesses, building up popular support by kidnapping notoriously corrupt individuals and returning them unharmed as soon as ransoms were paid, hijacking milk and food trucks and distributing supplies in poor neighbourhoods. They scored a propaganda victory after stealing 6 million pesos from the Carrasco Casino and returning a stash of employee tips which they had taken by mistake.

The government crackdown was merciless. It was illegal to even mention the words *Tupamaro, cell, commando, political* or even *subversive* and all left-wing newspapers were shut down. The mainstream press referred to the Tupamaros as 'the ones with no name'.

The Tupamaros built a radio transmitter to deliver their own news and developed their own underground press. They staged a series of situationist pranks, spraying the walls of a nightclub with slogans, like 'Everyone dances or no one dances', and charged into cinemas, cafés and theatres, where they handed out leaflets and harangued captive audiences with revolutionary speeches.

The CIA set up offices in Montevideo and under its tutelage, torture was refined and became so painfully effective that the bravest detainees were unable to hold out for more than a couple of hours. Waves of arrests wiped out whole cells, fellow travellers and anybody who had ever been suspected of thinking anything positive about the Tupas. Even after the organisation had been effectively eliminated, torture continued and Uruguay, which had been admired worldwide for its democratic traditions, became known as the 'torture Chamber of

Latin America,' with the highest per capita ratio of political prisoners in the world. One in fifty-four of its citizens was questioned, incarcerated and tortured.

After Raúl Sendic and the rest of the Tupamaro leadership were arrested - including José Mujica, known affectionately as 'El Pepe', who became the president of Uruguay over thirty years later - young, inexperienced hotheads took over running of organisation and the more playful aspects and the policy of nonviolence towards hostages disintegrated. Popular support drained away as random violence increased, and there was an outcry when Dan Mitrione, a CIA agent, was kidnapped and killed even though it later emerged that he had trained the Uruguayan military in the most sadistic of torture techniques.

Sitting on the top of a bus, soon after I first came to England, I saw a trail of docile people strolling down the road, escorted by uniformed police. Some were holding brightly coloured placards. I asked the woman sitting next to me what was going on. 'It's a demonstration,' she replied. I was astonished. What kind of resistance wanders around with the police?

***

José Mujica was jailed for thirteen years, almost all in solitary confinement, two of them at the bottom of a well. He spent two whole years, in a hole in the ground, all by himself. It makes me panic to even think about it - ten minutes would be tough for me, and as I write this, I feel my breathing getting shallow and the muscles tighten around my heart. Two years down a well. Mujica realised he didn't need much to survive.

When he was president of Uruguay from 2010 to 2015, El Pepe refused to move into the official residence and continued living with his wife on their ramshackle chrysanthemum farm, riding a sixty-year-old bicycle, driving an old Beetle, giving away 90 percent of his salary and refusing to take a pension when his term finished. This is how he addressed the United Nations:

> 'We are promised a life of consuming and squandering. But this is a countdown against nature, against future humankind. It is civilization against simplicity, against sobriety, against all natural cycles, and against the most important things: Adventure. Solidarity. Family. Friendship. Love . . . There's marketing for everything! There's marketing for cemeteries, for funeral services, for maternity wards, for fathers, for mothers, grandparents and uncles! . . . Everything is business! . . . The average man of our time wanders between financial institutions and the tedious routine of offices. He dreams of vacations and freedom. He dreams of being able to pay his bills, until one day, his heart stops.

People say El Pepe achieved very little during his time in office apart from legalising cannabis and same-sex marriage. They say he blew smoke out of his arse. He was criticized by the Left for being too willing to listen to everyone. But maybe this was still some kind of miracle. Che Guevara had dreamt of creating a 'new man' driven by moral instead of material incentives.

Mujica says, 'I haven't cultivated hatred in my garden for decades.' Power doesn't have to corrupt everyone.

***

El Pepe also said, 'Before we were here there were cattle'. I don't know why he said such a thing.

Even the most honourable settlers are wilfully blind. Before we were here there were other people.

We introduced the cattle.

***

We scrambled onto the school bus at 3.30 and the driver told us John Kennedy had been assassinated.

I was thirteen. I had developed zits with yellow heads on my chin and my forehead and finally started bleeding. We wore thin elastic bands that left angry red welts on our skin, with garters and safety pins to keep our sanitary pads in place. As the pad got soaked, it scrunched up and the blood spilled over the sides and onto your knickers where it dried dark brown and remained stained forever.

At the end of that year, Daddy was transferred back to Buenos Aires.

***

I spent the following year as a boarder at St Hilda's in Hurlingham, a western suburb of Buenos Aires and home to the Hurlingham Club founded in 1888 by John Ravenscroft, modelled on a classic English gentleman's club. Its current website urges sportsmen with scant regard for grammar to feel 'like a deep dishonour the mere suspicion of cheating and to carry with a cheerful countenance the disenchantment of a setback.' It has five polo fields, stables for two hundred and fifty horses, eighteen tennis courts, a golf course, swimming pools and cricket pitches. We couldn't afford the membership and anyway we lived on the other side of town.

St Hilda's School was set on extensive grounds with a large white schoolhouse where we ate our meals, did our lessons and homework and wrote a letter to our parents every Sunday evening. The rest of the time we hung out in our allocated houses dotted around the grounds. I shared a dormitory in St John's with two mean girls, my new best friend, Coggie Montague, and Susie Wiggins, another new girl. Susie was mercilessly bullied. This was truly terrible for her but a revelation to me. I discovered that not only was I no longer vulnerable, but even more thrilling, I was able to stick up for her without becoming a target myself. Susie Wiggins got in touch via Facebook several years ago and asked whether I remembered her. She said the bullying had been even worse than I had realised, she had been knocked over in the grounds one night, kicked around, and her shoes stolen. My attempts to help had not made any difference but she was grateful that I hadn't joined in.

There were no organised activities after lessons, so I ran around the hockey field by myself and read every book in the tiny, useless library. I decided I was going to be a writer or an artist and started by writing terrible poems and painting a series of faces of a weeping girl trapped behind a barbed wire fence.

I imagined two futures for myself. In one I am standing on a street corner, talking to three attractive young men; I have long hair and I'm laughing and carefree, flinging a long, striped scarf around my neck. I have dashed there from my studio, stacked with splattered canvases and pots of paint. In the other, I sit frozen at an oval dressing table with ruched frills and a polished glass surface with an ivory-backed brush set and a large tub of loose powder with a huge pink puff. I gaze into hinged mirrors, dressed in a strapless evening gown, my hair set firmly in an elegant, rippling coiffure, but my face is blurred. A double bed is reflected in the mirror and beside it there's the silhouette of a man in a dark suit with his head cut off by the mirror frame.

Some nights, after lights out, when the mean girls were taking a break from tormenting Susie, we lay on our beds and took turns picturing our wedding nights. I was fourteen but still vague about 'the facts of life'. I had never properly kissed a boy apart from one dry kiss inside a wardrobe during a game of squashed sardines and the practice with Jesús María, and we never even laid eyes on a boy at St Hilda's. A gaggle of girls followed the vicar around the school when he arrived to teach Religious Education, eagerly sniffing the faint sharp tang of testosterone that he exuded and speculating about his penis under those long vestments. Thin and red, I imagined. A cute male maths teacher appeared halfway through the year and the poor young man scuttled through the grounds with a permanent blush, collecting flocks of giggling girls chirping after him.

I warned Daddy that being a boarder was boring me to death and I was going to run away. He asked me to see the year out because he'd had to pay the fees up front, promising that I could attend a day school the following year. I agreed.

***

The only time we were allowed out of the school grounds was the promenade to St Mark's, the local Anglican Church, every Sunday morning.

After breakfast, we lined up sullenly in the assembly hall, kitted out in stout shoes, knee-length socks held up with elastic garters, white knickers, large baggy bloomers dragged over our knickers so that nobody would ever glimpse our knickers, even in a howling gale, a bra, a long vest, white shirts, a striped tie, heavy green serge pleated skirts with a sash at the waist, a green cardigan, a blazer with a St Hilda's badge sewn on the pocket, and a jaunty hat. Poppy-eyed, chinless Miss Briggs and a couple of her deputies strode down the line inspecting us head to toe. Every week the same furious sixth formers were ordered to wash off a smudge of eyeshadow or a lick of mascara, and they'd slouch back with murder in their eyes.

Off we tramped, two by two, in a crocodile, looking and feeling idiotic. The section we dreaded most was crossing a bridge with a small slum sprawled underneath. The teenage boys who lived in this *villa miseria* knew exactly when to expect the St Hilda's girls, and they'd leave their shacks and hoot lewd things up at us, waggling their hips and tongues, making me feel naked under all those dense layers, nipples pricking and something happening *down there.*

Down there was chaos and life, poverty and dirt, terrifying and inviting. We'd speed up, trotting briskly while Miss Briggs trilled out of her teeny mouth, *walk girls!* We scurried away as fast as we could but there was a part of me, a secret part of me, that longed to jump off the bridge into the unknown, into somewhere more alive.

***

Time was running out. I was bursting at the seams of my life.

From the minute I learnt to read, I read everything I could get my hands on. I hid a book on my lap at meals, read under a sheet with a torch after lights out, and Mum caught me reading under the shower with one arm held out. 'Penelope! You're the absolute limit!' I read Enid Blyton, Robert Louis Stevenson, Arthur Ransome's *Swallows and Amazons*, Susan Coolidge's *What Katy Did* and *What Katy Did Next*, Louisa May Alcott's *Little Women*, J. M. Barrie, *Gone with the Wind*, *Gulliver's Travels*, Arthur Conan Doyle, James Thurber, anything, as long as it was in English and took me somewhere else.

By fifteen I had become a more adventurous reader but still only in English. I read Mary McCarthy, James Baldwin, William Faulkner, J. D. Salinger, Alan Sillitoe, Keith Waterhouse, Dostoyevsky and T. S. Eliot. I refused to read the 'O' level set texts Wordsworth wandering 'lonely as a cloud' made me feel sick, and I couldn't be arsed with *Northanger Abbey*, which I have not read to this day. I liked *Macbeth* although, in my opinion, Birnam Wood was a total cop-out and Othello was alright despite Desdemona being such a drip. It never even occurred to me to read Latin American authors. I assumed *they* didn't have any. It was still always *them*. They were *locals* while we were, what? Tourists? Visitors?

I watched Antonioni's *Blow-Up* and *loved, loved, loved it*, although I had no idea it was based on a Cortázar story. I had never even heard of Jorge Luis Borges, Manuel Puig, Alejo Carpentier, Gabriel García Márquez or Mario Vargas Llosa.

I skipped a year and went into my 'O'Levels as a day girl at Northlands, which turned out to be just as boring as St Hilda's, but at least I could leave at the end of the day. I sat penned into the back left-hand corner of the classroom and plunged across the top of the desks and out of the door whenever I felt like it. I decided that being innumerate for the rest of my life was perfectly acceptable and refused to attend math classes. While everyone else was studying arithmetic, algebra and geometry, I went to the library and read novels. We didn't even have a laboratory at Northlands, so biology was the only science subject on the curriculum.

I sailed through six 'O'-levels without reading the set texts, which convinced me I was so clever that I didn't need to read any of the set texts for my A levels either. That turned out to be a big mistake I got a D in English even though it was my favourite subject. Mrs Wallace, the headmistress, correctly hissed, 'Penelope Woolcock, you're not as clever as you think you are'.

My friend Helen, who I am still friends with, claims teachers thought well of me. She remembered our strict English teacher writing *extraordinary* in the margin of an essay I had written, but I only remember Mrs Wallace saying I wasn't as clever as I thought I was.

Mum used to say, 'Penny's so clever, not like me,' which made me feel sad and guilty.

***

Calle Lavalle in Buenos Aires had a row of cinemas one after the other, and since I didn't realise that art house cinema was supposed to be difficult and good for you, I'd watch *Goldfinger* one day and Teshigahara's *Woman in the Dunes* or Sidney Lumet's *The Hill* the next, then *Lawrence of Arabia*, *Billy Liar*, *Doctor Zhivago*, *Le Parapluies de Cherbourg*, *Á Bout de Souffle*, and *The Graduate* promised there was a world out there I wanted to be part of.

As a small child, films terrified me. I had to be carried out screaming my head off as soon as Bambi's mother was killed ten minutes in and from Peter Pan as soon as the ticking crocodile appeared. I was convinced I'd be sucked out of my seat and trapped in the world of the film forever.

When I got too big to scream, I pretended I needed to tie up my shoelaces or affected an interest in the projector light behind me to avoid watching the film.

In Monty, when Mummy went to Argentina with Colin when her old aunts were dying, Daddy and I were left to our own devices, and one memorable Sunday we watched *Whiskey Galore*, *Duck Soup* and *The Gold Rush* one after the other. It was one of the best days of my childhood. Some Saturdays when it was too hot or too cold, we'd be dropped off at the local fleapit, the young kids eating crap and throwing popcorn at each other while teenagers sucked each other's faces in the back row. We'd watch a feature-length series of violent cartoons with a vulnerable mouse or bird meting out increasingly sadistic punishments to the cat or coyote, followed by a Western, followed by a comedy, followed by a film about a failing circus, followed by a pirate movie. We'd spill out onto the street six or seven hours later feeling sick with all the plots mixed up in our heads.

Mummy had her own film rating – PP, Prohibited for Peggy, because she only wanted to see *nice* films. We went to every Doris Day 'flick' as Dad called films, as soon as it came out because Doris was a Christian Scientist like Mummy and did pecks on the lips to a man she was married to with her pyjamas on. I loved Doris's soft-focus close-ups, Vaseline smeared on the lens to disguise her wrinkles, eyes wide and her mouth a little open circle of permanent surprise. *The Pyjama Game, That Touch of Mink, Calamity Jane, Move Over, Darling* and *Please Don't Eat the Daisies* - we enjoyed them all. Mum adored Rock

Hudson, so sexy in a nonthreatening way, until he died of AIDS, and then she never mentioned him again and would gaze into the middle distance like Mary Baker Eddy if his name came up.

Dad was game for anything and years later he and I enjoyed Ken Russell's *The Devils* and Derek Jarman's *Sebastiane*.

In the summer of 1964-1965, after I left St Hilda's and hadn't started yet at Northlands, neither Mum nor I had made any new friends and she convinced Dad to buy a television. After lunch every day, we watched a subtitled British or American film, *North by Northwest, Bringing Up Baby, A Matter of Life and Death, Some Like It Hot, High Noon* and *Shane*, all in black and white. It was many years before I realised many of them were classics and some of them were in colour.

It never occurred to me for a second, that I could make films myself. I thought actors made films.

When I was thirty-eight, living in Newcastle upon Tyne, working in a film cooperative, Mum and Dad came to visit and we all went to see Susan Seidelman's *Making Mr. Right,* about a woman who falls in love with an android. I had selected it thinking it was a harmless comedy, but at the end Mum pursed her lips and I could tell she'd hated it. The three of us went for a meal in one of the many mediocre Italian restaurants in town and while we were sitting around a Chianti bottle in a raffia basket covered in dripping candle wax, I begged her to tell me what had offended her.

Mum touched the bobbles on the coloured glass lampshade.

'Ayy, look at this lamp, isn't it pretty!'

'Mum! Please, tell me what upset you about that film.'

'Look at that little waiter's moustache.'

'Please, Mum, tell me.'

'This tablecloth. Linen isn't it?'

'Mum, come on . . .'

Mum gazed into the distance, changing the subject over and over.

I persisted until eventually Mum placed her hands on the table, looked me straight in the eye, and said clearly.

'The thing is, I'm on a different plane than the rest of you.'

'Speak to me! You're my mother!' I blurted.

Mum gave it to me straight.

'I'm not your mother.'

I experienced a brief moment of elation. An old weight lifted off my shoulders. Of course! That explained everything! I was adopted. I knew it! I had suspected as much until I saw a small black-and-white photo of myself as a baby with Granny Jessie at my christening, which had somehow persuaded me I was mistaken. That is why I was such a weirdo!

I let it sink in and took a deep breath.

'So, who is my mother?'

'God,' she replied promptly. 'God is your mother.'

I groaned and left it at that.

After Mum had gone to bed, Dad and I sat up late with a nightcap. 'I was interested watching you trying to talk to your mother. I gave up years ago.'

Mum was hermetically sealed. There was a great, whistling black hole inside her that Christian Science had filled up. She was hypersensitive, easily wounded, and rigid in her beliefs. She was also a lovely, kind person who would help anybody. Auntie Ethel told me that when her stockings had laddered before a special date, 'Peggy took off the pair she was wearing and gave them to me.'

Dad who had refused to buy a television in case the rest of us became couch potatoes, immediately became one himself and developed narcolepsy. He could fall asleep chewing a mouthful of food, as someone was speaking to him, as he was speaking himself, or holding a snack to his mouth. It horrified me. When I saw him dropping off, I'd start talking in a very animated way to jolt him out of it. I saw it as my job to keep him awake, and often it worked.

***

By 2009, ten years after Dad died, Mum was losing the plot, having breakfast at 3 a.m., handing her wallet over to shopkeepers and taxi drivers and haemorrhaging more money than her generous pension could provide. Colin and I prevailed on her to move into BABS, the British and American Benevolent Society Home where all the British community ladies went after their husbands died. I felt bad about this because Mum loved her little flat. She died less than a year later. I flew out to see her twice and was shocked to find that she no longer read her Lesson, showed no interest in going to church and had forgotten all about her Christian Science.

What was all that about? Surely religion is meant to be helpful when you die?

I googled Mum and Dad to check if they were out there in the aether, but despite Dad being a pillar of the British community and serving on so many committees, there was no trace of him; but there is a Christian Science Sentinel podcast with Mum telling her story about the miracle of Carrefour, her familiar little voice ringing from beyond the grave.

> Peggy Woolcock: 'My husband and I, quite a number of years ago, were driving home one evening and I said, "Oh I need to go to the supermarket" and we hadn't been there for two or three minutes and suddenly there was a tremendous noise!'
>
> Male Christian Science interviewer: 'What was the noise? What did it sound like?'
>
> Peggy Woolcock: 'Well, screaming! Three young men walked in and one of them came in with a machine gun he was about two metres away from me and he was pointing it at me and everybody else, saying to hand over our handbags and they wanted our money and they were holding up the supermarket!'
>
> Christian Science interviewer: 'How did you feel at that stage?'
>
> Peggy Woolcock: 'Well, I was terrified! But then when I heard them say they wanted our handbags I thought, "I wonder if I can, without this man with a machine gun looking at me, I wonder if I can get the money out of my handbag and hide it somewhere in a pocket or something you see before they

take it", it was money that I needed! Well suddenly I thought, I refuse to accept this picture, and I bowed my head, and I started to repeat the Lord's Prayer trying to think of every word with understanding as I went on.'

Christian Science interviewer: 'What did that do to help you?'

Peggy Woolcock: 'Well, it put me into contact with God, shall we say, I felt that God was close to me when I was repeating the Lord's Prayer. The moment I started to pray I felt that everything was all right, you know, that er . . . I felt quite calm about it. I suddenly thought to myself, something I'd read that morning, which was a quotation from one of Mary Baker Eddy's books, which is 'no evidence before the material senses can close my eyes to the Scientific Proof that God, Good, is supreme.'

Christian Science interviewer: 'Now what did that mean to you at that time?'

Peggy Woolcock: 'Well, I felt that God was looking after us all you know, that God was more powerful than the scene in front of me. Evil seemed to be present and it's as if it was more powerful than good and I felt that through praying that it was the other way around, you see? That good was present and that was what was going to prevail. I really felt peaceful, and I wasn't terrified any more, and while I was praying, I noticed a little girl crying in a cart just next to me.'

Christian Science interviewer: 'How old was this little girl?'

Peggy Woolcock: 'She must have been about five and she was very frightened, I put my hand on her arm and I said to her, 'don't you be frightened because God is right here' and so, you know, she stopped crying then. After that I looked up again and I saw that the two young men had gone into a room, where apparently they kept a safe, and they came out again complaining! They said there was no money in the safe and they went off! They said the hold-up wasn't really worthwhile. After the whole thing was over and these three young men had disappeared, I saw one of the cashiers there, a young girl who was absolutely hysterical, so I went over to her and I said 'calm yourself because you can go home this evening and tell your family about what happened, and that you're perfectly all right! You see you have to thank God because you're safe'. And so she looked at me, and she said, 'D'you know you're right!' She was sitting on the counter and she jumped off and quite happily she ran off, you see?'

Christian Science interviewer: 'What did that experience mean to you looking back on it from today's perspective?'

Peggy Woolcock: 'I felt that what I'd learnt in Christian Science, what one knows about God and Man, I was able to put into practice there and that it

> was effective. What's that saying? . . . 'What blesses one blesses all'. Well, that was proved to be true that day because I was blessed but everybody else in that supermarket was blessed in one way or another.

Bye-bye, Mummy. My omnipotent little mother. When I watched that small coffin carried up to the crematorium in the Cemetery of the Dissidents at Chacarita, I felt so sad; she was a brave, little, fat thing and she always did the best she could.

***

Apart from Helen, I had another close girlfriend, Ruhana Geffen, daughter of the Israeli consul in Argentina. She announced that Arabs were lazy and cowardly, fleeing in large numbers as soon as they saw a single Israeli, and that the Jews had *made the desert flower.* I had watched *Exodus,* a Hollywood movie starring Paul Newman and Eva Marie Saint, and they proved Ruhana right.

I wonder whether Ruhana is still alive, in her seventies like me, and whether she is applauding the sickening genocide in Gaza and the West Bank. I wonder whether she now sees there is always a desert, a desert that is not a desert, in these settler stories.

On April 8, 1948, fighters from the far-right Zionist Irgun and Lehi groups invaded Deir Yassin, a Palestinian village, rounded up all the inhabitants, men, women and children and killed them. News of the massacre spread to other villages so Palestinian civilians fled as Zionist troops advanced, never thinking that they would not be allowed to return. On November 2, 2022, the openly fascist, far-right coalition, led by the criminally corrupt psychopath Benjamin Netanyahu, won an outright majority in a national election. The atrocities pile up. I pick three days at random since October 7, 2023. On October 9, 2023, Israel's defence minister Yoav Gallant said, 'We are fighting human animals, and we fight accordingly' continued killing civilians in Gaza and cut off electricity, fuel, food and water. On August 8, 2024, Israeli Defence Forces waded through a lake of blood and bombed a school as children were playing football. March 20, 2025, Israelis killed eighty Palestinian children in the space of fifty-one minutes and dropped leaflets over Gaza saying nobody cared whether they lived or died. Trump wants to make Gaza the 'Riviera of the Middle East'. The people who live there have to disappear. They cannot resist. This today and today and today, this permanent present, washes away all the yesterdays. Settler nations are built on violence. I repeat this until I bore myself. We used to call people who repeated the same thing over and over, scratched records. But I have to keep repeating because I am in a constant state of forgetting, as I walk across Times Square in Manhattan, watch *Waiting for Godot* in Melbourne, or cross the railway tracks at Martinez Station, forgetting these are contested sites. And in the metropolis, in the belly of the beast, we have colonies within, reservations, shanty towns, prisons, designated spaces where inhabitants are subjected to continual violence.

The original violence is forgotten over and over; it's the void at the centre of the house of horrors.

A young woman from Gaza lives in my house. We laugh a lot. We cook and hug and resist despair. We do not pretend the horror is not happening. But we can't do anything about it.

***

Since I had decided I was too clever to study for my A levels, I had plenty of time on my hands, so I organised a school concert and persuaded Ruhana to help me. We recruited girls of all ages to sing, act and recite, and I reserved a spot for myself to tell a story I had written specially for the occasion. I was very proud of it. The protagonist was Junior Jesus, a flamboyant shyster who drove from town to town in a beaten-up Chevy, declaring that he was the 'Son of God' and warning that his death would be the 'End of Times', the sun would cease to shine, and the world would end. His preaching made him very rich. But he went too far and Christian citizens enraged by his blasphemy, crucified him on a lamppost. As Junior Jesus took his last breath, a cloud drifted over the sun and the world went dark. The gathering crowd were terrified, fearing they had made a terrible mistake. His followers wailed.

The cloud floated on its way and the sun shone as before.

On the eve of the public performance, Mrs Wallace and the entire teaching staff attended a dress rehearsal in the assembly hall. When it was time for *A Story by Penelope Woolcock,* I walked onstage carrying a tall stool and perched on it confidently in the style of Dean Martin or Victor Borge, who I had admired on television, and confidently launched into my performance. Right from the start, Mrs Wallace and her deputy, the elderly Miss Johnson, looked increasingly horrified while the remaining teachers shifted uncomfortably in their seats. I ploughed on, and when I finished describing the crucifixion in gory detail there was a dead silence, broken only by Miss Johnson snivelling until Mrs Wallace sprung out of her chair with surprising agility and pointed a finger at me as Diana Beare would do years later. 'Penelope Woolcock, you are a blasphemer. Miss Johnson is a devout Christian and you have made her cry. Not a word of this execrable filth will be heard again in this school.'

I picked up my stool and stalked offstage, back straight. None of the girls hovering in the wings would catch my eye. I ran to the bathroom and burst into great hacking sobs at the end of a long row of basins. A girl in the year below me who was what bitchy girls called a 'slut', was the only one to console me. She put a kind hand on my shoulder and whispered, 'I thought it was very good.'

I used a Biro to scratch out *A Story by Penelope Woolcock* on our mimeographed programmes and performed a rip-off version of Victor Borge's phonetic punctuation instead. It went down very well but my heart wasn't in it.

I wanted to tell my story.

***

The Lord, not any Lord but The Lord, also known as God, Jaweh or Jehovah, summoned Moses to Mount Sinai. Moses obediently legged it up the mountain for forty days and forty nights, leaving the Lord's chosen people under the care of his brother Aaron. While he was away, the chosen people lost faith in The Lord and begged Aaron to make them a golden calf to worship instead. When Moses came back down the mountain, lugging two massive stone tablets on which The Lord had carved some instructions, he found his people having a whale of a time cavorting around a golden calf. Moses threw a massive tantrum and smashed the tablets, but the Lord replaced them and gave him a portable tabernacle so he could carry them around more easily. Charlton Heston stood on a ledge in full technicolour bellowing out Cecil B. DeMille's *The Ten Commandments.* Edward G Robinson yelled his head off and the writhing masses wailed as they toppled down a deep ravine straight to Hell, where they belonged. Moses went on to become a prominent Republican and President of the National Rifle Association, and now he is dead.

Christian Zionists believe that in the fourteenth century B.C. a place called Shiloh -now known as Kirbeit Seilun on the West Bank in Palestine - was the capital of ancient Israel and the Lord had promised that the Jews could rule over it until the end of times. Scott Stripling, a Christian evangelical pastor from Texas, currently heads an archaeological dig, searching for the remains of the tabernacle with the two stone tablets the Lord gave Moses. If they find it, Israel claims it will prove this is their promised land and Palestinians are the interlopers.

In 2004 I was invited to show my film of John Adams's opera *The Death of Klinghoffer* at the Ramallah Film Festival. As I walked across the checkpoint a young Israeli conscript ordered an old Palestinian man to hurry up. The old man was unable to walk faster so the young soldier smashed him on the head with the butt of his assault rifle. The old man staggered forward, blood pouring down his face and splashing his white robe. Two family members held him up on either side and helped him walk a bit quicker.

I was the only person who was shocked.

***

Many filmmakers enjoy showing their work, but I am always apprehensive. My first attempt at public storytelling with Junior Jesus had ended in tears. As I walked into the Side Cinema at the end of the screening of my first film, *When the Dog Bites* about unemployment in a former steel town. I thought I was making a creative film about resilience, with escapologists and drag queens occupying the space that paid work had previously filled, but the audience thought I was mocking them. I heard a woman scream 'shoot her!' and a man shout, 'Bang!' I made my way apprehensively to the front of the auditorium to face the audience and the woman stood up and yelled, 'Why don't you crawl back into the gutter where you belong?' Years later, in 2003, at the Jerusalem Film Festival after the screening of *The Death of Klinghoffer*, I was chased around the cinema by several irate audience members, one of them a European Holocaust survivor, shaking her walking stick at me. When we crossed the checkpoint to show it in Ramallah, the Palestine Liberation Front threatened to firebomb any cinema that screened my film because it depicted a botched action while they were holding the front line in Jenin. The film starts with depicting the Nakba and provides a context to the execution of an elderly Jewish man during the hijacking of the *Achille Lauro* cruise ship in 1985. Then, as now, any attempt to understand and depict the source of Palestinian resistance, leads to accusations of antisemitism. A month later, at the London Jewish Film Festival, people queued up politely to take it in turns to spit out how disgusting and antisemitic they thought I was.

I've never got used to it. If you are telling stories people don't want to hear, they let you know.

***

The fifth Argentine coup was on June 29, 1966, in the middle of my last year of school. I woke up to military music playing on all radio stations followed by the announcement that the democratically elected President Arturo Ilia had been replaced by General Juan Carlos Onganía: 'I am convinced that it is essential to bring about a fundamental change in the Republic, a real revolution that will return to Argentines, their faith, their trust and their pride.'

He dedicated Argentina to the Immaculate Heart of Mary. Mary was immaculate because, like her son, Jesus, she was not the product of sexual intercourse.

Doctor Arturo Illia, a medical doctor nicknamed *La Tortuga,* The Tortoise, was a mild-mannered moderate, lampooned on television comedy programmes for being slow and ineffectual. But in 1963, Illia's first act as president was to lift bans on all proscribed political parties, including the Communist Party, the right-wing Movement for Integration and Development, and Peronist factions, who repaid him by ganging up with the military against him. Illia passed legislation issuing penalties for racial violence, invested in a national literacy plan, established a minimum wage, wrestled control of oil production away from foreign contractors and regulated pharmaceutical companies, all of which alienated the military, powerful landowners and the business community. In 1965 he angered the United States by refusing to send in troops to invade the Dominican Republic to oust a left-wing president. Not such a tortoise.

After he was deposed, Doctor Ilia returned to his hometown in Cordoba and continued practicing as a doctor, attending to poor patients for free.

Onganía presented himself as the dynamic leader the country needed. He was what Mum called 'a different kettle of fish', an admirer of General Franco and Mussolini, convinced that liberal democracy and left-wing ideology invited moral degradation and corroded traditional Catholic values. He led a faction of nationalist military officers who called themselves the 'last aristocracy', answerable only to God and History. They used metaphors of sickness to describe disgust at a body politic infected by liberal ideas, rotting its entrails and spreading cancer. The only cure was a Christian crusade to restore moral purity and restore the body back to health.

One month into his administration, Onganía ordered the federal police to invade the Faculty of Sciences at the University of Buenos Aires and in the Night of the Long Batons, police officers formed two lines and ordered the dean, the assistant dean, several professors and hundreds of students to run the gauntlet, battered by rifle butts and batons.

In 1966 the new minister of economy and work, Adalbert Krieger Vasena, a wealthy steel magnate, decreed a wage freeze and devalued the peso by 40 percent, throwing workers into extreme poverty, suspended the right to strike and encouraged foreign companies to exploit Argentina's national resources. Still oblivious to anything going on around me, I attended house parties, dancing to the Supremes, and one night I slow danced to The Righteous Brothers singing 'You've lost That Lovin' Feeling' in my new cashmere sweater with Vasena's nephew, a *niño bien*, a posh boy with floppy hair who grabbed my hand and put it on his throbbing penis. I was shocked and pulled it away.

Krieger Vasena was responsible for the El Chocón Dam that flooded vast lands in Patagonia to generate electricity in Patagonia. German settlers who lost land they had paid a pittance for, were handsomely compensated while the Indigenous Mapuche, who could not provide title deeds to their ancestral lands, were offered minimal or no compensation.

Central to Onganía's *Argentine Revolution* was a crackdown on all forms of 'immoralism', including miniskirts, men with long hair, and avant-garde artistic movements. I scoured Buenos Aires for artists in my short skirts without a care in the world. I could do whatever I liked.

***

I enjoyed being a teenager, dancing and smooching at parties, all just practice for the real thing. One night, Peter Duffel drove me home and we groped in his car; I felt a surge of desire but decided I didn't want to go *all the way* with him. He was indignant but I knew he wasn't *the one* I was waiting for. That night I dreamt that an enormous wave rose and froze like Hokusai's painting before turning into a one-dimensional façade of a street propped up like a Hollywood film set. Then I found myself walking on a thin ledge with lions prowling on the other side of a ravine. I went to a family dinner at my friend Robin's and regaled them with my dream. There was an awkward silence and then his elder sister's psychology-student boyfriend informed everyone at the table that I was sexually repressed. I went bright red and strongly denied it. Robin's Dad was a vicar and he pretended he hadn't heard, and Robin's Mum quickly asked whether anybody wanted second helpings. I passed over my plate. 'It's delicious, what is it?' Robin's Mum told me I was eating brains and I gagged.

School was over at last. I was sixteen and I had no prospects. I had no qualifications to go to a local university, bad A levels and no funding to go to England. My best friend, Helen, went off to art school in Exeter and Robin was doing compulsory military service because his father refused to bribe his way out of it like most middle-class boys. I was left to my own devices and after eating that chocolate biscuit at the Bar Moderno, I was open to everything. I was delighted when a tall man with shoulder-length dirty-blond hair accosted me on the corner of Florida and Uruguay, holding a stack of books. 'I'm Barzac and my poetry is going to change your life.' Now that really was an offer I couldn't refuse.

Barzac invited me for a coffee, adding that I would have to pay because he didn't have any money, and I knew my real life was finally beginning. Over that first coffee, Barzac explained he had rewritten *Hamlet*, a play which needed rewriting in my opinion, and we made plans to set up an artist's workshop and an independent publishing house.

I wrote to Helen every few days in a state of great excitement, letters she kept and gave to me.

> *I am AT LAST widening my circle of friends to include Argentines and the ones I have met are mature, interesting, intelligent and really good to know. People who only deign to speak to people whose parents they know etc deserve to be shot. . . but I feel I am limited by my tremendous lack of knowledge.*

I was meeting new people every few days. Apart from Barzac there was the Buddhist Bobby Curto who took a photograph of me for the cover of a magazine *Juventud Nueva* and wrote me poems.

> *Beauty my beauty*
> *our voice, your skin, your nails*
> *Beauty my beauty*
> *Yourself, your light, your shadow*
> *Beauty.*

I was finally clawing my way out of the suburbs. Two of my paintings were selected for a proper show in the city centre and I was meeting other artists, men who followed me around saying, *you really interest me.* I felt powerful and desirable. Walking down Goodge Street in Central London today a group of girls in their late teens swagger towards me, flaunting bare-flat tummies, clear skin, hair swinging in the sunshine, and I remember what that felt like. These days I would be completely invisible if I didn't smile at random strangers. But I do smile at strangers. And they smile back.

> *Dear Helen,*
> *Everyone is suddenly pushing and screaming grow up grow up and I want to do something great and assert myself as a person before I can give that little island of loneliness and one-ness and me-ness and dreams to anyone. Helen, it's awful because everyone I am in contact with is so impressed with me and it's very, very bad for me, I can't bear it so please write me a criticising letter.*

I genuinely tried to help Barzac sell his books, but nobody wanted to buy them even though a review in *Clarín* called him 'one of the most representative young poets of the thrusting young generation'. When I told Robin about Barzac, he said he sounded like a fraud. I was outraged.

> *Dear Helen,*
> *Robin is dead to me. I live only in the present and he is far behind. I am miles ahead, perhaps because I am now conscious of my responsibility as an artist and a mature person.*

Barzac smelt a bit, but I was dazzled by the things he said and when he offered to help me lose my inhibitions, I leapt at the chance. I asked my friend Susan Peters whether we could both lose our inhibitions in her house because I knew her mother and sister were going away for a few days. I met Barzac at Olivos Station. He stepped off the train, threw his arms open and yelled, 'I love you Penny, te quiero! Te quiero!' at the top of his voice. Everyone in the station was looking at us, I was mortified and herded him off to Susan's as quickly as I could. He bellowed about how much he loved me all the way there.

He limbered up by drinking the entire bottle of wine I had bought for the ritual and a lot of Susan's mother's gin before instructing us to clear a space in the sitting room. We obediently pushed the sofas to the side and he lit a candle in the middle of the floor and ordered us to sit down and focus. Susan and I sat on the couch watching him crawl around, gazing intently at the flame, then panting and howling like a wolf *Whoooooo!* This set off Susan's Labrador chained up in the garden and soon all the other dogs in the neighbourhood were barking like crazy. Barzac bayed and keened and lifted up a leg, and for a horrible moment, I thought he was going to piss on the floor. I noticed that he had rotten teeth and although I didn't want to die a virgin, I decided I couldn't face *going all the way* with him either.

***

I told my mother I wanted my room painted black but she ignored me and had it decorated pink. I loathed pink. I painted the lightbulbs green and black with gouache and my room smelt permanently of scorched paint, toxic smoke wafting everywhere.

> *Dear Helen,*
> *I just started painting and got so worked up that I started screaming and had to lie on the floor to relax and then had to walk twenty thousand times around the house clapping my hands and screaming – I haven't painted for three weeks and it was like untapping this bunged up energy which just exploded!*

***

I wrote what I was convinced was earth-shattering poetry.

I eat
Feet
I eat
Velocity
I eat
I eat
Eat
Velocity.

Penny at 15, Buenos Aires, (Family album), 1965.

I painted furiously, late into the night. What I lacked in talent I made up for with enthusiasm. Poor Mummy would come in the next day and say nervously, 'Oh, it's very modern, Penny. Very good.'

Dear Helen,
Today I felt that very near me was the essence of the truth and sitting cross legged on my bed with Edit Piaf singing La Ville Unconnu in the background, I tried to find it.

***

Helen, now Helena, came to visit me in London recently. She lives on the Pampas with her husband, Nick, who has a beard, as accurately predicted by a teenage Ouija board session at Jenny Potter's house when we were fifteen. I tell Helen I am writing about the Conquest of the Desert and the genocide of the Mapuche and other Indigenous people. She shrugs and mutters that remnants of the Mapuche tribe have started petitioning for their land, 'which is ridiculous because they stole that land from the Tehuelche.'

Helena and I have nurtured our friendship for sixty years despite choosing such paths. I love her still; she's an oddball who doesn't fit in with other rich farmers' wives. She met Nick after art school, and they returned to Argentina from London in 1978 in the throes of the last, and most murderous dictatorship. To this day, they say they had no idea what was going on. I believe them.

We didn't meet during that time.

Are European settlers only the most recent in series of players pushing other people off these fertile plains? Was the Conquest of the Desert another dreary chapter in an inexorable cycle of colonisation and land expropriation perpetuated by one group after another?

***

The semi-nomadic Mapuche were celebrated weavers and only one of many ethnic groups on the Pampas. The Tehuelche were a fully nomadic tribe until Roca's Conquest of the Desert in 1878, hunting and foraging across vast lands from the Santa Cruz River in the far south up to the Rio Negro in Northern Patagonia on the southern border of the Pampas. After the Spanish introduced horses to the Americas, the Tehuelche and the Mapuche became magnificent horse riders, roaming over extensive territories, capturing feral horses and trading textiles and meat with European settlers. The Tehuelche were often over six feet tall; the Spanish called them *patagones*, or 'big feet', because their *guanaco* skin moccasins left enormous footprints that led to exaggerated reports about a race of giants.

The past is always contested territory. In Helen and Nick's narrative, the Tehuelche are the docile 'good Indians', happy to cooperate with whites. The Mapuche, also known as Araucanos or Manzaneros, are cast as villainous Chilean invaders who brutally slaughtered the lovely Tehuelche. In this gobbledegook version, Roca's Conquest of the Desert was a noble attempt to rescue the Tehuelche from their persecutors. When I asked Helena where she got this stuff from, she sent me an article by Gustavo Cairo, an amateur historian from the right-wing

PRO Party, *Propuesta Republicana.* Cairo proposes that the Mapuche were 'sangrientos malones', bloodthirsty raiders, who strangled Tehuelche women and babies. He argues that Roca's Conquest of the Desert was a mission of mercy, saving thousands of prisoners from murderous Mapuche barbarians, and he rounds off with a rose-tinted view of Argentina as 'a country open to all who want to live in peace and thrive. . . an example to the world, of social integration without racial or religious problems.'

White immigration is enshrined in the 1853 Argentine Constitution. Juan Alberdi sponsor of article 25 expanded on it like this: 'In order to civilise by means of the populace it is essential to do it with civilised populations; in order to educate our America in liberty and industry . . . there are foreigners and there are foreigners'. We knew exactly what kind of foreigners we were.

Great-grandfather Alfred Lovett & his wife Annie on the left.
Buenos Aires, (Family album), c.1890.

Cairo quotes George Chaworth Musters, an English Royal Navy commander, who wrote a memoir about spending 1870 riding from Santa Cruz to Rio Negro with a group of Tehuelche.

I was so anxious to read it immediately that I threw my principles out of the window and signed up to Amazon Prime for a same-day delivery of *At home with the Patagonians*, anticipating a racist Victorian travelogue. To my surprise, Muster is respectful of both the Tehuelche and the Mapuche/Araucanos. He forms friendships, praises their intelligence, kindness and good nature, notes the absence of wife beating and is particularly struck by their indulgent attitude to child-rearing, probably in contrast to the emotional coldness and physical cruelty suffered by English public-school boys like himself. He touches on their suspicious attitude towards white Christians: 'Nor, considering the treatment, treacherous cruelty and knavish robbery, experienced by them at the hands of the invaders and colonists alternately, is this to be wondered at.'

Muster admires the negotiating skills of the caciques in resolving feuds between Tehuelche family groups as well as with other tribes. He witnesses several encounters with Mapuche groups and describes welcome ceremonies followed by horse racing and drunken feasting. He notes instances of intermarriage before both groups go their separate ways after days of festivities. Muster writes about the precise period during which Cairo claims the Mapuche were strangling Tehuelche women and babies and slaughtering the men.

Cairo also invoked José Bengoa's *History of the Mapuche* to make his case. Bengoa has always been a passionate advocate for Mapuche rights, sacked by the Pinochet regime from his university job in Chile for speaking out against the privatisation of their ancestral lands. In Bengoa's account, borders were much more porous, Indigenous people including legendary Mapuche caciques like Calfucura and Mangín travelled back and forth freely before arbitrary borders were drawn between Argentina and Chile.

My head spins. Every text mentions the names of different tribes, the Pehuenche, the Rangueles, the Pampas, the Picunche and the Huilliche, Chiriguanos and Mocoví; some share a language, others don't, and Mapuche groups seem to change names according to where they are.

***

It dawns on me, more forcefully, that all of us Argentines, unless we are Indigenous, we are all immigrants, and there is tremendous hubris about the way I place us, the British, at the centre of the story. This was a global Pan-European project of enslavement, looting and genocide that attracted amoral marauders from across Europe, people who were prepared to stop at nothing to get what they wanted. We looked down on our compatriots, the people we called Argentines, but we were all as Argentine and not as Argentine as each other, mucky immigrant settlers with blood on our hands, killing and erasing Indigenous people to this day. When we didn't do the killing ourselves, we looked the other way. In some ways we were worse than the others, living in an insular, gossiping community that refused to speak the same language as anybody else, reducing Spanish to a language of instruction *una cerveza por favor* while our English remained in stasis: *Stasis*: 'reduced mobility of the intestines with retention of faeces'. We were full of shit. And the people we called locals were no more local than we were.

***

The Anglo-Argentine community was very supportive of right-wing military coups, but I assumed we were not directly involved in any of the killing. We preferred drinking a nice cup of tea ignoring what was going on.

Patagonia, south of the Pampas, was historically viewed as a vast inhospitable desert, always a desert, inhabited by barbaric tribes with a coastline continually ravaged by Atlantic storms with no safe ports.

These days Patagonia has been reinvented as paradise on earth, rich in natural resources, home to docile Natives who are happy to cooperate with mining, ranching, fishing, sawmills, oil distilleries and hydroelectric plants. Despite the recent irruption of massive industrial projects, the landscape is fetishised. No longer bleak and desolate, it is considered stunningly beautiful, compared favourably to the Swiss Alps and the Lake District. Tierra del Fuego has become a prime hiking destination and niche travel companies offer an 'authentic experience' for the discerning international tourist.

On the Beagle in 1839, Charles Darwin pointed out that Patagonia was worth fighting over. He was rather shocked by the cold-blooded murder of 110 Indigenous men, women and children but was reassured when he was told that very small children had been spared and given away as slaves. He concluded, 'The war of extermination, although carried on with the most shocking barbarity, will certainly produce great benefits, it will at once throw open four or five hundred miles in fine country for the produce of cattle.'

***

A large Welsh community settled in Trelew in Southern Patagonia and at Northlands prefects monitored the corridors and playgrounds at break times, barking, 'Speak English, girls!' at the rich Argentine girls who preferred speaking Spanish and the Welsh girls, for whom English was a third language.

My friend Guy asked, 'Were the Welsh any better than the English?'

Welsh settlers arrived in 1865, part of the same great wave as my great-grandfathers, looking to protect their culture and language from the predations of the English. At this time, the Argentine State was seeking to consolidate its sovereignty over land south of the Rio Negro, focus of a territorial dispute with Chile, regarded as *tierra de nadie,* nobody's land. The Argentine Minister of the Interior, Guillermo Rawson, offered the Welsh financial inducements to settle and paid the Tehuelche three hundred thousand pesos and a quantity of goods and liquor to refrain from molesting the new arrivals. The Tehuelche were simultaneously there to do a deal with, and not there.

The first Welsh settlers arrived armed to the teeth. They had read Robinson Crusoe, heard about hostilities between European settlers and *Red Indians* in the United States and been alarmed by articles in the Welsh press claiming that the Tehuelche were giant cannibals. They arrived in winter and almost starved.

On the day of a Welsh double wedding in the Chubut Valley, the settlement was visited by two Tehuelche on horseback carrying a letter in Spanish which the local cacique had dictated to a Swiss naturalist. Neither the Welsh nor the Tehuelche spoke more than a smattering of Spanish and they were communicating in broken Spanish and sign language when one of the officers of the colony shouted, 'That's enough! These wild animals have come to spy so they can kill us later. Kill them both!' And that might have been the end of it.

But a wedding guest at the back of the crowd cried out 'No!'

Another supported him. 'That man does not have a savage face!'

Instead of killing the visitors, they painstakingly translated the letter cacique Antonio had given his grandson Francisco to deliver:

> *I and my people are contented to see you colonise on the Chupat, for we shall have a nearer place to go in order to trade... If your traders do not cheat us, we shall always negotiate with you.*

The cacique laid out clear terms about what they could offer and what they wanted in return. He explained they were on Tehuelche land so the Welsh should deal directly with him and not with the Argentine State. He was reluctant to travel to Buenos Aires to negotiate with the state because the city was full of diseases that were dangerous to his people:

> *In this way have died friends of mine last winter who went to prefer claims for land likewise. This is the reason why I did not go.*

A mutually beneficial trading relationship was established: precious ostrich feathers for decorating women's hats in Buenos Aires, Paris and London; guanaco wool, meat and skins, and textiles woven by the neighbouring Mapuche were exchanged for yerba tea, flour, bread, biscuits, tobacco and liquor. George Musters observed that the Welsh were 'pleasanter and safer' than what he referred to as the 'other Christians'.

Perhaps it only needs one opposing voice to stop the slaughter. And a second voice to make the tide turn.

This relationship was not genocidal but always within the white supremacist logic of the colonial project. 'The Handbook of the Welsh Colony' condescendingly advises new settlers:

> Defeat the Indians through kindness . . . we cannot disregard the rights of the Indians of the land . . . but should attempt to make friends of them, giving them whatever is honest whatever is just . . . let us treat the Indians as we treat each other and even

> extend to them, as we do to children, the leniency due to ignorance.

The new Welsh settlement only survived the first tough years because 'ignorant Indians' saved them from starvation by teaching them to break and ride wild horses, hunt ostrich and guanaco with bolas, and forage for wild plants for food and medicinal use. Welsh settler journals and diaries testify to the kindness and patience shown to these raw 'gringos' by the cacique Francisco and his people. In Wales, hunting was the exclusive preserve of rich English landlords but it could be freely practiced in Patagonia. These settlers never questioned their own right to occupy the land they wanted but the Tehuelche were always carefully to distinguish them from the rest of the *colonos,* settlers, referring to the Welsh as *hermanos,* brothers, never as the hated *Cristianos.*

In 1883 when the Conquest of the Desert spread its slaughter south of the Rio Negro, leaders of the Welsh settlement in Chubut wrote this feeble letter to Colonel Villegas:

> *Without wishing to interfere in any way with the measures which you saw wise to adopt we hope that you can show them every compassion and assistance that are consistent with your obligations. On our own part we take the opportunity to state that we have received much kindness at the hands of these natives.*

Some of the settlers were reduced to tears seeing their hunting companions herded into concentration camps and made futile efforts to release them.

By 1890 the Tehuelche had been swept off their land. The Welsh community survives to this day.

***

Benetton is the largest landholder in Argentina, owning nine-hundred thousand hectares of Patagonia and it makes a fortune out of livestock, farming, fossil-fuel extraction and logging. I visit the Benetton website and am immediately tempted to buy myself a green midi skirt for £59.99.

Next to pictures of beautiful, young people wearing colourful clothes, I read about how Benetton is a 'Greenpeace Global Detox Leader' and makes sure all its suppliers adhere to a code of conduct based on respect for human rights and environmental protection. Benetton fashion collections 'Respect the environment with the goal of creating a brighter future for all humans.' Fine words but Benetton fashion is just window dressing for a giant exploitative corporation. I decide not to buy the green midi skirt.

In 1899, after the British-funded Conquest of the Desert spread south from the Pampas and down through Patagonia, the Argentine State, set up shop again in Argentine embassies in Paris and London and sold the land off at knockdown prices. The London-based, English-owned, confusingly named, Argentine Southern Land Company snapped up nine hundred thousand hectares and expanded the railway system from Puerto Madryn to Trelew in the far South. They built up a profitable export trade in sheep and wool until 1975, when they sold the company to three Argentine businessmen, Menéndez, Ochoa and Paz, who sold it on to the Benetton fashion company in 1991.

I remember those pioneering Benetton posters in the 1980s, featuring models of colour in the days when that was unusual, presenting a utopian image of a world of social integration without racial or religious problems - cool kissing bishops and bold images of David Kirby dying of AIDS when that was taboo.

In 2002 a Mapuche couple, Rosa Nahuelquir and Atilio Curiñanco petitioned the court using the principle of terra nullius to reclaim a piece of land on which she'd been born, and which Benetton were not farming. They received no response, so they occupied 385 hectares on which to build themselves a house and raise crops and a few goats and chickens. But terra nullius doesn't apply to 'Indians', so Benetton prosecuted the couple, and they were promptly evicted by police, brandishing title deeds from 1899, 1975 and 1991. Rosa and Atilio didn't have a title deed, neither did any of the Indigenous people who had occupied the land for thousands of years until it was sold from under their feet. It's the same dreary story in the United States, Australia, New Zealand and Tasmania. And of course, Israel.

Then Nobel Prize-winning activist Adolfo Pérez Esquivel got involved and Luciano Benetton, worried about bad publicity, offered Rosa and Atilio land from another part of Patagonia. The couple refused, that was not their ancestral land with its own *nehuenes*, supernatural spirits connected to specific families.

In 2017 two hundred gendarmes attacked the Pu Lof Mapuche community occupying other ancestral lands bought by Benetton in Patagonian Chubut. An Amnesty International report states that they beat women and children, pulled their hair, and burnt their possessions. In our batshit-crazy, settler-logic world this led to designating the Mapuche as 'terrorists'.

Benetton responded by founding the Leleque Museum to celebrate local culture and polish their progressive credentials. The museum refers to the arrival of foreigners after the Conquest of the Desert as the 'Age of Progress' and to the Mapuche as 'invaders from Chile'.

The Mapuche are currently being pushed out of land nobody previously wanted in order to make space for the 'Vaca Muerta' the Dead Cow, a massive site exploiting oil and shale gas.

Every year thousands of tourists throng to the unspoilt Puerto Madryn to watch orcas and elephant seals and walk along designated paths admiring penguin colonies. Nature is a wonderful thing.

***

In 1973 I returned to Buenos Aires to see Mum, Dad and Colin for the first time since fleeing in 1968. Dylan had just turned four and although I'd had a bumpy ride, I never regretted leaving. This was just a visit. Mum rushed towards Dylan in the airport, arms open, desperate to hug her grandson for the first time. He hid behind my legs the way children do when strangers lunge at them, but soon they adored each other; he was a sweet little boy, and she was a great success as a grandmother. He loved everything about her: her big soft body, her cakes, the way she let him win at games and bought him anything he wanted. She and I had always struggled to connect with each other, she would often tell me with tears in her eyes how she had dreamt of dressing me on my wedding day, a day that never came. And she quite rightly blamed me for causing so much unhappiness by running off with the entirely unsuitable Raúl.

I was out of place in Buenos Aires; I had lost touch with everyone and my one encounter with an Anglo-Argentine school friend was excruciating for us both. She chatted about how outrageous she and her friends were because one liked coffee with milk, one liked it black and another preferred tea, and it made me feel like a right freak. She was appalled when she visited London, it was hard to find anybody who spoke English because it was full of Black people. Neither of us suggested meeting again. I told her nothing about my own life. I didn't know where to start.

Nine days earlier, Perón had returned from exile and there was a feverish atmosphere in Buenos Aires, layers upon layers of political posters plastered over every building in Buenos Aires and large numbers of *descamisados,* Evita's 'shirtless ones' were camped outside the Olivos presidential residence where Perón had dallied with Nelly eighteen years earlier, playing drums and chanting, 'Perón! Perón! Que grande sos!' Perón, Perón, how great you are!' El General had returned, and they wanted to be close to him.

I went for a walk one siesta time down an old railway track and stumbled across a makeshift shack on a bit of wasteland, a piece of yellow tarpaulin bolstered with rags and cardboard. I crept up and peaked inside. It had been made lovely: A shrine to Evita with orange sunlight shining onto crumpled pictures of her beautiful face stuck on every surface. I was intruding on a person who had felt seen and appreciated by this dead woman.

***

In 1955, President Stroessner was unwilling to guarantee Perón's safety in Paraguay, so he left for Venezuela where he was hosted by the dictator General Pérez Jiménez until Jiménez was deposed and he sloped off to Panama. Perón, now sixty, shagged around like an international playboy until he met a twenty-four-year-old nightclub singer and dancer, María Estela Martínez, always known as Isabel or Isabelita at the trendy Pasapoga Club in Panama City. Perón fell madly in love again. Unlike Nelly, Isabelita wasn't an actual child, but in newsreel footage and photographs, she looks like a prepubescent little girl, all gussied up as if a grown-up has helped her get dressed and plonked a bouffant wig on her head. She was pretty in a mousy sort of way, but not a patch on the glorious Evita. Dad called her 'that dreadful woman', and as time went on her enemies called her *la puta,* the whore, one of the few things she was not.

I wonder whether Perón, with his dyed, jet-black hair and vulpine teeth, ever spared a thought for Nelly, the *nenita* he abandoned? Did she come into his mind late at night when he strained to button his pyjama jacket over his growing paunch and picked up his own slippers?

Perón was tired of drifting, so he gratefully accepted a warm invitation from yet another fascist dictator, the Generalissimo Francisco Franco. He and Isabelita settled happily in Madrid until his return to Argentina in 1973. They initially lived in the exclusive El Viso neighbourhood, but they became very irritated by the frequent noisy parties of the Hollywood actress Ava Gardner. Perón built himself a three-storey house in a quiet suburb and that is where the seeds were sown for the real horrors to come.

Perón was safely under the protection of a dictator who had murdered over a hundred thousand of his own citizens. He loved being recognised on the street or in the supermarket and held court in Madrid to delegations from both left and right of the Peronist movement. He even hit it off with Che Guevara, remarking fondly that Che 'is an immature utopian... but he's one of us.'

***

Che Guevara distanced himself from Fidel Castro when he saw the ideals of the Cuban revolution pragmatically watered down. He was a radical egalitarian, believing that a new kind of human being would emerge under the right conditions: Instead of each of us striving to be richer than the next person, we would all be happy to work for the good of the wider community. Che was not soft, never hesitating to put a bullet in a traitor's head himself, but he believed it was possible to create a society based on love where all work would be equally valued, and highly qualified professionals, including medical doctors like himself, would be happy to earn the same as cleaners and care workers.

Thousands of Cuban professionals were not content and immediately fled to the United States, seeking better remuneration, and Castro pragmatically moved away from utopian idealism. Che left Cuba to start revolutions in other countries. It was an altruistic mission; he aimed to provoke 'two three many Vietnams' to take the pressure off the Viet Cong by forcing the United States to spread its resources across several fronts and create the conditions for international socialism.

In the early days of the revolution, every able-bodied Cuban had to take turns cutting sugar cane, backbreaking work that had been done by enslaved people before abolition in 1888; Fidel, Che and all government officials took shifts like everybody else. This practice ended after 1968 when the Soviet Union invaded Czechoslovakia to suppress the Prague Spring. Alexander Dubček, the first secretary of the Communist Party, removed press censorship and reduced the powers of the secret police: 'Socialism cannot mean only liberation of the working people from the domination of exploiting class relations, but must make more provisions for a fuller life of the personality than any bourgeois democracy.'

The Soviets rolled in the tanks.

I want to believe a story I heard years ago. Fidel was out in the fields taking his turn cutting cane leaving his brother Raúl in charge. Raúl condemned the Soviet invasion of Czechoslovakia. Out on the open seas, Soviet oil tankers on their way to Cuba immediately turned back. When Fidel returned to his office, he realised that Cuba would starve without Soviet oil and swiftly took to the airwaves to welcome the invasion: 'We had no doubt that the political situation in Czechoslovakia was deteriorating and going downhill on its way back to capitalism and that it was inexorably going to fall into the arms of imperialism.'

By then, Che had failed to jump-start a revolution in Congo, thwarted by the combined forces of white South African mercenaries, the Congo National Army, anti-Castro Cuban pilots and the CIA. He was also foiled by presuming that he knew what was best for everybody else. In his diaries he wrote: *The human element failed. There is no will to fight. The [rebel] leaders are corrupt. In a word. . . there was nothing to do.*

Che refused to buckle. He was a revolutionary not a gasbag. President Nasser of Egypt warned him to 'stop behaving like Tarzan,' but he ignored him and took a small team of dedicated guerrillas, both women and men, to Bolivia to kick-start a revolution there. He still believed in lighting a spark of discontent that would spread into local insurrections and explode into revolution. Guevara, who had been such a brilliant military strategist in Cuba, failed to do basic research and he and his team arrived having learnt to speak Quechua in an area where Indigenous people spoke Guaraní. Those close to Che loved him, but local 'Indians' resented what they saw as these white saviours.

On October 9, 1967, Che was tracked down by Bolivian army general Gary Prado with intelligence support from the CIA. Sergeant Mario Teran was selected to kill him in what he describes as the worst moment of his life. Guevara looked straight at him and said, 'Calm yourself and aim well. You are going to kill a man!'

***

Two years after Che's death I became a mother. It's unremarkable these days so it's hard to remember what a scandal it was to have a child out of wedlock. As far as I know, at that time, I was the only unmarried mother in the Argentine British community. Even in England, unwed nineteen-year-olds were pressured to give their babies up for adoption. But this was no accidental pregnancy. I became pregnant at eighteen because Raúl airily announced, 'I am thirty, it's time I had a son', I threw away my birth control pills without thinking twice. I had absolutely no idea what I was doing, but it was a choice.

Nearly nine months into my pregnancy I had not yet seen a doctor, and nobody had ever asked how I was or offered to help me with anything. After wandering around Spain, France and Holland with other Argentinian drifters, Raúl and I rented a bedroom in a flat in Barcelona from Bibs, a sweet Swedish lady with alcoholism, Greta Garbo cheekbones and alabaster skin. Bibs only left her bed once a week to replenish her stash of brandy. She'd roll out of bed, take off her grubby nightie, slip into one of her beautifully tailored suits, comb her hair, apply a slick of red lipstick that hinted at the beauty she had once been and set off a little unsteadily. She spent the rest of her week drinking litres of brandy by herself. I knew she was desperately unhappy and made her jam sandwiches and offered her plates of brown rice, but I didn't know how to help her. I had enough problems of my own.

None of the loose itinerant group we were part of had jobs and, looking back, I have no idea how we survived. In Paris we scrounged leftover vegetables at night around the old Les Halles market. In Barcelona I painted an Inca sun on a bedsheet and sold it to a design shop and used the money to buy two baby grows, some nappies and a Moses basket. I never had enough to eat and I was always hungry. Raúl sneered that I was '*una lima nueva*' a new file, working my way through any food that came my way. He never lifted a finger through the whole of my pregnancy. I just accepted this was how things were. I was very skinny and in the wake of that time, I have very poor bone density in my seventies. Palimpsest.

Every night into the early hours, Bibs lay in her bed silently drinking Fundador brandy de Jerez and when I got tired I retreated and lay on a mattress on the floor in the bedroom next to hers while Raúl and his new friends played guitar and laughed loudly in the sitting room. Among the frequent visitors was the very sultry, beautiful, dark-haired Elizabeth who was rumoured to have had a torrid affair with El Cordobés, the legendary bullfighter, and now only had eyes for Raúl. I lay seething, a jealous, skinny teenager with a big bump.

Raúl and I were in the bathroom together when he announced that he was leaving to tour a puppet show with Elizabeth. Raúl was a gifted puppeteer, but I knew nothing about this tour. 'Please don't go', I begged him. 'I'm having the baby so soon.'

Raúl glared at me in disgust. 'You've always been a coward.'

I usually didn't argue, but this time I plucked up courage. 'Are you having an affair with Elizabeth?'

Raúl was enraged. 'You're a coward and you have a dirty mind!'

I begged him to forgive me.

He refused until I was on my knees, weeping into the bidet. 'I'm sorry, I'm sorry, I'm sorry.'

Eventually he relented and said he would let it go.

***

And that is why I was on my own with Bibs passed out on her bed, when I went into labour. One of the bohemians visited and noticed that I was in a lot of pain; he later admitted he knew I was going into labour but rushed off anyway to catch the boat to Ibiza. Two hours after he left, the front bell rang, and two young Americans, Bill and Steve, presented themselves. They had run into Raúl and Elizabeth in Valencia, and he had told them they were welcome to crash at his place in Barcelona. I let them in and took myself off to lie on the mattress. Bill, a shaggy bear of a man, and dark-haired Steve heard me squirming and they got worried and squatted on the edge of my mattress. Steve suggested I needed to go to hospital. Bill, at a loss, proposed marriage.

'No, thank you,' I replied.

Steve was more practical. 'Shall we get a taxi?'

I barely believed I was pregnant, despite this little kicking creature in my belly, but eventually I agreed that I would go to hospital if the *I Ching* confirmed this was the correct decision.

The *I Ching* is an ancient Chinese divination text that was very popular with hippies. Traditionally yarrow stalks are thrown to reveal patterns, but we threw special coins, which represented a hexagram corresponding to a specific text. Poor bewildered Steve and Bill watched me throw the coins and draw a pattern with broken-and-single lines in between excruciatingly painful spasms. The *I Ching* was usually very vague, but this time it was clear. A small dark stranger was about to arrive! Steve quickly called a taxi, and they bundled me off to the general hospital. When I told the porter at the gate how frequent my labour pains were, I was rushed straight into the labour ward.

***

I was given an enema, shaved, and a red liquid was painted on my pubes. And I was laid down on what I remember as a marble block, it can't have been a marble block, with a bare light bulb dangling above it, and immobilised with my legs wide apart and my feet strapped high-up into stirrups. A large nurse advanced on me with a very large syringe.

'What are you doing?' I squeaked.

'Putting you to sleep,' she replied.

I remembered Mum's story about how awful it was being unconscious while giving birth to me and I resisted strenuously. Eventually she relented as long as I promised to be quiet.

We don't want you making a noise and disturbing the other patients.' I promised faithfully to give birth quietly.

I hummed and missed my Mum. A load of medical students piled in to observe their first birth with a conscious mother. Nobody asked whether I objected to having an audience, although to be fair, I was too far gone to have an opinion. When the baby slipped out, quacking like a little duck, the students cheered and clapped, and I felt very clever. He bellowed as he was whisked off. They presented him to me all cleaned up. Baby stared at me with dark, shiny black-button eyes. I stared back. I don't know whether to call this love, we didn't know each other then, but it was a fierce commitment. *There is nothing between you and the wild world but me,* I thought as we both stared at each other. *And I am going to protect you.* Baby studied me intensely. None of that otherworldly stargazing of the newborn. *Don't even think about going anywhere.*

'What is his name?' I didn't know his name. But I was afraid that if I admitted that, it would prove I was unfit to be a mother, and they would take him away from me. 'Dylan,' I said firmly. I had read and loved *Adventures in the Skin Trade* by Dylan Thomas and you could pronounce the name easily in English and Spanish. Everyone assumed he was named after Bob Dylan and years later there was a dozy rabbit called Dylan in a children's television series, and Dylan bitterly resented being teased over that.

***

I informed my parents that I had a baby when Dylan was four months old. Poor Mum wrote to say: *I worried that you were cold and hungry but I never dreamt you would be jumping into bed with strange men.* Of course, Raúl had been having an affair with Elizabeth and I tried leaving him when Dylan was two weeks old but he made a huge fuss and threatened to kill himself. It took me about a year to leave him but I did it.

I didn't see Mum for five years, but Dad flew to London in 1971 when I wrote to tell them that I had left Raúl. He invited Dylan and me to return to live with them but that was never an option. Dad was amused by the West London bohemian flat I shared with a group of anti-apartheid white South Africans avoiding conscription. It was a chaotic household, we turned all the sofas upside down with their feet in the air and sat on their backs eating macrobiotic food, smoking grass, dropping acid and listening to Frank Zappa, Cream and Captain Beefheart while Dylan toddled around peacefully. Dad understood why I preferred this messy life to the one I had fled. It was precarious but I could breathe.

Dad visited his father to break my disgraceful news. Grandpa Gordon Woolcock had returned to England as soon as he retired and bought a tiny, detached house in Worthing where he lived a modest and highly regulated life after Granny died. He set the table for the next meal as soon as he had washed up and put away the dishes of the previous one, watched the news and smoked one Senior Service cigarette after dinner. Dad worried that the unvarnished truth would kill Grandpa, so he softened the pill by informing him that I had married 'an Argentine blighter' and had a child with him. Instead of having a heart attack, Grandpa checked his watch and muttered, 'What? Oh, what, what, what? We're going to miss the six o'clock news.' For the next four years, whenever we met, he inquired whether I had divorced 'that Argentine blighter' I had never married and eventually I agreed the divorce had come through

When I returned to Buenos Aires in 1973, Mum and Dad were living in the small flat in Martinez, which Mum and Teresa cleaned to within an inch of its life every single day. The blowsy chrysanthemums print still hung on a pale-grey wall next to the framed pictures of Mary Baker Eddy and Jesus and a kitsch silver painting of Paris that I had insisted on buying when I was fourteen. There were two incidental tables adorned with tiny bunches of porcelain flowers, shepherdesses, little silver bowls and a large, cracked vase painted with a misty rural scene. Dad had his large blokey armchair and Mum had her chintzy one for reading her lesson, there was a three-person sofa and a vitrine with a large selection of crystal glasses and bottles of spirits. On the other side of the room there was a polished oval dining table and a set of chairs.

The bookshelf had vanished.

And that's why I pile my house high with books and paintings and photographs, casting a spell to keep the suburbs at bay. For forty years I couldn't even set foot in a suburb without being slain by torpor and nausea. As soon as I got out, it would lift again.

At night, metal shutters were lowered and floor-length flowery drapes were drawn over lace curtains. Dad sat on his armchair gripping the remote control, fast asleep, only waking up aggrieved if anybody tried to change the channel. *I'm watching this!* Mum felt lonely and neglected and she cried a lot. Colin was thirteen when I ran off and he says the atmosphere at home was so miserable that when he was back from boarding school he stayed over with friends as often as he could. He and Mum blamed me. I knew they were right. It had been my job to entertain Dad, keep him interested and awake and at home.

Then find a nice boy and marry him. I just couldn't do it.

***

Dad, Mum, Dylan and I boarded a tiny plane from the Jorge Newbery City Airport to visit the Iguazú Falls. It was a horrendous flight, blown around the skies like a paper plane, the air hostesses strapped in, eyes wide, white faced, clutching each other while Dad tried not to look frightened. Mum stared into space denying the reality of the storm that was tossing us about and I kept my fear at bay by consoling Dylan who was seven or eight. Our nerves were shredded by the time we arrived at Puerto Iguazú but none of us said a word about the fact that we had nearly died. Naturally Mum was convinced she had saved the entire plane with her Christian Science 'work'.

It was eight o'clock at night, dark but boiling hot, and the shiny marble floor outside the arrival hall was covered in hundreds of huge iridescent beetles lying on their backs, waggling their legs in the air. I began frantically turning them over to help them crawl away, but they flipped back again immediately. Other passengers sniggered at me, the Beatle Saviour in a yellow Liquorice Allsorts dress. Dylan was embarrassed. 'Mum, stop it, stop it! Mum!' But I couldn't help myself.

The Devil's Throat is more gigantic than anything you will see in your life, an ocean crashing into a ravine with a deafening roar. The Iguazú, 'great water' area, was occupied for tens of thousands of years by the Eldoradense and then the Guaraní until the conquistadores arrived. The Guaraní story is that Naipí, a beautiful Native woman, rejected a jealous god and was canoeing down a river with her human sweetheart when the spurned lover sliced open the river and created an eternal waterfall to keep them apart.

When we visited, there was one solitary Guaraní man with long hair selling bracelets. Dylan asked me to take a picture of him next to the 'Indian'. It was excruciating, and a few years later Dylan found the photograph and asked why I had agreed to take it when it was so obviously wrong. I was embarrassed and threw it away.

I went to Iguazú knowing what to expect and it still blew my mind. But Álvar Núñez Cabeza de Vaca, a sixteenth-century explorer, set off for the Americas only forty years after Columbus and stumbled across the falls without having seen any tourist brochures.

***

Cabeza de Vaca, Head of a Cow, not only had a fabulous name but he was able to think for himself. He was second in command of a fleet of five vessels commissioned by Charles V to conquer territory stretching from the Gulf of Mexico to what is now Florida. His commander, Pánfilio Narváez, boasted about presiding over the murder of an entire village whose inhabitants had come out to welcome his company with food. When Narváez asked Bartolomé de Las Casas, a horrified eyewitness, to comment on this slaughter, Las Casas told Narváez he was going to hell. An

Indigenous tribe, known as the 'Safety Harbour People', sent Narváez away assuring him there was a mythical place called Apalachee, that was rich in gold. Narváez became obsessed with finding it. His expedition was an abject failure with only four out of eight hundred men surviving, including Cabeza de Vaca.

The four survivors spent eight years travelling through what is now Texas, New Mexico and Arizona, encountering Indigenous cultures on their way; Cabeza de Vaca called them the Roots people, the Fish and Blackberry people and the Fig people, depending on their main food source. At times the resourceful Cabeza de Vaca and his companions became servants to those who fed them, at others they traded between tribes until they became known for shamanistic healing, breathing on the sick and muttering prayers. It is likely that they infected those they met with deadly diseases because even the most well-intentioned of us are members of a death cult that wipes out everyone in our path.

Cabeza de Vaca wrote about his adventures and his account fully acknowledges the humanity of all those he encountered. After suffering a series of calamities, half-starved and having lost more of his companions, the group reencountered a group of 'Indians' they had befriended earlier. '*Upon seeing the disasters we had suffered, our misery and misfortune, the Indians sat down with us and began to weep out of compassion for our misfortune.*' Initially when the 'Indians' offer hospitality, Vaca's group fear being sacrificed to their idols and eaten. Eventually they are so cold, hungry and exhausted that they agree to accompany these 'Indians' back to their village where they spent a sleepless night waiting to be roasted. But like the blameless biscuit I was offered in the Bar Moderno, their fears were groundless, many strangers cared for them tenderly. On his return to Spain, Cabeza de Vaca reported to his Majesty:

> *In two thousand Leagues we travelled on land, and by sea in boats, and in the ten months more after our rescue from captivity that we untiringly walked across the land, nowhere did we come across either sacrifices or idolatry.*

He didn't see cannibalism, didn't invent any, and quarrelled bitterly with his fellow Christians who 'want to make slaves of our Indians'.

Cabeza de Vaca encountered many forms of social organisation. There were hierarchical and egalitarian societies, hunting and foraging groups, settled agricultural communities and some that moved seasonally between the two. The reductionist evolutionary view that grimly follows the progress of humanity from hunting and foraging through agriculture to industrial neoliberalism is just a story. There are so many ways to live, and this billionaire shit show is just one of them.

***

Perón was a chameleon, pleasing everyone, supporting completely contradictory ideologies. While he was in Madrid these contradictions started imploding. For years the movement had staggered on, bloated and confused, with Perón smiling and nodding, smiling and nodding, embracing visitors from all sides and sending them home convinced that he supported them. A formal split finally occurred in 1970 when left-wing Peronists, who identified with Evita's politics, broke away from the trade-union-based right wing and formed the Christian socialist Movimiento Peronista Montonero, known as the 'Montoneros', committed to social justice and the armed struggle.

In Madrid, Perón warmly encouraged left-wing visitors like Rodolfo Galimberti from the Montoneros and Envar El Kadri from the Fuerzas Armadas Peronistas, but when they went home, he welcomed the right-wing general secretary of the Confederation of General Workers, José Ignacio Rucci, and his ally, Norma Kennedy, and reassured them he was really on their side. More worrying to the old egotist, was the rise of a tendency led by Augusto Vandor, a leading figure from the usually loyal Confederation of General Workers that proposed Peronism without Perón. Perón didn't like the sound of that at all, so he sent Isabelita off to Buenos Aires to investigate this heretical faction. During this fateful visit Isabelita was introduced to the fanatical José López Rega, a retired police corporal obsessed with the occult. Isabel was mesmerised and returned to Spain with López Rega in tow and appointed him as her husband's personal butler and astrologer.

To begin with, López Rega rented his own digs in Madrid and Perón's staff sniggered at his bizarre practices behind his back; but in 1965 he moved into the Perón residency and the laughter stopped. López Rega expelled Isabelita's spiritual advisor and anybody else he perceived as a threat. He listened in to Perón's telephone calls, opened his mail and vetted all his visitors. Isabelita called him Prophet Daniel, and Perón, who loved an infantilising nickname – Potota, Evita, Nenita, Isabelita - called him *Lopecito.* Others referred to him as 'El Brujo', the Witch. López Rega was a devotee of Alice Bailey, an English esoteric writer who claimed that all twelve turgid volumes of her oeuvre had been telepathically dictated to her from beyond the grave by Djwal Khul, a Tibetan master of wisdom. Bailey explained that the Second World War was 'the greatest spiritual event which has taken place since the fourth kingdom of nature' and that the dropping of the atomic bomb on Hiroshima was 'the broom of the Father of all, sweeping away obstructions in the path of his returning Son'. López Rega regarded himself as the reincarnation of the archangel Gabriel and believed that Perón was the chosen emissary for a new era of spirituality, for which Bailey coined the phrase 'the New Age', which has become a potpourri of mindfulness and crystal gazing.

Lopez Rega was a member of Anäel, a right-wing secret society with a potent brew of mystical Rosicrucian, fascist, racist and anti-Semitic beliefs which he expounded in *Secrets Revealed*, a mind-numbingly boring 758-page volume. He was very thin-skinned and could hold a grudge. Many years after journalist Pedro Leopoldo Barraza had published a scathing review of *Secrets Revealed*, he was

Isabelita, Perón, & Lopez Rega, Madrid, Spain, c.1970.

shot dead by the Triple A, the paramilitary Argentine AntiCommunist Alliance.

Once López Rega was ensconced in the Perón home, he shared their company with Isabel's twenty canaries and Perón's beloved poodles, Puchi and Kimona. He had already fulfilled the first of his own prophecies by becoming the most powerful man in Argentina without even being there. From that time on, in every single photograph and newsreel, you see López Rega standing close behind the Perón couple with an odd, little smirk, his beady eyes fixed on the back of Perón's head. If he was the spider, Perón was the fly.

In 1971 Eva Perón's embalmed body was finally returned to her widower in Madrid and López Rega spent weeks stretching Isabelita out on a long table with her head touching Evita's coffin while he performed magic rituals intended to shift Evita's soul from her corpse into Isabelita's body.

On May 25, 1973, nine years after General Onganía's Argentine Revolution, his successor, General Lanusse, announced democratic elections. Lanusse declared that he was prepared to do anything for his country, including speaking to Perón, which he called 'swallowing the frog'.

***

For the first time in eighteen years, the Peronist Party was allowed to participate in an election but without Perón as their candidate. Héctor Cámpora, a left-wing dentist, won a landslide victory with the slogan Cámpora for President, Perón to Power. Mum and Dad were horrified: 'The man's a bloody fool'. Cámpora immediately granted amnesty to all political prisoners, restored diplomatic relations with Cuba and, under pressure from Perón, called for new elections, this time with Perón as the candidate. The revolutionary Montoneros who Perón was calling 'These marvellous young people' committed themselves to the democratic process after years of attacking prisons and barracks demanding his return. The Peronist right seemed to be losing ground.

On June 20, 1973, Perón, Isabel, and López Rega set off for Argentina. President Cámpora travelled to Madrid to pick them up, and there's a newsreel showing López Rega hovering solicitously as Perón and Isabel fondly embrace their staff and slide into the back of a black Rolls-Royce. López Rega slips into the front seat, and they cruise off, a little Argentine flag waving on the wing mirror, to Barajas Airport, where a full military escort and a band was waiting. Isabel hugs Franco's sister, her darling friend Pilar, Perón shares a long, fond embrace with General Franco himself and they fly off to establish the New Age.

***

Perón was coming home.

The Montoneros had mobilised the masses to welcome Perón: 'a Ezeiza compañeros a recibir un viejo

Montonero!', off to Ezeiza comrades, to welcome an old Montonero. Over a million people turned up to welcome Perón home, and the atmosphere was festive, with drummers and dancers and a crowd singing about how great he was. But a man in a little Fiat Torino was driving around shouting warnings. 'Cuidado! Be careful! The right is planning something.'

That morning, ambulances packed with weapons had left the Ministry of Social Welfare for the airport, snipers from the Peronist right concealed arms in musical instrument cases and took up positions by the huge stage. As the crowd surged forwards, they were mown down by machine-gun fire. People scattered, screaming, running for their lives. Impoverished young men, who had climbed nearby stumpy trees to get a better view, dropped out of the branches like little birds, and Ford Falcons with no number plates drove straight into the crowd, guns firing.

As people fled towards Highway 205 dragging blood-stained bodies, eighteen thousand doves, a thousand for each year of Perón's exile, were released from the stage area. Terrified birds flapped across the sky as snipers advanced, shooting, stabbing and clubbing anybody in their way, targeting men with long hair and anyone wearing jeans.

A group of workers were interviewed by a television news crew near the 205.

'It's the Communists!'

'You blame the Communists?'

'Of course. Of course, it's always them, causing trouble. We're here for Perón.'

But Perón was nowhere to be seen.

Professional snipers, positioned on the highway overpass, shot people in the back as blood-soaked doves smacked into them as they fled. Mutilated bodies were strung up on the stage, others were shovelled into ambulances and were never seen again. Most of those killed were illiterate shanty-town dwellers, so their names were never recorded.

Farther down the road, confused people milled about.

'Where is he?'

Perón and Isabel had flown into Morón, an airport fifty kilometres away, where all was quiet and peaceful.

Nine days later when Dylan and I arrived at Ezeiza, I asked Dad about the burnt tree stumps around the airstrip. He said it was something to do with those 'bloody Peronists'.

***

Back in 1967, aged seventeen, I didn't think about these things.

General Onganía was still in office. Not that I cared, politics was a shambles that had nothing to do with me. I wrote to Helen airily, *I don't know whether I told you, I have become an anarchist. Some people feel the need for an organised government, but I find the idea repellent for a number of reasons.* I didn't tell her what the number of reasons were because I had no idea what they were.

A few weeks after I met Barzac, I had realised that he was not a ticket to anywhere I wanted to go. I met him to return a stack of his unsold poetry books, and he suggested we audition for a play, *Libertad y Otras Intoxicaciones,* Freedom and Other Intoxications.

The director, Mario Trejo, and three or four cast members sat in the empty auditorium of a run-down theatre. Barzac did his barking-dog act and was summarily dismissed. I was pushed on stage with a piece of paper in English and told to read it out.

> I am Stephania, Birgitta, Marie Claire, Ivanka, Manuela, Chang, Jane, Fatima, and Uma and I have been fucked in Stockholm, fucked in Berlin, fucked in Paris, fucked in Moscow, fucked in Madrid, fucked in Peking, fucked in London, fucked in Karachi and fucked in Delhi.

The trouble was that the word *fucked* stuck in my throat. I twisted one leg behind the other.

'I have been, I have been . . . f . . . I have been . . .

When Mummy was really cross, she had been known to say 'blooming' something or other. When I was very annoying, Daddy occasionally said, 'damn the girl! Mummy would object 'Ayy, John!' And he would apologise. But not even the naughtiest boys I knew said *fuck*. I was mortified. I tried again.

'I have been . . ,'

I just couldn't do it. 'I had never been. . . I have been . . .'

Mario Trejo and his cohort laughed, 'Say *gaga* then. Say I have been gaga in Stockholm, in Moscow, Madrid.'

I said gaga.

Mario stood up. 'Fine. See you at the Instituto Di Tella tomorrow at ten. We're rehearsing in the theatre. We open in two weeks.'

I went home and wrote one of my terrible poems.

I must leave the weak behind
In order to break
Break the chains
That shackle me
To the old, old slimy umbilicals
Out of date and past my time

I never saw Barzac again.

A couple of years later, Raúl and I were living in Ibiza, a sleepy island a few years before clubbers invaded it with ecstasy-fuelled house music and live sex shows. We smoked hash, dropped acid, played Cream and Blind Faith and lapped up the tales of bedraggled travellers returning from Marrakesh and Kabul, dreaming of enlightenment. I was nineteen and a new mother. It was a warm evening. I was swinging in a hammock on a terrace next to Dylan asleep in his Moses basket, cicadas were buzzing and Steve Winwood was singing about trying to find his way home. Jorge, who had just arrived from Morocco, piped up.

'Che, do any of you remember Barzac?'

Eyes were rolled, clearly everyone thought Barzac was a bit of a joke. I remained silent.

'He's dead. He was seen walking into the sea at Essaouira. Suicide.'

I had dropped Barzac like a stone and now he was dead. He had opened a door for me, and I never looked back to see how he was. Now he was dead.

***

After Ezeiza, there was no longer even the pretence of a unified Peronist movement. Cámpora was prevented from investigating the massacre and the Montoneros took up arms again, swearing revenge on the traitors who had laid this murderous trap for them. Portraits of López Rega, Jorge Manuel Osinde, Juan Manuel Abal Medina, José Rucci and Norma Kennedy, with the strapline 'Responsible for the Ezeiza massacre', were flyposted all over town.

Perón never condemned the airport massacre, but he became very unwell soon after. His doctors suspected he'd had a heart attack but López Rega announced that although ordinary mortals needed X-rays, he was able to inspect the inside of Perón's body with his naked eye, and his heart was in excellent shape.

López Rega instructed Isabelita to give President Cámpora an ultimatum: If he did not resign the presidency and call new elections immediately, she would fly her husband back to Madrid. Cámpora was quickly replaced by López Rega's son-in-law, Raúl Lastiri, who appointed López Rega as his minister of social welfare. A date was set for a general election with Perón as the candidate.

Perón needed a running mate. Picking the ever-loyal Cámpora would align him to the Left, but choosing a right-wing candidate would drain all support on the Left. With López Rega's voice in his ear, the wily old fox made a brilliantly counterintuitive choice: his wife Isabelita, the nightclub dancer who had no opinions of her own.

Perón-Perón, a truly magical ticket, was elected by another massive landslide in September 1973.

The New Age had arrived.

After the election Perón was often too sick to function, leaving Isabelita in charge. But Isabelita was no Evita. Evita was uneducated and inexperienced, but she was smart, she was political, and she believed in something.

Isabelita was dim, uncharismatic, and unimpressive.

And she was completely controlled by El Brujo.

López Rega had already squirrelled money from the Ministry of Social Welfare to fund his secret paramilitary organisation, The Argentine Anti-communist Alliance, The Triple A, during Lastiri's presidency; in attendance at the initial meeting was the core group that had carried out the Ezeiza massacre – the minister of the interior, the deputy chief of the Argentine Federal Police, several provincial governors and López Rega himself. The Triple A set about systematically torturing and murdering not just those engaged in the armed struggle, the Montoneros, the FAP and the Trotskyist Ejercito Revolutionario del Pueblo, the E.R.P. – but anybody loosely associated with them, as well as left-wing journalists, liberals, nuns and priests, anybody who dared speak out. Later, during the Dirty War, the Triple A and its leaders, including the sinister Scottish- heritage Anibal Gordon, were absorbed by the SIDE - Secretaría de Inteligencia del Estado - the state intelligence service, where their murderous skills were put to good use.

Under López Rega's direct orders, the Triple A killed fifty people every single day between July and September 1974. A Morality Commando assassinated prostitutes and bodies riddled with bullets were found at the side of roads with their hands chopped off. Some were political activists, others included a couple and their daughter who were killed because their son had been involved in left-wing activities, and the son of the former rector of the National University of Mar Del Plata was dragged out and shot while his house was firebombed behind him.

The Montoneros stepped up their activities and on September 23, two days after Perón was reelected, they gunned down one of Perón's most loyal supporters, José Ignacio Rucci, a key leader of the orthodox wing of the Peronist Party and general secretary of the CGT, the Confederation of General Workers.

The Montoneros and the ERP funded their weapons and activities by kidnapping executives of multinational corporations, many of them British or American, and holding them for ransom. They kidnapped Ronald C. Grove from the Vestey Group, Norman Lee from Coca Cola, Frank Victor Brimicombe from the British American Tobacco company, Enrique Nyborg Henderson from the Bank of London and South America, David Wilke from Amoco, Eduardo Oxenford from Alpargatas, Charles Roberts and Frank Ingrey from the Roberts Merchant bank group, John

Swint from the Ford Motor Company and Jorge and Juan Born, which goes some way towards explaining, if not forgiving, why the British community was so willing to turn a blind eye to the Dirty War. Charles Agnew Lockwood, an English merchant banker, was kidnapped twice.

Dylan and I were on our way back to London from Buenos Aires when we had an unexpected eight-hour layover in São Paolo. We were sitting next to Charles Lockwood's wife. I don't remember how I knew who she was but she took a shine to us and rented us all a hotel room. We hung out for hours and she paid for everything and neither of us mentioned her kidnapped husband. I thought about saying something, but I only had platitudes to offer, and Dylan, who was about seven, was doing a good job of distracting her. When we finally arrived at Heathrow, I watched her collapse into the arms of a man in a suit who was waiting for her.

Years later a lot of people pretended they had been against the dictatorship from the start, but at the time they just wanted the chaos to stop.

***

I nearly became a kidnapper myself while I was pregnant and living in abject penury with Raúl in Barcelona. Rafael, a friend from a wealthy Spanish family, suggested we pretend to kidnap him and demand a ransom from his parents. I was very enthusiastic about this plan and would have absolutely gone ahead with it if Rafael had not got cold feet. I was the only one who kept pressuring him to change his mind. It did not occur to me to spare a single thought for how upsetting this would be for his parents.

***

A few months into his presidency, Perón was spending long hours in bed with his poodles, physically ill and slipping in and out of senility. Then, in a rare moment of lucidity, he realised he had made a terrible mistake. He summoned Isabelita, López Rega and his technical secretary, Gustavo Caraballo, to his bedside and gave them all instructions that if he died, Ricardo Balbín, leader of the centrist Radical Party, should succeed him rather than Isabelita Caraballo. López Rega was incandescent while Isabelita remained silent. A few days later, under intense pressure from Lopecito, Perón recanted but begged his wife not to make any decisions without consulting Balbín if she became president. López Rega informed Caraballo that Perón had gone crazy and blocked all access to him. In order to intercept intruders, he installed a microphone on Perón's bedside table and rushed to his side whenever he heard him calling out.

***

When we performed *Libertad y Otras Intoxicaciones* at the Di Tella Institute, the centre of the contemporary art world in Buenos Aires, I felt I'd really arrived. I wrote to Helen

> *I have so much energy that is continually exploding, I'm full of love and fireworks. I aspire for uninhibition*

> *to reach out and sock the viewer in the face and leave him gasping, perturbed and worried.*

I desperately wanted to be taken seriously, and it worried me that men in the theatre company kept patting me on the head instead of treating me like a serious artist.

Libertad y Otras Intoxicaciones was a series of fragmented scenes with no overarching narrative. I thought it was marvellous. The only plays I had ever seen were by the amateur 'English Players', who produced enthusiastic versions of *The Importance of Being Earnest, The Mikado* and *The Pirates of Penzance*, the memory of which still brings me out in hives.

Director, Mario Trejo, had recently returned from France where he'd worked with the founders of the legendary Living Theatre, Julian Beck and Judith Malina. Europe! I eagerly lapped up the talk about dissolving the fourth wall and Antonin Artaud's Theatre of Cruelty where 'the purpose of theatre is to drain the abscesses of society' by making jets of blood and cockroaches crawl out of a woman's vagina. Mario explained that the purpose of this new theatre was to shock the audience out of their complacency, and I was certainly shocked out of mine. They admired Isidore Ducasse, the Count of Lautremont, who extolled the joys of sinking sharp fingernails into the body of a live baby and ripping its heart out. I found this very worrying but didn't dare say so.

***

Raúl Martinez, 1969.

La Polaca was the only other woman in the company, as young as I was, but more worldly wise. She rarely spoke and we avoided each other. There were nine men, Geronimo who was funny and camp, Pepe who supported the Montoneros and had a magnificent aquiline nose, handsome Cacho who lived in an artist's warehouse in the Boca, five others I have forgotten and then, then there was . . . Raúl Martinez. The other men understood that I was out of my depth and were amused by my naivety. At seventeen I was afraid that at this rate, I might die a virgin, and I knew most of them would have been happy to leap into bed with me, even Geronimo, who could go both ways as we said at that time. But I was waiting for the *one*.

Raúl had dark-olive skin, black curly hair, beautiful brown eyes and a full mouth, and I was in awe of him. In one scene Raúl and Pepe took turns pretending to torture each other, which I found very profound. Raúl had a solo where he stood on the stage and pulled a taut invisible band out of the middle of his chest, straining at a magnetic force until the veins on his temples bulged and throbbed and his entire body quivered. The first couple of times I couldn't even watch, a bit disgusted and terrified that he was going to explode, but gradually I was bewitched. I couldn't keep my eyes off him but he completely ignored me, which made him even more attractive.

I wrote to Helen.

> *My father came into my bedroom late last night. I was tremendously touched, he said 'Penny I just get a glimmer of something, I'm beginning to realise I can't protect you anymore. I will have to just stand by and watch while my daughter who I have watched grow up all these years, gets hurt and I can't help her'. By the way I am crazy about T. S. Eliot at the moment.*

One night, after the show, a group of us were crossing the busy Avenida Libertador, and as I stepped out carelessly in front of a car, Raúl grabbed my hand to pull me back and didn't let go until we reached the other side. I felt a tremendous whoosh between my legs, in my *down there,* my concha, my chucha, my tush. And the whoosh spread all over my body, to the tips of my fingers and toes and up my spine.

He let go of my hand and walked on. Nobody had noticed but I was head over heels, orgasmically in love. *Helen, I have never been conscious of my body and now I am. Are you aware of yours? If not, I'll tell you how when I am more peaceful.*

Raúl barely knew I existed.

I was obsessed.

***

The Marriage of a Queen and the Bandit is an Italo Calvino folktale about a Princess who refused to marry. Desperate to get her fixed up, the King and Queen organised a procession of suitors and the Princess watched a line of wealthy Kings troop past, followed by fancy Princes with fancy hair and fancy clothes and fancy jewellery, followed by less impressive Barons and a trail of ordinary Knights. The Princess yawned. She knew exactly what her life would be like if she married any of them. And she didn't want to know.

At the very end of the procession was a professor astride a small pony, his long legs dangling almost to the ground with a rucksack full of junk on his back. The Kings and the Princes and the Barons and the Knights had smiled winsomely at the Princess, but this fellow acted as if he couldn't care less whether she chose him or not. The Princess pointed: 'That one. 'The King and Queen were very unhappy about her marrying so far beneath her station, but she had always been stubborn so they knew there was no point trying to change her mind.

The Professor insisted on carting his new bride off straightaway so the King hurriedly appointed a retinue of soldiers and servants to accompany them. The landscape got bleaker and more desolate, but the Professor refused to stop for food or rest and gradually all the Princess's companions headed back home. The Princess suspected she had made a terrible mistake, but she was too proud to admit it. Eventually the Professor stopped at a desolate spot and tapped his staff on the ground. A trapdoor opened and he threatened to kill the Princess if she didn't climb down a deep shaft. To her horror she found herself in a cave full of dead bodies. Her new husband explained it was her job to stack the dead bodies upright against the wall to make space for all the others he was going to kill.

The Princess realised the Professor was really a bandit.

This life, stacking dead bodies all day long, continued miserably until a dove flew out of a little chest of drawers and the Princess was able to deliver a message to her father.

The Princess was rescued and soon remarried the more suitable King of Siberia. The Bandit was furious and locked himself inside a picture frame. The King of Siberia bought the picture believing it was the portrait of a saint and hung it above the marital bed. The new Queen was alarmed by its likeness to her former husband, but the King told her not to be so silly. That night the Bandit undid the bolts on the frame, crept out and whispered in the Queen's ear, 'Put your head on the pillow so I can cut your head off.' The King woke up and sounded a trumpet and the Bandit was finally slain.

I understood the Princess. I rejected all the nice men too.

I never regretted it or blamed anybody else. I did what I wanted to do and, like the Princess, I refused to listen to any warnings.

***

After a brief run in Buenos Aires, we took *Libertad y Otras Intoxicaciones* on tour to Mar Del Plata, a tourist resort on the Atlantic Coast probably not the ideal location for avant-garde theatre. In Argentina, at that time, the age of majority for women was twenty-five and I was only seventeen, so I needed Mum and Dad's permission to travel without them. Mario Trejo and Pepe visited our Belgrano flat and, while I squirmed, explained how essential I was to the performance and how tenderly they would watch over me.

Audience numbers in Mar Del Plata were poor after the full house excitements of Buenos Aires. Only six people turned up for one performance and all of them left halfway through an unappealing scene when the cast crawled around the auditorium and pretended to vomit all over them. We continued performing to an empty theatre. I thought this was marvellous and wrote to Helen that *I loved it, loved, loved, loved it.*

I was having the time of my life, despite being half-starved and sharing a room with La Polaca that had grubby, crumpled sheets and a rusty shower that spat out trickles of tepid water. Mario Trejo was less delighted; he was out of pocket, having paid for the theatre and our digs. He secured the necessary permits from the municipality for us to stage a 'happening' in the town centre to drum up an audience. When it got dark, I was hoisted up and stretched out on four of the actors' shoulders and carried down the middle of the street like a corpse, escorted by the rest of the cast parading behind with enormous church candles. We set off down the middle of the high street, and I looked up at the night sky and the stars feeling the wonder of it all until I heard a lot of shouting. I turned slightly to see the tops of an angry mob who seemed to have no interest in experimental theatre.

***

The men carrying me were jostled, but we somehow made it to the entrance of the shopping centre, where the cast formed a circle and hummed 'Om, oooommmmmmmm', as I ran around with a ball of string, tightly binding them into a bundle while the crowd jeered abuse: 'Degenerate faggots, hippies and whores'. When I had completed immobilising the cast, the mob attacked. I punched one of the assailants and before anybody could stop me, I indignantly marched over to a row of uniformed policemen who were nonchalantly leaning against their cars. 'You should be protecting us!' The police immediately responded by bundling us all into two vehicles and driving off. I attempted to give them directions to our disgusting hostel while Raúl, Cacho, and Pepe hissed, 'Why the fuck did you do that?'

In a flash I realised that I had stepped over an invisible line. I was no longer one of the people the police had a duty to protect. Minutes before, I had been on the inside, refusing to read *Northanger Abbey*, now I was outside the pale, I had slid down the long Ludo snake and skittered off the game board into the danger zone.

La Polaca and I sat on a concrete slab in a bare cell with four gaunt sex workers. Both of us had green spittle on our clothes and in our hair. I was no longer 'one of us'.

I was one of them.

Mario Trejo sprung us out of jail after a few hours, brandishing a stack of good reviews, proving we were a legitimate theatre group and there would be consequences if we were not released. The following day there was a picture of me on the front page of the main tabloid captioned: *flamante peliroja sin corpiño,* 'shameless braless redhead' with a bunch of 'deviants' who had been attacked by 'healthy youth'.

Back in Buenos Aires, Teresa arrived at Mum and Dad's flat to do the ironing, waving her copy of the *Crónica.* 'Señora, no es la Penny?' Madam isn't this our Penny?

Finally, whatever was going on politically had come to my door.

I was very lucky. A few years later we would have all disappeared.

***

By May 1, 1974, Perón was referring to the Montonero youth as 'useful idiots'. Their armed struggle had pressured the military into calling the election that had led to his return but now he wanted them to step back and do nothing. He repeatedly exhorted his supporters to 'Go from home to work and back home again'.

But they just wouldn't listen.

On International Workers Day, Union bureaucrats and orthodox Peronists were at the front of a massive crowd gathered outside the Pink House. The Montoneros, The ERP and the rest of the smaller Left parties were massed behind them. Lopez Rega infuriated Perón by showing him photographs of graffiti accusing Perón and Isabelita of being sell-outs and traitors, graffiti widely believed to have been instigated by Lopez Rega himself.

Perón walked to the balcony, site of so many triumphant rallies with Evita at his side. But this time it was Isabelita trotting beside him, wearing a belted shirtdress, and along the way, he remarked, 'Doesn't my wife look pretty? What do you think of her dress?'

Isabelita stood next to Perón looking like a good little girl who had been told to stand up straight. López Rega, grey hair neatly slicked back, hovered behind Perón's right shoulder with his signature smirk, suggesting he was in on a secret. Isabelita presented the pretty Queen of Labour and her two princesses with their crowns. But the Montonero group were growing restless, shouting, 'No me rompas las pelotas, Evita hay una sola' - don't break my balls, there's only one Evita, which rhymes and sounds a lot better in Spanish.

A furious Perón accused the young crowd of being 'stupid, beardless brats.'

The Montoneros ramped it up, 'What's going on, General? Is our government full of gorillas?'

The Right Wing started a counter-chant: 'Ni Yankis ni marxistas, somos Peronistas.'

The Montoneros went for the jugular. 'Vea vea vea, que manga de boludos, votamos a una muerta, una puta y un cornudo', 'Listen, we're just a bunch of arseholes who voted for a dead woman, a whore and a cuckold'.

They had gone too far.

Perón praised the 'true patriots' at the front and accused the Left of being 'agents of foreign countries, double agents and mercenaries.' The Montonero contingent, over half of those present, flooded out of the square.

For the first time in his life, Perón watched the masses turn their back on him.

This was war.

***

It was time to leave Mar del Plata. We had gathered in a café with our suitcases, and my lift was leaving after Raúl. All I knew was that he had a sullen girlfriend called Marta who occasionally picked him up after rehearsals in Buenos Aires. I had no idea where he lived, and I was terrified he'd be swallowed up by the city and I'd never see him again, doomed to spend the rest of my life wondering, *What if?* What if he was the true love of my life, my one chance at happiness? I had to do something.

I tapped his arm.

Raúl followed me out. We walked for half a block, I looked him straight in the eye, took a deep breath and declared, 'Te amo!'

I love you.

I'd said it.

Raúl nodded and said nothing. We walked around the block and returned to the café in silence. I was elated. I had done what I needed to do. I had taken control of my destiny and if I never saw him again, it didn't matter.

When my lift arrived, I sat in the back next to a handsome young man studying to be a psychoanalyst and fell asleep on his shoulder. He was left-wing, thoughtful, handsome, bookish, funny, solvent, and he evidently really liked me.

But I loved Raúl. The Professor.

I was very itchy when I returned home and discovered tiny little creatures crawling around my hairline and my *down there*. I showed Mum, who showed Teresa, who diagnosed lice! Mum rushed off to the chemist and informed him that her maid had *piojos* and he sold her a bottle of a black, viscous, poisonous lotion and a fine-toothed comb. As I combed my long hair, dozens of little black bugs dropped into the white bath, wriggling they disappeared down the plughole.

***

A few days after returning to Buenos Aires, the phone rang. It was Raúl. 'I have finished with Marta. Do you still love me?'

'Yes! Yes! Yes!'

A million times yes. Yes! Yes! Yes!

I broke off my date with the aspiring psychoanalyst and raced off to Retiro to meet Raúl.

Raúl had arranged to borrow a bed from Enrique, a fresh-faced student with tousled hair. Enrique gave us the key to the apartment, told us his parents were away and explained that his bedroom was easy to identify because he was the only Jew in the building with a poster of Yasser Arafat on his wall! Another bomb went off in my brain. Clearly here was another side to the story Ruhana had told me and I was determined to find out what it was. But first I had to have sex.

Raúl and I took all our clothes off. I lay obediently naked on the bed and Raúl stuck his penis inside me without any foreplay. I was curiously unengaged. No whooshing. After some thrusting Raúl threw his head back and gasped, 'Penny, te amo! I love you!' I found his performance fake and ridiculous - *is that it?* I pushed that thought away. I told him it was my first time, and he seemed pleased. It was a week after my eighteenth birthday. When I stood up some liquid leaked out of my *down there* and I assumed I'd caught a venereal disease.

Raúl sat naked in the hallway and ignored me and I tiptoed around, wondering what was wrong. I wrote to Helen.

My parents hate him because he is twenty-nine, divorced, an actor, has a beard and no money. Anyway, you really can tell when you fall in love, so I don't understand why everyone gets so het up. Raúl (I love him so much it hurts.) Raúl seldom gets angry but when he does he can explode and can kill someone so I had better be careful.

All the warning signs were there.

The aspiring psychoanalyst wrote me a note accusing me of being false and a hypocrite. I didn't care.

***

My new friends claimed the Bar Moderno was frequented by piece of shit anarchists and all serious revolutionaries and intellectuals frequented Confitería La Paz on the corner of Corrientes and Montevideo with its big double doors that swung inwards like Western saloons in the movies. I was living a charmed life with the most interesting people in Buenos Aires, but I had swung from being a too chatty big head to a dumbstruck dummy, afraid of opening my mouth in case I said the wrong thing and annoyed Raúl. In this new upside-down world, the Viet Cong were heroes, the Americans were bloodsucking imperialists, the Israelis had stolen land from the Arabs and the British Empire had been a genocidal nightmare. All of which turned out to be true.

One night at La Paz with Raúl and a few others, Pepe strolled in scowling. He had a new girlfriend with delicate, beautiful features like a Modigliani painting. Lucía was new on the scene, like me, and we steered clear of each other in case we caught something. Pepe flung himself down at the table and growled that he and Lucía had gone to the cinema. 'They put on a newsreel about Vietnam before the main film. I could hear Lucía sobbing and, I'm not going to lie, I had a tear in my eye as well. I was feeling great about having a girlfriend who felt the same as me about the world and I put my arm around her. And you won't believe it, but she sniffled, "Pobre Americanitos". Poor little Americans!! Well obviously, I walked out and left her there!' Everyone laughed. Pepe was indignant. 'It's not funny. What the hell was I doing with that little fascist?'

Lucía was crying for the wrong people! I giggled treacherously. I could have so easily have made the same mistake myself. Lucía was never seen again but I continued to be tolerated by my new community who found it amusing when I insisted that I was poor. Relative to my school friends who had big gardens and swimming pools, I was. Compared to actual poor people, this was risible.

In August 2022, I googled Confitería La Paz and discovered that it was in the throes of being replaced by a sushi bar.

Everything I had grown up thinking about the world was falling apart, but it is only in my old age that I question why none of us ever gave a thought to the genocide, only eighty years earlier, that had made space for us all.

***

The two months after I returned from tour in Mar Del Plata were a living hell.

I fought with Mum and Dad day and night. One terrible evening they forbade me to see Raúl and I refused to go out on a date with a nice St George's boy. My father locked the front door when I tried leaving. I warned him, 'If you don't open the door I am going to scream, 'papa no me pegues!' 'Daddy, don't hit me!' Dad didn't believe me. I ran out to the balcony leaned over and screeched at the top of my voice: 'Papá no me pegues!'

They knew they were beaten. They unlocked the door, and I was gone. Am I proud of this? Not really. Dad had never laid a finger on me.

Being with Raúl was just as fraught. We had nothing in common, he didn't understand why I laughed at things he didn't find funny, in fact he didn't find anything funny and accused me of being pathetic and bourgeois. He used the silent treatment to punish me for things I didn't know I had done. Mum had always used silence as a weapon, so it made me wretched. But I continued pursuing Raúl single-mindedly, he was my one-way ticket out of the British community because he would never belong there. The alternative was a wedding and life going on and on until I died inside then killed myself.

I ran away from home and Raúl and I slept all over town, in artist warehouses in La Boca and in special hotels prostitutes rented by the hour, including one that allowed a couple to stay until 6 a.m. if you arrived after midnight. Sex was a lot more fun now as I relaxed into my body and started having orgasms. I thought about sex all the time but sometimes in the throes of fucking, I imagined the facade of the hooker hotel sliding off and surprising passersby, Dad always among them, gazing horrified at couples going at it in every room.

This went on for about three weeks, I must have worn the same clothes every single day, until Daddy rang me at work – I had a secretarial job - and asked me to meet him at the English Club that evening. Mum had made me take a typing and speedwriting course to give me 'something to fall back on' until I got married. I was a terrible typist and bored to tears working for a ball bearing company. I explained to Dad that since I was spending eight hours a day doing something I didn't want to do it was only fair that I spent another eight doing what I wanted, which was certainly not staying at home, having supper and watching television with them. Years later Dad said he envied the sexual freedom I had enjoyed, and I was embarrassed and shrugged him off.

February is a sweltering month in Buenos Aires and the Calle Veinte y Cinco de Mayo was noisy: street sellers yelling 'Laponia! Laponiaaaa heladooos!', 'Clarín, Clarín, Diarioooo' and the usual cacophony of beeping cars. A beggar, bare feet encrusted with dirt, asked me for 'una monedita', 'a spare coin' and a man leaned out of a car window, fingers bunched, shouting, 'Qué hacés boludo?' *Boludo* is an insult Argentines use all the time, it literally means 'big balls', suggesting stupidity, not bravery, like the *Viz* character Buster Gonad who has *unfeasibly large testicles* he pushes around in a wheelbarrow. Arsehole. I opened the door of the English Club and stepped in.

An eerie hush.

A uniformed porter took my name at a polished desk under a gigantic oil portrait of Queen Elizabeth clutching an orb, resplendent on a golden throne, with a magnificent crown on her head, festooned with a diamond, emerald and ruby studded necklace, a blue sash across her tight embroidered bodice, her dress cinched tightly at her tiny waist and billowing into clouds of white lace. Halfway up the wide marble staircase, I passed an enormous painting of Princess Margaret Rose perched on a chestnut horse, her midnight blue velvet robe tumbling over its glossy flanks. I was glad Raúl wasn't with me.

Daddy and I knocked back two whiskies each, and he told me that if I agreed to come home, he and Mummy would pay for me to go to England.

I agreed and immediately began making plans to buy Raúl a ticket too.

***

Perón was rapidly losing the plot and on July 1, 1974, only eight months after winning the election, he gasped for breath a few times, cried out, 'I'm going! I'm going!' and dropped off his chair, stone-cold dead. Isabelita remained blankly unresponsive as his monitor flatlined, but López Rega raced in screaming, 'The General died once before and I revived him!' He grabbed Perón by the ankles shrieking, 'My Pharaoh, don't leave us!' Doctors, secretaries and nurses stood and watched Lopecito waving his arms wildly over Perón's dead body, 'Wake up, my Pharaoh!'

Perón remained dead and El Brujo blamed the doctors and nurses for distracting him.

The dim-witted Isabel was now president of Argentina, the first woman in the world to assume that post. And El Brujo shifted into the centre of the frame.

I just read this passage out loud to my friend Chloe and she said, 'Did you just make that up?'

'It's all true.'

We both laugh.

But governments with jokers at the helm are not hilarious.

What followed was a period of colossal ineptitude and bloody violence.

The Triple A continued its murderous missions, and Isabel was lampooned as *la sonsa, la boba, la puta,* silly, nitwit, whore. Pundits predicted that Isabelita would be a figurehead president, but with El Brujo pulling her strings, she gripped tightly onto the reins of power, signing decrees of annihilation by the dozen and ramming through an authoritarian right-wing programme. There is a bizarre piece of newsreel showing Isabelita screeching from the balcony in her shrill little voice with Lopez Rega beside her, silently mouthing the words he had written for her.

William Rogers, secretary of inter-American relations, visited Buenos Aires to speak to Isabel about surging levels of violence and the disastrous Argentine economy. He describes a surreal encounter with Isabelita sitting on a chair on a raised platform in front of a closed curtain. Whenever he asked her a question, Isabelita paused and leaned back, as if lost in thought, before replying. After half an hour, Lopez Rega emerged from behind the curtain and Rogers realised he had been whispering answers into her ear.

Grenadier Jorge Sosa Molina reported that a young officer had entered Isabelita's office and found López Rega slapping her, hard around the face. The shocked young officer drew his pistol and asked the president what she wanted him to do. Isabel waved him off quietly, 'No, No . . . leave it . . . he is revitalising me. I get confused sometimes.'

It's hard to muster any sympathy for Isabelita. She was clearly in what we would now call a coercive, controlling relationship, one that led to the torture and murder of tens of thousands.

The game was finally up when López Rega's protégée, the Minister of the Economy, Celestino Rodriguez decreed a walloping 160 percent devaluation of the peso, prices soared, and people's savings were wiped out. A two-day general strike was called by the usually supportive Peronist unions, the metal and textile workers, sent a delegation to the Pink House demanding López Rega's head. Isabelita refused. Finally, moderate Peronists and chiefs of the armed forces held a meeting where they concluded that López Rega was an insane and dangerous individual who was manipulating the president. Brigadier Héctor Fautario sat next to Isabelita at an official dinner and explained that the army hierarchy was unanimous, López Rega had to go.

Isabelita refused, 'Brigadier, I can't do that!'

Fautario was adamant, 'This is out of my control; Madam, I am just the messenger, I believe you have no option.'

Isabelita, lost without her puppet master, fell into a deep depression. She couldn't eat or sleep and fainted frequently. Cabinet meetings took place in her bedroom while the streets spun out of control. The Triple A had lost its leader and although the leadership of although the leadership of both the ERP and the Montoneros had been annihilated, the killing machine was a beast that needed feeding.

Isabel was packed off for a holiday in Cordoba and the nurse assigned to take care of her recalled that she read magazines and watched movies and showed no interest in the outside world. When she returned to Buenos Aires she carried on as before, screaming in her little-girl voice, promising to make the Argentine people happy.

***

Everybody knew that a coup was imminent, and it had widespread support. In January 1976, the son of Lieutenant General Julio Alsogaray, Juan Alsogaray, nicknamed The Hippy because of his long hair, cracked opened his father's safe and stole detailed plans for the coup, including the precise date it would take place. He passed them on to Rodolfo Walsh, the head of Montonero Intelligence, who informed the Montonero leader Mario Firmenich. Firmenich welcomed the news, believing as so many revolutionaries had before him, that a repressive military dictatorship would alert the working classes to the true nature of the state, provoking the masses to rise up and lead the glorious revolution. Robert Cox, editor of the small-circulation English-language *Buenos Aires Herald*, had a contact in the army who told him on the 21st of March, 'The taxi is going to roll, not tomorrow but the day after.'

***

The sixth coup took place on March 23, 1976. General Videla of the armed forces replaced General Laplane who had answered to El Brujo. Three senior officers politely asked Isabel for her handbag, extracted a small revolver, and informed her she was under arrest. Videla took power alongside Admiral Massera and Brigadier General Orlando Agosti Commander in Chief of the air force.

Junta sworn in, Genera Videla at the centre, Buenos Aires, (Photographer unknown), March 1976.

General Videla, married to the English heritage Alicia Raquel Hartridge, always reminded me spookily of Dad, with sensitive, slightly protruding eyes, a small chin and a prominent Adam's apple, his hair always neatly gelled in the Argentine way with a tiny curl at the nape. He made an announcement that played across all media outlets.

> We advise the nation that from today this country finds itself under the operational control of the Junta. We order all residents to adhere strictly to all legal provisions and directives emanating from our military, police and security forces.

Every mainstream newspaper came out in support of regime change and military sources boasted that it had been a *decorous coup*. Ricardo Balbín of the Radical Party approved because, 'Without peace we can't do anything.'

In his editorial, Robert Cox wrote in the Herald:

> *The armed forces have done everything they could to uphold the constitution. Their patience knows no parallels in recent Argentine history. Yesterday it became clear that whatever happened, the government was dead. The only problem that remained was to get rid of a corpse.*

That same day, the *Herald,* which knew its readers, also ran a long article about Roddy Llewellyn apologising for any embarrassment he had caused the Royal Family by his affair with Princess Margaret, adding a message from Idi Amin in Uganda, remarking that the break-up of their affair 'will be a message to all of us not to marry ladies in very high positions'.

Mum and Dad and their friends were mightily relieved. Senior management at Lever Brothers, where Dad was chief accountant, put out a supportive statement:

> *The Videla government is about the best we are likely to have . . . this is the first opportunity we have had in three years to restore the economic viability of our business.*

Spain, Perú, Brazil, Malta, Ecuador and Chile rushed to recognise the new government and informed sources whispered that Washington had been given advance warning of the coup and raised no objection. The British Labour government held back but as soon as Margaret Thatcher was elected three years later, she restored diplomatic relations with the junta and closed a Labour programme that had welcomed political refugees from Pinochet's Chile.

Three Roman Catholic cardinals blessed Videla's inauguration and throughout the Dirty War Videla nurtured close relations with both Admiral Massera's tennis partner, the country's papal nuncio Pio Laghi and Cardinal Raúl Francisco Primatesta.

A large arsenal was found at López Rega's Ministry of Social Welfare: crates of pistols and dumdum bullets, hand grenades, machine guns and car licence plates. Newspaper columns called it 'boots with a human face', announcing that Videla was ushering in 'an era of hope'. The *Herald* said the army deserved a blank check to get on with cleaning up 'putrefaction'.

The Junta consolidated by replacing every provincial governor with a military officer, political parties were dissolved, workers were instructed to go to work as normal or be punished under the military code, and ten-year prison terms were instigated for anybody 'propagating subversive material which might be offensive to the armed forces'. General Videla made his position clear: 'As many Argentines as necessary must die to ensure security.'

Strict media censorship was imposed. In response the Montonero, Raúl Walsh created ANCLA, a clandestine news agency that used an information chain, a system of hand-to-hand leaflets, with instructions:

> Reproduce this information, circulate it by any means at your disposal: by hand, by machine, by mimeograph, orally. Send copies to your friends: nine out of ten are waiting for them. Millions want to be informed. Terror is based on lack of communication. Break the isolation. Feel again the moral satisfaction of an act of freedom. Defeat terror.

Walsh's surviving daughter, Patricia, said she kept a mimeograph in her wardrobe, although there was nothing to print because the writers had all been disappeared. As the Montonero organisation crumbled there was little anybody could do openly. 'We used to write Down with The Dictatorship with lipstick on bathroom mirrors in bars. That could cost you your life, but we did it anyway.'

Instead of the socialist uprising the Montoneros had hoped for, tens of thousands of people were tortured and killed. They say that Jorge Lizaso from the Peronist Youth was skinned alive. Being disappeared is different to disappearing.

Although their leadership had been decimated, the Montoneros continued the armed struggle as long as they could. On July 2 they bombed the dining hall of the security branch of the federal police, killing twenty-one police and wounding sixty-three. Two days later this was followed by retaliatory madness from the Right: three priests and five seminarists were murdered 'for our dynamited police comrades, dedicated to those who poison the minds of our virgin youngsters', even though none of the murdered priests had any connection to left-wing Liberation theology. An unidentified young man was gagged and shot dead by a firing squad with his hands tied behind his back in front of the Obelisk on 9 de Julio and Corrientes. Thirty more bodies were torn apart by explosives outside Pilar.

If we are playing a numbers game, the Montoneros, the ERP and other left-wing guerrilla groups killed up to 1,366 people, almost all policemen or soldiers. That's a lot.

The Triple A and the military tortured and murdered around thirty thousand.

The Montoneros claim that five thousand of their supporters were killed, only some of whom were directly involved in or even supported violence. Most of the Montoneros who were tortured and killed were small fry, known as *perejíl*, parsley, and many of whom had disagreed with taking up arms. Another two or three thousand ERP supporters were killed. That leaves about twenty thousand dead who were not involved in, or in favour of, the armed struggle.

Victims included sixty schoolkids from Manuel Belgrano secondary school who were ordered to be tortured and killed by senior Police officer Miguel Etchecolatz, for campaigning for subsidised transport. That became known as the Night of the Pencils.

***

Back in 1971 I wandered into the Glastonbury Festival with Dylan. No computer crashes, no tickets, just a few people in a field listening to Hawkwind, Traffic, Arthur Brown and Melanie. I had no money, no shoes and no food but these trivial concerns didn't worry me. I read that sentence now and wonder how I fed Dylan? I did. But how? I really wanted to be enlightened. I had seen Maharaj Ji at the Conway Hall, a plump little boy with a squeaky voice pronouncing confidently that if you wanted to know the time, you looked at your watch, and if you wanted the Truth, you kissed his feet. I wasn't impressed. I wanted to find a proper teacher. I had forgotten all about politics, navel gazing was my mission now. I was more like Mum with her belief in Mary Baker Eddy and 'knowing the truth' than I liked to think.

I scooped up two-year-old Dylan who was hanging around hopefully by the ice-cream van and we came across a tall man in a long rustic-brown robe surrounded by an enthralled group. This man was staring intensely at the young woman in front of him. He moved his hand horizontally very slowly up from her crotch to her belly and declared, 'Your Kundalini has risen to here.' He addressed the rest of us. 'As you know, the Kundalini is a coiled snake that lives at the bottom of your spine, and it needs waking up. Some people's remain dormant their entire lives, it just lies there, snuggled up forever. But, if you find your path, the snake stirs and unfurls through your chakras until it reaches the top of your head. That's when you discover untold power and unimaginable bliss.'

I was mesmerized, and desperate to know where my Kundalini was. I suspected it was fast asleep but I sidled closer hoping the tall man would give me some encouragement but after a couple more inspections he announced that working on the celestial plane was exhausting and he needed a break. 'We are setting up a spiritual community in Gloucestershire. If you'd like to join us, go to Christopher Clarke's antique shop in Stow on the Wold and he will direct you to Swyre Farm.'

'Who are you?' asked the first girl. 'I mean, like, who are you?'

'I am no one. I am everyone.'

'Do you have a name?'

'Some people call me Reshad.'

A dark-haired, surly woman stepped out. 'Reshad needs to rest now.'

I was exhilarated.

***

I left my boyfriend and the remote cottage in Wales where we were living and hitchhiked, barefoot, to Swyre Farm with Dylan on my hip. We were welcomed by about thirty young

Penny & Dylan, Ibiza, (Family Album), 1970.

truth seekers on a ramshackle farm. I learnt that Reshad was spending time in Turkey with his Sufi teacher, Bulent, and would be back in a few weeks. His previous name had been Tim Feild, he was from a very upper-class family one of the very few who could trace their origins back to William the Conqueror, had been schooled at Eton and served in the Royal Navy before becoming a successful pop star in the early 1960s with The Springfields with 'Son of the Preacher Man', Dusty Springfield. I was even more intrigued.

Life in the commune was curiously asexual and uneventful. We gardened, worked as amateur builders restoring the farmhouse, meditated twice a day and waited for Reshad. I also hired myself out to a local builder, doing dry stone walling and plastering and heaving boulders around building sites to prove something or other.

I was meditating on my own one evening and heard rustling, which I believed was an angel paying me a visit, but when I opened my eyes it was only a little mouse nibbling at the bowl of rice the candle was stuck into and I ran away.

Finally, the great day arrived. We were told that Reshad and Siddiqa, who we all called Sid, his right-hand woman, had landed in London and would be blessing us with their presence that evening. They swept in like visiting potentates in their robes and were welcomed with a lot of shiny-eyed adulation but luckily no foot kissing. Reshad was very animated at the long table over dinner, and I longed for him to notice me with his beautiful warm brown eyes. We were advised that he would be making individual appointments with each of us over the following days. I was longing for my special time but anxious that I might be one of those destined to return to the primordial slime after a brief sojourn on the conscious plane. My name did not appear on the list for three days. The chosen ones floated out after their sessions and revealed their new Arabic names, where they were on the spiritual ladder and the special meditations they had been assigned. They were told they had to 'live in the question, live in the breath, give up all transient material concerns', and I nodded sagely wondering what it all meant. Reading it now, it sounds a bit like Christian Science!

I was the very last to be summoned.

I went in convinced that he would suggest I leave because of my low level of spiritual advancement and bad vibes.

Reshad was sitting cross-legged on a cushion. He pointed at a spot in front of him. I sat obediently and he smiled, his beautiful eyes crinkling at the edges.

'Penny.'

I nodded.

'Penny, I have been watching you'.

There was a long pause. I became more concerned.

'Your name is Nur.'

I was disappointed. Nurrr. The way he said it didn't even sound like a name, more like clearing your throat.

He gazed and eventually told me that I was very special. I had my own special path to the Light, to what some call God. 'There are very few souls in the world with that gift.'

I was astonished.

'You know what that means. Don't you?'

I really didn't.

'It means you don't need a teacher. You don't need an intermediary.'

Reshad looked at me intensely. What was he talking about?

'Of course, a teacher can never . . . be. . . with a pupil. That would be quite wrong.'

I began to see where this was going. He explained that he and I would be at the head of founding a spiritual community, the male and the female creating what the New Age needed.

It was a surprise, but I wanted so much to believe it that I almost did.

He stood up and opened his arms. I walked in and there was an awkward embrace that went on far too long. I could feel his penis tapping at the door of his robe.

When I came out the others were eagerly waiting as usual. 'What did he say about you?'

I decided not to tell. 'Not much.'

'What's your name?'

'Nurrrr.'

'What? Nothing else?'

'Just the name'

I didn't dare tell them I was enlightened. I didn't think they would believe it.

I was moved out of the attic dormitory into a room of my own and Reshad made nocturnal visits when Dylan was asleep. We were to get married and live in the gatehouse and Dylan would to be sent to Eton while we travelled around spreading knowledge. I picked blue tiles for the gatehouse kitchen feeling like a complete fraud.

I felt I was going mad. Turning to stone.

A few months later Reshad went back to Turkey for a refresher session with Bulent.

I felt a huge wave of relief. I ran away the following day.

Again.

I googled him after writing this and discovered that Reshad had been an acolyte of Alice Bailey's like López Rega and died in 2016. I was twenty-one when he told me I was spiritually advance and I remember thinking he was absolutely ancient but he was only about 36, and the whole episode was more like bullshit than grooming. Still, according to Wikipedia, after me, he married a woman named Penny who he renamed Nur.

That's quite weird, right?

***

I was completely lost. I had run away from one world, but I had no idea where I belonged. I was floating around nowhere, anywhere, rootless. I wasn't anybody from anywhere. I had shed the Anglo-Argentine accent so quickly that nobody has ever asked me where I am from. The colour of my skin and the way I speak says I am English, but I'm not. Not really. I'm not Argentine either. I'm a bastard, from a depressed and psychotic settler community. Unmoored. It took me a while to find my feet, making it up as I went along, and I'm still doing that.

***

It was illegal to mention the Montoneros or the ERP by name. In the *Herald* the ERP are referred to as 'the non-Peronist terror group' and the Montoneros as 'Marxist terrorists' or 'the Marxist unmentionables' or the long-winded and ungainly 'Argentina's other guerrilla organisation that helped put Perón in office and was later disowned by Perón'.

In Uruguay the Tupamaros became 'the ones with no name'. What we say matters. What we don't say sometimes matters even more.

***

I always imagined that torture took place in dark dungeons, but the Naval School of Mechanical Engineering, the ESMA, is an imposing white building with white pillars on the Avenida Libertador, an impressive boulevard inspired by Baron Haussman's modernisation of Paris and named after General San Martín, who liberated Argentina, Chile and Perú to free it up for settlers. It's the road that connects the mainline Retiro Station terminus with the middle-class northern suburbs.

It was hiding in plain sight. Thousands of people walked and drove past it every day.

The coercive state finds ways to inspire terror. Many years ago, I came across paintings in the Prado depicting the auto-da-fé, the interrogations of the Spanish Inquisition and I was astonished to see they were held in wide-open squares before huge audiences. For four hundred years, often in the presence of royalty, cruel and sadistic punishments were meted out in full view to heretics and apostates, a warning to all. In Argentina's Dirty War, people were 'sucked up' openly, while passersby pretended not to notice. They had to see and not see. That was the point.

The ESMA was the most notorious prison for the 'disappeared' but there were others in Buenos Aires with inoffensive names like Hotel Sheraton, the Little School House and Olympus, and another six hundred prisons that were open secrets across the country. Some, like the ESMA, were run by the navy, others by the air force or the army, but their bloody business was the same.

***

Argentina brags about being the most cultured country in Latin America. The navy prides itself on being the most exclusive and civilised of the armed services, 'Gentlemen of the Sea'. Admiral Massera, handsome with black bushy eyebrows, identified the three twentieth-century evil ideologies that must be obliterated in order to protect Western Christian values and the sanctity of the family: Those of Freud, Einstein and Karl Marx.

Prisoners gave naval officers nicknames; Abdala, Luís D'Imperio, would visit his *chupados* in the basement of the ESMA after they had been tortured and bring them *alfajores con dulce de leche*, delicious soft cookies made with corn starch. I don't have a sweet tooth but as I write this I salivate. Where can I buy alfajores in London? I stop thinking about torture for a minute and guiltily trawl the internet. There's an Argentine deli in Borough Market; I dash there, make a purchase and eat the whole packet.

Chupar means 'suck'; a *chupado* is 'someone who has been sucked up'. This was the slang used by both prisoners and officers, the officer *sucks* the *chupado* off the street, and the prisoner is ingested into the belly of the state.

***

Never Again. *Nunca Más*.
Never again. Never. Never. Never. Never.
Until the next time.

In December 2023, Javier Milei, a reality television personality was elected president of Argentina. He had revelled in insulting guests on his television show, his hyperbolic bullying lauded as plain speaking, telling it how it is. 'I'll break your nose you washed up old man . . . you don't understand anything you fool . . . you donkey, you idiot . . . I'm going to wipe the floor with your face . . . you useless, bloodsucking, parasitical shit . . . stick your political correctness up your arse.'

He charged around the campaign trail with a chainsaw to illustrate what he would do to public services and presented a grinning Elon Musk, with his own chainsaw, side-splittingly funny unless you are among the Argentines affected when Milei hacked thirty thousand government jobs as soon as he got into office. Extreme poverty levels have risen massively but his approval ratings continue to rocket.

Politics as spectacle. The only sin is to be boring.

López Rega is long dead, and Isabelita has been a recluse for years, but they reappear reflected a thousand times in this crazy hall of mirrors. Milei's detractors compare his closest confidantes, his sister Karina and the journalist Carlos Kikuchi, to Isabelita and López Rega. But Javier's most trusted advisor has always been his bulldog mastiff, Conan, his 'little four-legged son'. When Conan got sick and left his physical body to sit at the right hand of Number One, also known as God, Milei cloned him six times. One puppy died and Angelito, the Little Angel, apparently provides a corridor of light for his doggie brothers, each named after a neoliberal economist and responsible for their own government departments. They issue instructions on policy through the services of Celia Liliana Melamed, a medium, who specialises in *interspecies communication.* Celia claims she can communicate with rabbits, cows, cats, birds, spiders and mosquitoes, revealing on air that she'd had a reassuring conversation with the coronavirus. Milei himself has seen the resurrection of Christ three times, 'But I couldn't tell people in case they say I'm crazy'. It was Number One who advised him, through his dead dog, to leave show business, enter politics and became president.

The dog was right.

Liberty Advances is a rubber-stamp party with very few members and sings from the right-wing playbook. It has declared war on feminists who they always call 'feminazis', promotes climate change denial and claims that trans-rights activists advocate cutting off the testicles of five-year-old boys. Milei's vision is to privatise all public services, dollarize the economy, legalise selling children and human organs and increase spending on intelligence.

And in this settler-colonial country, it is 'foreigners', a dog whistle for nonwhite and LGBTQ+ people, who are to blame for a corrupt and decadent society that needs another clean sweep.

According to Milei, it is a myth that thirty thousand people disappeared after the last dictatorship and anyway those who were murdered deserved to die, because 'in a war it is legal to kill the enemy.' Vice President Villaruel's father was a military man proud of fighting subversion, and Milei himself worked for Antonio Bussi, who was accused of eight hundred kidnappings.

Never again. Until the next time.

***

The hierarchy of the Argentine Catholic Church condoned the eliminating of prisoners but insisted it be done 'humanely'. Prisoners who were 'sent upstairs', the military euphemism for killing people, were stripped naked and given Pentothal, a strong tranquiliser, flown over the River Plate and dropped into the sea, where their lungs swiftly filled with water because they were unconscious.

Only about a hundred of the five thousand prisoners in the ESMA emerged alive. These survivors were the only living witnesses when some of the military personnel responsible for the horrors were brought to justice. There was no logic. Some of those who had collaborated enthusiastically with the military as *marcadores*, markers, those who drove around streets with officers identifying people to be sucked up, were 'sent upstairs' along with those who had refused to betray anyone.

***

I circled back to politics in my early twenties after the hippy-dippy mystical bullshit and this time it stuck. First time around, I had enthusiastically adopted revolutionary left-wing views, because I was desperate to ingratiate myself with all the cool people I was meeting.

My upbringing and education had only prepared me for marriage to a nice Anglo boy so when I finally managed to leave Raúl, I found myself in England, a nineteen-year-old single mother with no idea how to make a living. I didn't want to get married, and I didn't know how to support Dylan and myself. I had hated being a secretary, and anyway, I'd completely forgotten the speedwriting, which I'd been crap at in the first place, so I slid down the social ladder and woke up with a bump. For about ten years I did low-paid menial jobs. I worked as a waitress, in the Harrods chocolate department, as a farm hand, a cleaner, in a printed circuit board factory and in a hospital kitchen. I wasn't slumming it by choice like Simone Weil; I couldn't think of anything else to do. These were happy years. I was poor but it didn't define me. I loved being a mother, apart from parents' evenings, where I was younger, poorer and more dishevelled than the other North

Oxford mums with their Jaeger outfits and their big houses. I had friends and lovers and I made art out of anything I could salvage. I played John Coltrane's *My Favourite Things* and Miles Davis's *Sketches of Spain* over and over again. It was the life I had chosen.

My stint in the printed circuit board factory was an eye-opener for a middle-class girl. At that time, Dylan was five and we were living a couple of miles from the Welsh border in a cottage in the middle of nowhere, no electricity and one cold-water tap, cooking over an open fire and trudging through mud every morning to school and work. The factory owners paid us pennies and we were forced to do unpaid overtime until the business went into profit. One morning our three bosses rolled up in new Mercedes-Benz cars. That lunch time I called everyone to a meeting and announced that if they could afford to buy themselves expensive new cars, they could pay us to work on Saturdays. The bosses called their own meeting at the end of the working day. They said that if anybody wanted to leave, they were welcome, the door was open and there was a queue of people out there who were desperate for work. Nobody moved. 'Everyone can go home now. Except Penny.' And they sacked me.

I was completely helpless.

Next, I found a job winding blackcurrant brambles around wire fences on a vast farm producing fruit for the Ribena soft drink. Blackcurrants have tiny spiny thorns that easily pushed though the inadequately thin leather gloves they gave us. My hands felt like pincushions, so I removed the gloves and stood pulling out the spiny thorns for a couple of minutes. Richard Green, the owner of Wittern Farm, popped up on the other side of the fence. 'I don't pay you to pull the thorns out of your hand. Do it in your break. '

I walked out.

These are the things that happen when you're a nobody.

***

On arrival at the ESMA a *chupado* was referred to as a 'packet', given a number, stripped naked and handcuffed to a bed. The *picana,* an electric prod, was applied to their genitals, their nipples, mouth, nose, eyes, ears and anus and a plastic bag was repeatedly tied over their heads and removed just before they choked to death. After a session, torturers would chat about football and the weather and return to their wives and children.

The Mariano Moreno National Library is a free online archive of oral testimonies. I dived in. Survivors talk very quietly, without crying or expressing any emotion, often the more horrendous the description, the quieter their voices. The psychologist Marta Haydeé García de Candecoro was 'sucked up' by the air force and taken to a detention centre known as *La Cueva,* The Cave. On arrival, she was punched in the stomach for being 'a whore, like all psychologists'. Her husband, Jorge, was there too and she was forced to listen to his screams as he died. She described one subofficer, Gregorio Molina, nicknamed Charlie, who raped women after he tortured them. He raped Marta several times and when she asked, 'Why this?' Gregorio replied, 'Because you're a lady, and I know that outside of here you wouldn't look at me twice.'

Another witness was kept in a room for soldiers to rape or masturbate over whenever they felt like it. She was *una cosa, a thing.*

Enrique, Cachito, Fukman, a big bear of a man, was given a *milanesa* sandwich by his torturer when he said he was hungry, the torture resumed after he finished eating. He and several others spent months in the room they called *capucha,* hooded and shackled on their beds apart from when they were escorted to the bathroom. He says that Teresita, one of his female comrades, was raped every time she went to the loo, so she held it in as long as she could. Sometimes bored guards would dangle prisoners from beams and use them as punchbags or force them to do callisthenics until they collapsed and then kicked them around. Prisoners got to know the different guards on shifts; those who *gave* beatings but allowed them to speak to each other, guards who didn't *give* beatings but enforced silence, and the best of all, guards who didn't *give* beatings and allowed them to speak.

Ana Testa yawned when she talked about her worst experiences. I found this strange until she explained that she had been able to go away somewhere in her mind so that she wasn't really present when they hurt her. She said it was a lie to pretend that they had all had been heroic under torture; she herself had given the name of one of her comrades and she was grateful that he was alive and had forgiven her.

Another woman admitted she had asked her torturer to hold her hand when she was in extreme pain. He did.

In terrible times people take a scrap of kindness wherever they can get it, from whoever will give it, from the person who is hurting them.

It was a crazy world. When one prisoner arrived at the ESMA with a broken leg after being 'sucked up', the ESMA doctor fixed him up and put a cast on it.

Then they killed him.

***

In 1690 the first person, I mean the first *European,* old linguistic habits die hard, to set foot on the Malvinas archipelago on the South Atlantic, was the English John Strong, who named it the Falkland Islands. Long before then Yamana canoe people had dropped in from time to time but never settled. The Argentine name Islas Malvinas derives from the French Îles Malouines, the name given to the islands by French explorer Louis-Antoine Bougainville, who visited in 1764. Around that time, some Spanish settlements were attempted but they failed to thrive, and the following year, a British captain, John Byron, left a plaque claiming the Falkland Islands for the unhinged King George III, a madman who foamed at the mouth and spouted rubbish for hours at a time.

The islands remained uninhabited, genuinely terra nullius, visited by fishing ships and Yamana in bark canoes, until Argentine independence in 1816, when Argentina purchased the Malvinas from Spain.

On November 6, 1820, the Buenos Aires federal government offered Ludwig Vernet, also known as Louis or Luís, a Huguenot entrepreneur, who variously claimed to have been born in Hamburg or France, and wherever he was from, had recently emigrated to Argentina, taken citizenship and accepted the concession to hunting and fishing rights on the Isle of Solitude, part of the Falklands/Malvinas. The Argentines promised Vernet tax exemption as long as he established a settlement within three years. After a couple of attempts, Vernet managed to repair the ruins of former garrisons, import some horses, and attract 150 settlers, a few Europeans, some gauchos from the Pampas, a group of Tehuelche, with whom he had established good relations, and fifteen adolescent enslaved Africans, who were promised their freedom. Vernet gave each settler a parcel of land, seed and tools and by 1829 the settlement was doing quite well despite the predations of overfishing by North American whalers and sealers. In 1833, with the approval of the Buenos Aires federal government, Vernet seized three North American ships. The British backed the Americans, invaded the islands, threw out the Argentine settlers and established British rule.

The British shipped in a few hundred of their own settlers, destitute people from Wales and Scotland, and their descendants are now the tiny homogenous population of 1,840 people who claim self-determination as 'natives' of the Malvinas.

Dad was always splenetic about the fighting over 'these godforsaken islands in the South Atlantic, why would anybody want them?' He was wrong. There are plenty of reasons to seize a useful base in the South Atlantic surrounded by fish and oil reserves. On the Argentine side it has become a potent symbol of neocolonialism, Argentina always in complete denial about its own colonialism. There was one phenomenally profitable product that could flourish in this windy inhospitable place: sheep. After the Industrial Revolution, the new mechanised mills in the North of England grew huge maws for slurping colossal quantities of wool for crafting into carpets and curtains, coats and sweaters, suits and blankets, socks and gloves and hats and skirts for export all over the world.

Back in 1516, Thomas More had issued a warning,

> *Your sheep that were wont to be so meek and tame, and so small eaters, now, as I hear say, become so great devourers and so wild, that they eat up, and swallow down the very men themselves. They consume, destroy, and devour whole fields, houses, and cities.*

From 1750, commercial agents working on behalf of absentee English landowners evicted Scottish Highland crofters from their ancestral lands to make way for sheep. After these sheep had chomped their way across Scotland the British began shifting surplus flocks to Australia, New Zealand and the Falkland Island. They multiplied and gobbled their way across the islands, so the British Falkland Island Company shipped flocks over to Tierra del Fuego and Patagonia on the Argentine mainland.

The great devourers had arrived.

***

Pieces of the settler jigsaw keep slipping into place and things I didn't understand and then only half understood slowly come into focus. There were stages of attrition in the very south of Argentina, and it was the British with their cuddly, vegan, woolly ruminants who delivered the coup de grace on this ghost train of horrors.

The first wave of colonisers and missionaries delivered to the inhabitants of Patagonia and Tierra del Fuego the same devastating cocktail of raw violence, bad faith, germs and Christian conversion that Columbus and Cortés had dished out in Central America and the Caribbean.

In 1519 when the explorer Ferdinand Magellan was making his way down the coast of Patagonia, he encountered a group of Tehuelche and invited two young men onboard, plied them with gifts and food, tricked them into trying on leg shackles and sailed away with them against their will.

They died on the voyage to Spain along with Magellan and most of his crew.

There were encounters where shipwrecked sailors were sheltered by Indigenous people and left once they had mended their ships. But there were many more heartbreaking meetings of such monumental bad faith that the Selk'nam hid away for the next three hundred years, warning each other of the arrival of Europeans by lighting fires, which is how Tierra del Fuego, which literally means 'Fireland', got its name.

Sailors interpreted these fires as threats from cannibals who wanted to roast them alive. Actually, they were warning each other about us.

For over three hundred years explorers saw nothing they wanted in this frozen land, so the Selk'nam and Yamana, the Alcaluf, the Hausch and the Kaweskar were left more or less in peace, apart from missionaries, whalers and sealers, until, in 1883, placer gold was found there, gold that can be sifted by individual miners out of sand and rock, triggering a gold rush that attracted hordes of rapacious Europeans, mainly English, Scottish and Croatians, who indulged in an orgy of sexually enslaving women and killing Indigenous men. James Radburn known as El Jimmy relates to his biographer:

> The miners camped on the island also raided the Indian camps for women, and after the usual scrubbing they lived with them until they made their 'pile' of gold and left the island; or until the women were so notoriously pregnant that they should be left. . . . Once all of the women of a mining camp, but one, fled. The men shared her until she was expelled when almost ready to give birth.

The scrubbing referred to sheep dip.

This woman, passed around like a *thing,* like the women in the ESMA, kept finding her way back into my mind however hard I pushed her away.

Looking into where I come from has been more disturbing than I anticipated. There were weeks when a grainy black-and-white photograph of a dead, naked man lying in long grass became imprinted on my eyelids as soon as I tried to go to sleep. I'd wake up sweating a few hours later. By this time, the photograph had become a fragment of moving footage, with a shadowy figure shovelling a spade into the man's naked body. Drenched in sweat, I'd get out of bed for a pee and go back to sleep. When I woke up again, the fragment was still playing on a loop and so it went on until I was afraid of going to bed.

I came across a photograph that had shocked me so deeply I buried it deep in my unconscious. In 1897, thirty-year-old Julius Popper, born into an affluent Jewish family in Bucharest, was issued a permit by the Argentine government to mine for gold in Tierra del Fuego. Popper claimed that eighty Selk'nam had attacked his miners on El Páramo Beach, so he gathered a group of men armed with Winchester rifles to teach them a lesson. He engaged an official photographer to document this 'Indian Hunt', producing a series of pictures with Popper and his men posing triumphantly like big-game hunters over dead Selk'nam.

Julius Popper 'Indian' hunt, Tierra del Fuego, (End of the World Museum), 1886.

These images returned to haunt me.

***

Popper did not pretend he was killing people who were less than human.

> *They have been graced with elevated and noble humanitarian sentiments, they are reasonable, magnanimous even to the point of forgiving their enemies, they disdain revenge even returning bad with good, even becoming protectors of the race which persecutes them, taking shipwrecked victims to places where they can get help . . . they are not cannibals or the savages depicted in modern ethnographies, but rather affectionate men who are loving towards their children as children are towards their parents; they mourn their dead for a long time with faces painted black.*

Then he killed them. 'Indian' hunts did not end when the gold ran out and the prospectors left. British gentlemen were on their way. My people.

***

After the hideous violence of the gold miners and overfishing had reduced access to vital food supplies, the final nail in the Indigenous coffin was the privatisation of Patagonia and Tierra del Fuego. In 1881, Argentina and Chile finally settled their ongoing territorial dispute by drawing a line straight down Patagonia and Tierra del Fuego, cutting through Tehuelche, Selk'nam and Yamana land, mountains and rivers. Argentina was granted everything on the

East, and Chile got the West. The Selk'nam and Yamana found themselves stranded on both sides of this new arbitrary border.

Chilean and Argentine governments sold concessions to the land they had seized to new settler citizens at bargain prices, authorising owners to clear their lands of the Native population and its flora and fauna 'by any means necessary'. 'Clearing land' was a euphemism for internment and genocide of the people who lived there, sanctioned by the state and carried out by civilians.

***

My great-grandparents and most of the British community lived far away from the open violence. They settled in the southern suburb of Quilmes.

Quilmes is the name of the most popular Argentine lager and these days you can find it in hipster bars in London, Bar Chick, Bar Kick and Barrio Soho in Shoreditch. If you question the etymology of the name, an invisible door springs open and spins you back to the seventeenth century. The Calchaquíes were a Diaguita tribe famous for their fine pottery and bravery. They fought Spanish colonisers for 150 years but when they were eventually defeated, the last eleven thousand were force marched 1,400 kilometres to the south of Buenos Aires, most dying of hunger and exhaustion along the way. The land they were displaced onto was named Quilmes after their original home in Tucumán. The survivors died or were assimilated, their descendants are probably still there in the marginalised *barrios* or in domestic service. In

1890 a German immigrant founded a brewery on the site and called it Quilmes.

And the quicksand swallows them up again.

***

The Argentine state granted Dawson Island, off the Fuegian coast, to Giuseppe Fagnano's Salesian Order to establish a mission. The Salesians had proved themselves trustworthy: They had accompanied General Argentino Roca on his bloody Conquest of the Desert in the Pampas. '*We must adapt to love or force; in this circumstance, the cross must go behind the sword.'* The Salesian website explains that since they were founded by Saint Don Bosco in 1859 the brothers have devoted their lives to his dream of saving souls. *Give me souls take all the rest, Genesis 14.21.*

In 1895 Peter McClelland, one of the founders of the Sociedad Explotadora de Tierra del Fuego, wrote a letter to the landowner Moritz Braun explaining that Fagnano had offered to take 'Indians' to live on Dawson Island for a pound a head. This is 'the cheapest way we can get rid of them short of shooting them, which is rather objectionable.' Indian Hunters, engaged by landowners, had two choices, the rather objectionable murderous option or packing 'Indians' off to Dawson Island. Bullets are expensive.

Between 1880 and 1910, about a thousand Indigenous people were interned on Dawson against their will. Most died from depression, overcrowding, infected clothes and forced labour in the Salesian sawmill. The Italian speaking Salesians didn't think it was necessary to learn Indigenous languages, contract a single doctor or provide medical facilities, despite huge death rates from measles and tuberculosis.

> The Yamana and Selk'nam traditionally coated their bodies with animal fat and wore cloaks of hide with the fur side out to keep dry and warm. Missionaries hated nudity and compelled them to wear clothes that carried lethal European germs and remained damp when they got wet.

Only the cemetery flourished.

Lucas Bridges, the third son of Thomas Bridges, visited Dawson Island to meet Hektliohih, a proud Selk'nam he had hunted with before he was interned. Hektliohih did not complain of outright mistreatment by the Silesians but said simply, 'Shouwe t-maten ya', the nostalgia is killing me.'

Adults died quickly and in such numbers that Salesian fathers stopped trying to convert them and concentrated on the children; one of the fathers explained they'd also given up on general schooling because children were dying so soon after arriving and restricted their work to religious education.

> Children became masters in the art of a Christian death. . . It was enviable, seeing them leave this world for eternity so well prepared, filled with faith and happiness as if they were going to a feast!

***

In the twentieth century, after the first 9.11 in 1973, General Augusto Pinochet overthrew the democratically elected socialist, Salvador Allende, and imprisoned and tortured his political enemies on Dawson Island. When Brazilian journalists were allowed to inspect it, there was nobody there.

The Salesian mission on Dawson finally closed on September 29, 2011.

***

I moved to Oxford with Dylan in 1976, full of revolutionary fervour after my experiences in the silkscreen factory and on the blackcurrant fields. It was the year of the Junta's murderous coup, so I imagine that Sylvia Pettigrew, my aunt by marriage, was full of revolutionary fervour too, but the consequences for her were catastrophic.

I rented a flat on Walton Well Road next to Port Meadow, got a job in the John Radcliffe Hospital up the road and immediately joined the National Union of Public Employees. I was the only middle-class worker in the diet kitchen, and I found it difficult to take part in the morning banter because my colleagues began every day gossiping about a group of people they all knew very well. Hilda, Dierdre, Trevor and Ena led very eventful lives, some of them were obviously really annoying, and my co-workers Beryl, Pauline, Vivienne and Victor knew all their comings and goings. After a couple of weeks, I dared ask how come they all knew the same people. They hooted. 'It's *Coronation Street*!' a soap opera they all watched.

I was mortified but it broke the ice. After that, they made fun of the way I spoke, la-di-da, and trained me to do my tasks as slowly to prevent our superiors from giving us more work. Viv, the head cook, was from St Kitts and told stories about arriving in England waving her little Union Jack flag expecting a warm welcome and being greeted by monkey noises and people lifting the back of her skirt to see whether she had a tail. Victor, assistant head cook and Viv's best friend, was a member of the National Front. Viv didn't seem to mind because Victor hotly denied being a racist. He explained that he admired Hitler for his commitment to public works, and building autobahns that were the envy of the world. Beryl was a Tory and mother of a policeman who was overlooked for promotion because of his low arrest rate, preferring to tell troublesome young boys to shove off home rather than locking them up. Pauline's husband was a fireman, and she was very pretty and very large. She loved peanut butter because it was the only fattening food she didn't like so she didn't need to eat it. They were all proletarian and although they showed no interest in revolutionary politics, I recruited them all to NUPE and became a very active shop steward across the hospital.

It didn't feel like enough. Getting tea breaks for my colleagues was all very well, but I wanted to overthrow the state.

And then the doorbell rang.

A hapless young man with thick, smeared glasses stuck together with Sellotape held up a copy of *Socialist Challenge* and announced that he was a member of the International Marxist Group. I practically assaulted him. 'I want to join, now!'

He backed off behind the rubbish bins, alarmed. I assured him I was all for the revolution, but he said he would be back the following week with things for me to read. I dutifully ploughed my way through a stack of tracts about how the ruling classes were perpetuating the capitalist system at the price of large-scale unemployment, mass starvation, bloodshed and the threat of nuclear war and that women were the slaves of the slaves. The only solution was not socialism in one country that had led to the repressive Stalinist Soviet regime but an international revolution. When the young man returned, I assured him that I agreed with everything the Fourth International stood for and he invited me to attend a cell meeting in a small, terraced house up the Cowley Road.

I cycled there in a state of great excitement. I don't know what I expected, but a dingy sitting room with grimy-brown swirly-patterned carpets scattered with piles of unsold revolutionary papers, collapsing sofas and tea-stained mugs was not what I'd dreamt of. Everyone looked exhausted. I was soon exhausted too. Being a revolutionary involved a massive amount of frenetic activity that was not visible to normal people. We held weekly cell meetings with our secret names even though everyone knew who everyone else was – mine was Davies - union meetings, campaign meetings, caucus meetings before meetings and dashing off to picket lines all over the country, sometimes spending all night huddled around fires in oil drums, and of course public demonstrations most weekends. On top of all this, I was Dylan's mother, and after he went to bed, if I was free from picketing duties, I stayed up until the early hours, making art to keep myself sane.

After a year in the IMG, I was frustrated, it was too middle class, too full of people like me, although I did at least have a working-class job. In 1978 I jumped ship and joined the Workers Socialist League, who published their own, much drearier paper, *Socialist Press*. The WSL had genuine working-class members in the British Leyland car factory, and we were very proud of them. The WSL had split from the Workers Revolutionary Party and then itself split three more times before dissolving in 1984, three years after I left. We were required to attend even more meetings than the IMG, and there was no interest in anything other than the class struggle. Race was not on the agenda, and the word *feminists* was always glued into one word: *petitbourgeoisfeminists*. During the nationwide steel strike in Thatcher's first term, I was approached by the WSL leadership, saying it would be very helpful if I hooked up with the convenor of the Corby steelworks, Roger had indicated that he was willing to join the organisation so long as he could have sex with me whenever he wanted. I refused and they didn't push it too much. This is how things were in those days, I never considered making a fuss about it. I mentioned it recently to Paul, an old WSL comrade I had been friendly with, and he was shocked, they had approached him first and asked him to persuade me to pimp myself out.

On one occasion I shared a revealing drive from Oxford to Middlesbrough with comrade Pat Lally, four and a half hours each way, to attend a pointless meeting about nothing, with six people in attendance. Whenever we stopped for coffee, Pat admired the identical Formica fittings and food in every motorway cafe, so you could be anywhere at all, but he strongly disapproved of the pointless individualism of customers wearing clothes in different styles and colours, something he was determined to forbid after the glorious revolution. I knew I wouldn't enjoy living in his version of a socialist paradise.

We completely ignored the Communist Party, who we called 'tankies' or 'Stalinists', but engaged energetically in factional infighting with other Trotskyist groups. The Fourth International was founded in 1938 by Leon Trotsky after most of his close friends and family had been killed, and he and his allies had been expelled by Stalin's Communist Party. By 1940, he was an old man living in Mexico City, looking after his rabbits and playing out a massive, apparently reciprocated, crush on Frida Kahlo. I say he was an old man, but he was only sixty, over a decade younger than I am now. His wife, Natalia, scratched out Frida's face from all the photographs of them posing with Diego Rivera and Frida, a poignant attempt at removing her from the frame, just as Stalin had removed Trotsky from Soviet portraits. Trotsky's dearest friends, his first wife and two of his sons, had been murdered by the KGB, one daughter had died of tuberculosis and his favourite, Zina, killed herself. Ramon Mercader, a strange young man who was dating Trotsky's secretary, insinuated himself into the household and on a warm day dropped into the library to see Trotsky wearing rainboots and a large raincoat *in case it rains.* Natalia heard a scream. Mercader had stuck an ice pick in the back of Trotsky's head.

Trotskyism started with the seeds of trauma, murder, and betrayal.

***

The missionary Thomas Bridges, who compiled the Yamana-English dictionary, became a farmer, and applied for land concessions, claiming he would hand most of it back to the Yamana and Selk'nam to continue their traditional hunting and foraging, protected from white settlers with bad intentions.

I believed he provided a chink of light in a litany of horrors. I was wrong.

***

Oddly enough, the *Buenos Aires Herald* was the only newspaper that reported uncomfortable truths about the Dirty War. Three months after the coup, which the *Herald* had welcomed so warmly, the newspaper was reporting on the continuing presence of Ford Falcons. '*The nightmare of the cars without number plates*' parked outside government offices.

On July 5, 1976, the editor Robert Cox wrote a long piece that began by condemning terrorism and critiquing those on the Left who only excoriate the brutality of the Right. Cox went on to report on the case of Carmen Beatriz Frascotto de Román. She came to his office to report that three Ford Falcons with no number plates had driven up to her house, men in plain clothes had jumped out, beaten her up, threatened to kick her eight-year-old son in the head if he didn't keep his face to the wall, and dragged her husband away. Cox writes, 'What happened to her could happen to any of us. She doesn't know what her husband is supposed to have done. She doesn't know who has taken him away . . . her predicament is shared today by scores, possibly hundreds of people.' Carmen de Román looked everywhere for her husband and became increasingly isolated. 'People are frightened to be seen near me. If I meet them in the street, they try to avoid me.' She told Cox her husband had been a union delegate between 1971 and 1973 but had no connection to the armed struggle.

Very few spoke out publicly, although in his Independence Day sermon the archbishop of Santa Fé, Monsignor Vicente Zaspe said, 'Argentine homes are being shattered by fear, by kidnapping, by murder and by the awareness that there is no authority to appeal to.'

Just as it is not true that all Indigenous people were wiped out and not every single coloniser was evil, it is not true that nobody spoke out. People did – not many. And it was too dangerous to listen to them.

***

In the secret prison camps, officers, soldiers and young left-wing militants were bound together in a macabre embrace.

Witnesses from the ESMA said their comrade Victor, had been strapped naked to a bed as they dangled his baby son upside down. When they gave the baby an electric shock on one of his chubby little legs and threatened to smash his little head against the wall, Victor named names. Nobody blamed him. People he named died. Victor didn't kill them.

In this nightmare world, officers at the ESMA would sometimes give the prettiest prisoners expensive perfumes, tell them to dress up and take them out to nice restaurants and then onto the Mau Mau nightclub.

***

When I was a teenager, the Mau Mau on Calle Arroyo, was the coolest nightclub in Buenos Aires. 'An elegant place for elegant people' according to *La Nación* newspaper. None of us had any idea the name was in spectacularly bad taste, named after the insurgent movement fighting British colonialism in Kenya. It had African patterns on the wall and served expensive drinks on little tables scattered around a shiny dance floor. I went on several dates to the Mau Mau with Eduardo Gnecco, who wore a suit and tie and picked me up in his own car. My mother approved of Eduardo despite him being *an Argentine* but I wrote to Helen that our dates were so sedate, and he was so *perfect* that I felt like screaming, kicking over all the tables and bashing people on the head. Sorry Eduardo if you ever read this, I was crazy. Eduardo tracked me down on a visit to London fifty years later and I learnt that he had his own biscuit factory and had married Marilyn, a nice woman from the Welsh community in Trelew with whom he had four children.

***

There were dates in the ESMA too.

Nilda Goretti, known as Manú, was selected for a special evening by her main torturer, 'Mariano'- Captain Raúl Scheller; a hood was placed over her head and she was pushed into a car. 'I was shaking from head to foot, I thought they were taking me somewhere to kill me.' When the car slowed down, her hood was removed and Scheller ordered her to get out. She found herself by the Costanera, a strip along the River Plate with *carritos,* food carts selling delicious take-away chorizo and *chivitos,* thin beef sandwiches, in front of fine-dining restaurants. Manú was escorted to a table set with a linen tablecloth and found herself sitting with ten other guests. 'How could I have dreamed they were taking me out to dinner?' She gradually realised that her fellow diners were officers from different torture camps with kidnap victims, pretty women like herself. It was two o'clock in the morning, and she was too nervous to be hungry, but Scheller ordered her to eat what he ate – a Russian salad, steak and chips, and a flan with 'dulce de leche' - while they chatted about nothing. It reminded Manú that there was a world outside and that she wasn't part of it. She was a ghost. After dinner she was driven back to the ESMA.

You think, of course you can't help thinking, why didn't she run away? But where would she run to? Was there anybody in that restaurant, who would have risked their own lives to help her? And if they had, wouldn't they have been 'sucked up' too? She didn't know whether they were military or informants or other prisoners and none of it made any difference anyway. She was out of the concentration camp, in a public place, and she was still trapped and helpless.

The Triple A had decimated the Montonero leadership and six months after the coup, the SIDE 'sucked up' the rest of the active membership, leaving what Manú described as *four crazy cats,* inconsequential rank-and-file members, each carrying a cyanide pill to avoid cracking under torture. Montonero Party infrastructure had been destroyed, there were no safe houses, no channels of communication, and Manú and the others didn't want to put their families in danger by asking them for help. Even if they managed to escape, they had no travel documents and nowhere to go. When Horacio Domingo Maggio escaped from the ESMA, he was caught, and prisoners were made to walk past his bullet-riddled, blood-soaked body.

Later on, a few trusted prisoners were allowed out to see their families, and on these visits, they did not say a word about where they were the rest of the time. They were there and not there. Visible and invisible.

Manú testified against Captain Scheller along with other officers but it's impossible for her to pin down exactly how she felt about him. They were the same age and at times they'd had real conversations. She remembered saying, 'How did this happen, how did we come to this, where you believe that, and I believe this?' Twice Scheller drove her forty miles from the ESMA to La Plata to visit her family. He left her with her mother and stayed overnight in a hotel nearby. Manú said nothing and her mother knew better than to ask. The following day, Scheller returned and ate lunch with her parents. Manú said that Scheller's invasion of her intimate spaces, her home, and her close family had been worse in some ways than the physical torture, worse than being tied naked to a bed with an electric cattle prod applied to the most sensitive parts of her body. Now there was nothing that they had not tainted.

The yawning Ana Testa believes that Miguel Cavallo, the one they called *Serpico* or *Marcelo*, a naval intelligence officer at the ESMA, was truly in love with her. He had no family and had never met anybody like her, so pretty, funny and intelligent. He drove her to celebrate the New Year with her family and stayed for dinner, polite and appreciative, asking her mother for the recipe of Cassata Brasilera, a delicious pudding she whipped up with condensed milk, cream, egg yolks, sugar, vanilla fingers and grated chocolate. Ana says at that time, she cast him as the 'goodie' in the movie and it had cost her a lot of therapy to disentangle the grisly mess in her head. Cavallo was later indicted on 228 counts of homicide.

At the head of the ESMA was Commander Jorge Eduardo Acosta, the Tiger. He turns and smiles straight down the lens, eyes sparkling, a better-looking version of Alec Guinness in *The Lady Killers,* the same long, thin face and nose, an interesting man who knows who he is and is happy about it, someone you'd think you'd enjoy meeting. The Tiger was personally responsible for the torture and death of thousands of people, a few were kidnappers, a few had laid bombs, but most of them had just protected someone or carried messages, fellow travellers or people who had opinions they voiced too readily, like the two French nuns Léonie Duquet and Alice Domon, one of whom had nursed General Videla's disabled son. Or Father Mujíca, a socialist priest who worked in slums and had never supported the armed struggle and yet was gunned down by a MAC-10 submachine gun. Or the Swedish teenager Dagmar Hagelin, scooped up in a case of mistaken identity. Or Azucena Villaflor, María Ponce and Esther Ballestrino, Mothers of Plaza de Mayo *sucked up* while silently protesting about the disappearance of their children. Some Montonero prisoners had supported the military strategy, but many others believed it had been a catastrophic mistake, including the Trotskyist PST, Partido Socialista de los Trabajadores and the PO, Partido Obrero, who argued that an armed struggle was premature and suicidal. The one thing all prisoners had in common is that none of them stood trial, no evidence was ever produced, no witnesses, no lawyers, no judge, no jury, no nothing. *Pff!* they simply vanished.

Like Sylvia.

The Tiger with his baby blue eyes was renowned for his sadism. He was an enthusiastic torturer and occasional rapist who enjoyed escorting the best-looking female prisoners to his favourite restaurants, Los Años Locos, El Globo and El Hispano. He was also a devout Christian who prayed every night, consulting Baby Jesus about who *should be sent upstairs*, and Baby Jesus obliged with a list of names.

***

In October 1976, the junta's Foreign Minister Cesar Augusto Guzzetti declared there was no such thing as right-wing subversion in Argentine.

> My concept of subversion refers to left-wing terrorist organisations. The subversion of the right is no such thing. The country's social body is contaminated with an illness that forms antibodies. These antibodies cannot be considered in the same way as the germ. As the government controls and destroys the guerrilla, the action of the antibodies is going to disappear . . . this is just the natural reaction of a sick body.

Torture and murder heal the sick body politic.

***

Having joined the WSL thinking it could jump start the revolution, it felt as frustratingly far away as ever, so I joined the Leninist Faction inside the WSL hoping that if we were more focused and organised we could push things along. In theory, we didn't have a leader, but our de facto leader was a bombastic young man, Mark Hyde, who stood with his legs wide apart, jiggling his balls, as he lambasted everyone for their incorrect positions on everything. He wrote our policy document accusing the WSL leadership of being 'amorphous, rambling and lacking in hard programmatic content'. Hard programmatic content sounded sexy.

In the summer of 1980, I went to Argentina to visit my parents with Dylan, and when he returned to school in

Oxford–I flat-shared with Kath, another single mother–I travelled to Bolivia to meet up with the Trotskyist Partido Obrero Revolucionario. The leader of the POR, the legendary Guillermo Lora took me to the tin mines on the Altiplano. It was stunningly beautiful up there, the air so thin that it was hard to breathe, the pinks, blues and blacks of the shawls and bowler hats worn by the women shone brilliantly as they raced around, while their miner husbands and brothers attended classes in Marxism where they dreamed of streaming classical music in their communal toilets and building an egalitarian revolutionary society full of joy. I saw with my own eyes that the things we only talked about were possible. It felt so real, so far from endless agendas and matters arising that even when Lora asked me to *chupame el pito,* suck his dick, at the back of the bus on the way back to La Paz from the Altiplano, it didn't ruin it. I was travel sick and anyway, I didn't fancy him. He whined a bit but didn't push it.

By the time I returned to Oxford, the rest of the Leninist Faction had secretly joined the Spartacist League without telling me.

The Spartacists were the weirdest group, a bona fide cult. Over the years I have occasionally caught sight of a couple of them on demonstrations, clutching *The Spartacist,* a slim paper with peculiar headlines calling for North Korea to have nuclear weapons and denouncing Afghans as 'goat fuckers'. Their primary aim was to smash all other Trotskyist groups so that the working classes, who as far as I could tell had no idea that any of us even existed, would no longer be distracted and appreciate that the Spartacists were the only lodestar, lighting the shining path to the 'Glorious Day'. I thought they were mad.

A special one-day conference was held, at which all five of us in the Leninist Faction were expelled by the WSL for being clandestine members of the Spartacist League. I was puzzled that my Faction colleagues all sat on their hands, leaving me jumping up and down on my own, protesting loudly that we were being unfairly accused. After the expulsion my Faction comrades asked me to meet them that night to discuss further plans. I took the bus from Oxford and climbed up narrow stairs to a tiny flat near King's Cross. Di, Pru and Mark were joined by other people I didn't know, smiling at me in a patronising way. I felt like a particularly slow child: 'We have something to tell you.' They revealed they had lied to me, and they were now all Spartacists, and I should join because they were really wonderful and I was going to love it. I felt utterly betrayed. At first, they tried to bulldoze me with their superior knowledge of revolutionary politics, then they became abusive and finally tried to physically prevent me from leaving the room. I panicked, pushed through the two spindly men blocking the door and ran down the stairs with the group yelling after me, 'You have blood on your hands.' Which is true in a way, but not in the way they meant.

The tube had stopped working so I walked to Victoria Coach Station from King's Cross.

I'd missed the last bus to Oxford. I sat there until morning, freezing cold, next to a few homeless people and pigeons pecking leftovers.

Years later one of the Leninist Faction members apologised. She told me Spartacist women were pressured into giving up their children to concentrate on party work, to have abortions if they got pregnant and encouraged to use sex as a recruiting tactic. Apparently, the American leader, James Robertson, enjoyed sitting in a corner watching party members having sex, bizarre if it's true. I hovered close to cult life with Reshad and the Spartacists, but I have Mum to thank for inoculating me against too much certainty.

***

Everything changed when I was awarded a large Southern Arts Council grant to concentrate on my artwork. I gave the WSL notice that I intended to leave my hospital job but they informed me that this was not my decision to make. Three male comrades were sent to coerce me into staying in that kitchen job for the rest of my life because I had a useful trade union position. They berated me until dawn when I pretended to give in because I wanted to go to bed. I left my job anyway and was suspended again for breaking party discipline. I'd had enough. Like alcoholics who have drunk their fill, I have attended enough meetings to last the rest of my life. It's obvious that neoliberal capitalism is a stupid, miserable system for living on this planet that we are so busy destroying, it is literally insane that tiny numbers of greedy white men have trillions while others starve, spending more and money on weapons to kill people instead of looking after them.

I truly believe we can choose to live together more generously and lovingly as brothers and sisters, I just don't want to sit in rooms fighting other people who believe in the same things.

Penny painting, Oxford, England, (Photograph Sharon Woodward), 1982.

Despite our best efforts, Margaret Thatcher won a landslide election, the racist National Front was in the ascendency, unemployment was rising exponentially, and a new, money-grubbing culture was rising in the ashes of old industries. The immensely wealthy wiped their arses with £50 notes and imported snow for their children's birthday parties. Despite all the silliness and some bullying, I am grateful for that period of activism. At least we tried. I still try. Intersectional feminism with its queer alliances is so much better than the old version and grassroots movements are springing up and doing things differently and despite the dark shadow of fascism swooping over us again there are communities that don't turn away, and I am with them. I don't know where hope lies but I know it's not by burying our heads in the sand.

Although my family lived apparently blameless lives, sitting tight, beyond the fort, beyond the wagon circle, there was another story.

***

In 1877, there were five hundred sheep in Magallanes, a decade later there were six hundred thousand, and by 1894, two million sheep were industriously gobbling their way across lands where the guanaco, the Alcaluf, the Yamana, the Kaweskar and the Selk'nam had roamed.

Sheep may safely graze and pasture
In a watchful shepherd's sight.
Those who rule with wisdom guiding
Bring to hearts a peace abiding
Bless a land with joy made bright.

***

Indigenous people lived in Tierra del Fuego before 8000 BC, when the archipelago was still joined to the mainland, but they were not citizens of Argentina. They were now living on land that farmers wanted for grazing sheep with a handful of skilled European shepherds and farmhands for herding, shearing and fencing.

Fuegian nomadic hunter-gatherers were plunged into starvation when wire fences imported from Britain enclosed their traditional hunting grounds, along with the extinction of the guanaco, a species of llama, which fed on the same grass as the sheep. The Selk'nam and Yamana retaliated by damaging fences, driving flocks into swampy areas, and cutting the tendons of sheep. Farmers regarded this as unprovoked violence. It was 'the Indian problem'.

The solution was simple. It's worth repeating. Sheep farmers paid a bounty of £1 for a complete skull or a pair of hands or ears of a Selk'nam, 'macho' or 'chunky' as they called them. A pair of women's breasts also sufficed as proof of their demise.

The main landowners who provided horses and money to clear the land of 'Indians' were Moritz Braun and José Menendez of the Sociedad Explotadora de Tierra del Fuego, known succinctly as La Explotadora, the Exploiter, the English Ernest Hobbs of the Sociedad Ganadera Gente Grande, the Welsh Mont E Wales of Phillips Bay Farming, and the German Rudolf Stubenrauch of Wehrhahn and Company and the Falkland Islands Company. The Indian Hunters who did the actual killing were Scottish or English.

A letter from GHC, a sheep foreman who arrived via New Zealand, relates that he was invited on an expedition soon after he arrived.

> *I said I was quite willing to go but that hitherto I had very little practice in killing Indians, nevertheless I was willing to see how it was done . . . they wanted me*

> *to have a revolver but I said it was not necessary as I could kill as many Indians as I require with a rifle.*

Indian hunter Sam Hyslop showed off horse hobbles he had made from the skin of a 'chunky' and the pile of money he had made from killing them. John Walker and his cousin Henry Edwards boasted about killing 'darkies'. One hunter was known as Dancing Dan, Norman Wood was another. Arthur Miller wrote this letter to his friend Edmund Goodhall on January 17, 1873.

> *You will have heard accidentally of the Indians down here. I will tell you as well as I can what is really true. There were a gang of fifteen on them in the Sierras robbing. An aférez (junior officer) came across and killed three, also losing a soldier I believe. They attacked Pavón and lost another. They came for Edward's trot horse and Walker shot one in the back and the farm-hands finished him. On the way Heralde met them on the other side of the Sierra and killed six, and yesterday I heard that some of them came back with some more and that they killed four. This I give you for what it is worth, I know it is the truth. We spent a very pleasant Christmas Day.*

Alexander McLennan, a former British soldier known as *el chancho colorado*, the Red Pig, was hired as Menendez's chief Indian hunter. Menendez gave an interview to *El Diario* in 1899 justifying violence because, 'The indios rob for the pleasure of robbing and love to destroy private property.' *Indians* were thieves. Everything belonged to us.

Waite Stirling, the English Bishop of the Falkland Islands described Indians as sunk in the depths of barbarism and when an English farmer explained that he had killed 'About twenty of them' because of what they had done to his sheep and would have killed more if he could, Stirling exclaims in his letter to the Society, 'And no wonder!'

In 1895 McLennan bragged about murdering a large group of Selk'nam in cold blood when they came to the bay to collect mussels at low tide. He and his posse lay in wait with repeater rifles, firing indiscriminately at men, women and children, some of whom drowned when they fled into the sea to escape. He told Lucas Bridges, 'It was really a most humanitarian act if one had the guts to do it.' He argued that these people could never live their lives alongside the white man; that it was cruel to keep them in captivity at a mission where they would pine away miserably or die from some imported illness; and that the sooner they were exterminated, the better. MacLennan took an arrow in his back before the slaughter and made it into a tie pin, which became one of his most treasured possessions. When McLennan retired, Menendez gave him a gold watch to thank him for his labours.

In 1898, Menendez's administrator, the English James C. Robins, went with MacLennan to take revenge on 'Indians' who had stolen some sheep. They rode up with fifteen soldiers, tied up their horses and approached an 'Indian' village silently on foot. In a chilling letter to a friend, Robins writes, *I'll draw a veil over the next five minutes and let you guess the rest.* James Radburn, *El Jimmy*, admitted that:

> *Indian hunts were not as romantic as you might think and you couldn't admire this system for cleaning the island of natives but it was part of the job and at the same time more exciting than anything I had done before.*

El Jimmy later married a Tehuelche woman and had several children with her.

The shepherd William Blaine grew up in poverty in Scotland, tried his luck in New Zealand, sailed from there to the Falklands/Malvinas, and then travelled with sheep to Tierra del Fuego in 1881, eventually returning to Scotland in 1898. Blaine records that he sent four men to look for lost horses and they returned with three 'Indian' boys.

> *Their introduction to civilisation was as follows – first with a pair of sheep shears their head was cropped as close to the skin as the shears would cut it. They were next taken alongside the dipper with shoe brushes, they were effectively scrubbed with sheep wash, non-poisonous of course, this was to kill the vermin – then they were finished up with soap and water. With old clothes from the men their nakedness was covered for the first time in their lives, they were very much afraid of the rifle, the consequences of clearing out was well impressed on their minds, in a short time they were quite at home among us.*

In 1895, there was a trial to determine whether the treatment of Indigenous people had broken the law. Eyewitnesses and employees of the great landowners testified about forced displacement, Indian hunting, the abduction of children and sexual slavery. John McRae, Alexander Cameron, Mont Wales and Moritz Braun were all cleared of any misdoing.

> *It is public knowledge that the Indigenous people of Tierra del Fuego were living in a state of barbarism, and that they were nomadic, feeding themselves through hunting and, mainly, with the sheep they came across; that regarding these Indigenous people, there is no provision for defining their legal status; that the preceding do not allow for criminal prosecution of any person for the humiliations that are said to have occurred against the Indigenous tribes that have lived in Tierra del Fuego and Adjacent islands.*

***

I started writing what I assumed would be an aggrieved memoir about how constraining life was for girls and women in the 1950s and 60s in the Anglo-Argentine community. I never gave a thought to the damage our tea parties were sitting on. Boredom often disguises horror, but I didn't know that then.

***

Thomas Bridges's son Luke Bridges, who had learnt Yamana and Selk'nam, relates that centuries of abuse had taught the Yamana to be wary, and when they paddled out and shouted 'yammerschooner, yammerschooner' with arms outstretched, irritating Charles Darwin and other visitors, they were asking visitors, 'be kind to us! be kind to us!'

A few years later the Patagonian Missionary Society pressured a reluctant group of Yamana, including Orendellico, once known as Jemmy Button and now a grown man, to take his family to Keppel, one of the Falkland/Malvinas Islands to establish a Christian mission. The Yamana were homesick and offended by being forced to work for food and constant accusations of thieving, so they rose up and killed the captain, his mate, a catechist, a carpenter and four able seamen. The ship's cook survived. The Yamana took his possessions, plucked his body hair as they did their own and taught him to hunt and fish. The cook described this mirror image of what Europeans did when they gave Jemmy, Boots Memory, Fuegia Basket and York Minster stupid names and made them conform to Victorian social norms, as torture.

Missionaries were astonished that Orundellico/Jemmy Button refused to return to England. 'It's not my country', he said. They did not understand why he preferred Tierra del Fuego to Walthamstow and/or why he refused to allow missionaries to take his children away for a Christian education. The Reverend Despard of the South American Missionary Society wrote disapprovingly that Orendellico *imagined Christianity to be just a custom of a different nation, instead of a privilege and a duty of every fallen man.* Missionaries were unable to see that the Yamana had their own culture.

The Yamana were nimble thinkers, quick to pick up English words, but anthropologists, settlers and colonisers always used the word *mimicking* for this talent, a word we reserve for describing monkeys, parrots and Indigenous people.

In 1884, four Argentine warships arrived in Ushuaia to claim Tierra del Fuego for the Republic of Argentina. The Yamana were initially alarmed, but Captain Augusto Lasserre promised Reverend Bridges they would not interfere with his mission or oppress the Yamana in any way. These friendly visitors raised the Argentine flag, built a new office, set up two reflecting beacons and departed. They left behind twenty men and the measles virus. Within a month, over half the Yamana died, and two years later, half of those who survived had died too.

Everything we touch sickens. We are the disease.

In the 2010 census, 2,761 people identified themselves as Selk'nam. After centuries of persecution for being 'Indians' there is now an obsession with racial purity, so they are written out of the story all over again. The French-Canadian anthropologist Anne Chapman, considered a great defender of the Selk'nam, would only interview someone who identified as Selk'nam if they spoke the language and had two Indigenous parents. The widespread rape of Selk'nam women by European men and the fact that Selk'nam children on Dawson Island were punished for speaking their own language counted for nothing. In 1973, Chapman recorded the death of 'the last Selk'nam', Angela Loij, and proclaimed the Yamana extinct. Indigenous people lose their identity if they change and use technology along with the rest of us. Unless they remain romantically pickled in aspic, they become nobodies all over again, we weep a few crocodile tears and forget about them and the land we stole from them.

In Patagonia, Bruce Chatwin claims that he met the very last Yamana, Grandpa Felipe, in 1977. He also tells a story about McLennan the Red Pig, in retirement with his wife Bertha, in full delirium tremens shouting 'Don't kill me' at Selk'nam warriors he hallucinated around his bed. He ran away and was found naked, eating grass in a bullpen. McLennan never married anybody so this might be pure fabulation. In 1986, the honour of being the 'last Yaghan' fell on Rosa, then there was Julia, followed by Ursula and then Cristina Calderón who died on February 22, 2022.

The Selk'nam activist Vanina Oheda refuses to accept the idea that the Selk'nam have been annihilated, 'We want to scream every day that we are still alive, and as I always say, as long as there is blood in our veins, we will continue living.'

There are still Selknam communities in Argentina and Chile and a small Yamana community in Ushuaia and another on Navarino Island, all strongly resisting erasure by the well-intentioned and the malevolent. There is also a hipster beer. Cerveza Yaghan is '100 percent artisanal with traditional flavours and an original taste.'

The Tehuelche, the Picunche, the Pehuenche and the Huilliche have adopted the Mapudungun language and organised under one banner, the Coordinadora de Organizaciones Mapuches, a united front against the incursions of settlers with their railways, their cattle, their army, their dams and their fossil fuel extraction.

They are still here.

***

In the seventies, second-wave feminism was in full flow alongside revolutionary class politics. I read Simone de Beauvoir and Germaine Greer, Kate Millett, Shulamith Firestone, Gloria Steinem, Marge Piercy and Marilyn French and many others. Novels were usually about miserably married women who made cupcakes and wanted to kill themselves until they shacked up with another woman and escaped the clutches of the patriarchy; it seemed inevitable that I would magically become a lesbian. On the corner of Walton Well Road where we lived, there was a women-only house. They were radical lesbians who believed that pregnant women should abort sons, that *penetration is rape* and that having sex with men was *collaborating with the enemy*. I was in awe of them, especially Spike, who had spikey hair and piercings and burped shamelessly and unapologetically. I visited the house a couple of times, obviously without little Dylan, who had a penis. The biggest poster in their sitting room said simply, Heterosexuality is the Cornerstone of Male Supremacy.

I was sleeping with Steve, a former welder who was studying at Ruskin, a college that prepared working-class trade unionists for university degrees. I only ever saw Steve late at night and he sloped off at dawn, which suited me perfectly. One evening we shared an avocado, a treat in those days, and he stuck the stone in a jar of water with a toothpick so it could grow into a plant. I indignantly accused him of trying to domesticate me and flung the stone in the bin. He was bewildered.

One morning he lingered instead of leaving as it got light. I was too embarrassed to ask him to leave, but eventually I had to go into town. As we walked up Walton Street, he flung his arm casually around me. I cringed. Spike and the political lesbians cycled past us, one at a time, waving cynically. *Fuck, fuck, fuck, fuck, fuck.* I wriggled out of his arm. 'Do you think you own me or something?'

Marriage terrified me. I had seen what it had done to Mum and Dad, and it's obvious that I chased Raúl relentlessly precisely because he was utterly impossible, and it was never, ever going to work. After Raúl, as soon as a relationship with a lover got serious, I ran away. Monogamous coupledom is not for everyone.

Friendships have sustained me through my entire adult life. Some have been short, some have lasted decades, women and men who have celebrated my successes and mourned my failures and I theirs. I adore you all, you know who you are, many still in my life, all the way to the very recent darlings you all stop me from slipping into stupor or despair. Thank you. And thank goodness I had a child when I was too young to know what I was doing.

***

Manú's was the first testimony that helped me put a face to the disappeared. She is an artist, with an attractive mobile face, her gestures and dress style remind me of my friend Helen. She survived the ESMA because she was recruited into what military double-speak called the 'process of recovery', a slave labour force, who were killed if they refused to work. Prisoners longed to become slaves, to move from the *capucha* torture chamber, where you could be killed at any time, to the *fish tank*, where you were useful and might survive. Slaves in the fish tank forged counterfeit documents for the military, drew maps, wrote whitewashing articles, and if they were bilingual, like Manú who grew up speaking both French and Spanish, they summarised what was being said about the regime in international newspapers and magazines. Slaves would try to help other comrades get out of capucha by claiming they had an essential skill but even in the fish tank, prisoners disappeared, and their comrades were informed they had been transferred to a farm in the South. Eventually, everyone realised that this 'farm' was at the bottom of the ocean.

Swim with the sharks or die with the fishes.

Admiral Massera was insanely ambitious and plotted to elbow General Videla out of the way and become president himself. He set up his own newspaper, *Convicción,* and recruited journalists, artists and intellectuals to write for him, including three of the ESMA slaves, who had their hoods and shackles removed every morning and were driven to work.

The editor Hugo Lezama knew that the best writers were left-wing and commissioned them to write for the culture pages about Marcel Proust, Andy Warhol, Günter Grass, Merleau Ponty and Jean-Paul Sartre, review films that were banned in Argentina, and produce articles about gay and lesbian rights. Naturally, *Convicción*'s editorials and news pages were fully in support of what they called 'legal repression', and any mention of human rights was forbidden.

Another way to survive was to have a useful skill. Mario Villani was good at mending things. He refused to fix the *picana,* the electric cattle prod used for torture, but when they replaced it with an electric transformer that caused even more pain, he relented and fixed it. Miguel Etchecolatz was the Federal Police commissioner supervising twenty-one concentration camps across the city, and Villani reports that after torture sessions, Etchecolatz would confide in him about his son's problems at school. Villani has a photographic memory and after the fall of the dictatorship, he was able to identify by name dozens of the ESMA torturers and guards. Graphic designer, Victor Basterra, was a slave counterfeiter, producing driver's licences, passports and identity documents for use by the military for their illegal activities. He hid extra copies of the photographs he took for documents in photo-sensitive boxes, later used to identify dozens of perpetrators.

A few lucky ones were allowed out to work, returning to the torture chambers of the ESMA every night. Manú worked on Calle Florida, just up from Harrods. I remind myself of the emaciated, shackled prisoners from the Dachau camp who marched through the town every day to work in factories alongside townspeople. Nobody knew and everyone knew. Manú was eventually allowed to live outside, but she continued doing what she was told, *home to work and work to home*; she remained compliant and silent. This lively, clever woman lived for years with a metaphorical hood on her head. The camp was not just a physical location, it was a state of mind.

Prisoners remained silent because they were afraid, afraid for themselves, for friends in captivity, for their families, and anyway, who could they tell and what could they say to them? Fear coiled tightly around their tongues and they said nothing. One woman was sent to Mexico where she could have easily gone to her aunt's house and asked to be driven to the German embassy to ask for asylum, but she kept quiet.

That's how it works.

When a senior officer gave Manú permission to leave the country, The Tiger screamed that she was betraying him by leaving. Her life was his to dispose of.

Captain Scheller took Manú to The Embers in Acassuso to eat onion rings.

The Embers, modelled on an American fast-food diner, opened in 1965, and Jenny Potter, Susan Peters and I would order milkshakes and chicken in a basket with fries and a side of onion rings, feeling like teenagers starring in our own movie.

Mum and I took Dylan to The Embers in 1979. Manú might have been there with Captain Scheller. They would have looked like anybody else.

***

Manú and Ana were not in love with their captors. They just wanted to live. But a few female prisoners formed intense romantic relationships, in which one partner had the power of life and death over the other.

Lieutenant Jorge Radice said he fell madly in love with Anita Dvantman because her bravery in the torture chamber blew his mind. He later claimed that officers and prisoners had all gone crazy. Anita became a *marker,* driven around town, voluntarily fingering former friends and comrades including her own former mother-in-law. Radice and Anita went on to have two children together. He was extremely bitter about female prisoners who denounced him for torturing and raping them, calling them 'ungrateful wretches' because in other camps like La Perla, Campo de Mayo and Tucumán, they killed all the women they raped.

Vice-Admiral Ruben Chamorro and the Montonera prisoner Marta Balzán got married and went on to advise the apartheid government in South Africa on effective torture techniques. Chamorro died before he could be tried for his crimes, and apparently Marta chose to follow a spiritual path after a visit to India and disappeared into LaLa land.

Then there is the chemist Mercedes Inés Carazo, a Montonero leader known as Lucy. She was tortured for three months but they couldn't break her. One of her torturers, Antonio Pernía, found out where her husband, El Monra, was holed up, and during the shootout Pernía brought their ten-year-old daughter, Mariana, safely out of the house before killing her husband. He took Mariana to the ESMA to visit Lucy before dropping her off with her grandparents and Lucy fell in love with him. Lucy told her cellmate

> You know about me and Antonio, right? It's horrible but I love him. Sometimes he looks at me and says, 'How can you love me? I'm a shit. I'm a murderous beast.' One time he screamed, 'Get out of my bed, you know I killed your husband!' But I love him. I don't know why, maybe because he gave my daughter back.

Carazo says she and Pernía ate out at the best places, the food was delicious, and the contradictions were stomach-churning.

Pernía's nickname was the Rat.

Carazo woke out of her nightmare and is now the national coordinator of the Peruvian Technological Innovation Centre Network in Lima. Unlike Marta Balzán, Lucy did not collaborate and used the little power she had to help other prisoners get jobs in the fish tank where they had a better chance of survival. Her relationship with Pernía ended when the dictatorship fell. Female survivors forgive Lucy. They do not forgive the 'mini-staff', those prisoners like the Kapos in Nazi concentration camps who were more brutal than the guards.

One female survivor who was 'sucked up' by the air force instead of the navy says she feels they were lucky to be incarcerated in places where they were behind bars. They didn't have the added anguish of being taken out to dinner by men who tortured them.

Journalist Miriam Lewin, very pretty with blue eyes and red hair, wrote copy for the military during the football World Cup in 1978. The Tiger once gave her a silver bracelet for her birthday saying, 'Michi darling I've never given you anything.' She lost it immediately.

Secret prisons were hot houses where poisonous plants bloomed. Officers often stayed over at the ESMA in the evenings and on weekends rather than going home to their wives and families. Manú once asked the Tiger why they didn't go home. The Tiger was indignant:

> It's your fault! With you we can talk about movies, the theatre, about anything. We can talk about politics. You know about raising children; you can play the guitar; you know how to handle a weapon. You know how to do everything! You are the women we thought only existed in novels and movies. It has destroyed our families. Because now what are we going to do with the women we have at home!

Captain Scheller said to Manú, 'I look at my wife and I think, I don't belong here. I'm sharing this history with all of you, not with her.'

***

During our second visit to Argentina in 1980, at the peak of the dictatorship, Dad, Dylan and I went to La Bombonera stadium to watch a Boca Juniors home game against Argentinos Juniors. The 'barras bravas', hardcore Boca Fans, were penned into a corner and as soon as the whistle blew they went ballistic, beginning with an outpouring of adoration for the club that meant everything to them. '*Boca, Boca de mi vida, vos sos la alegría de mi corazón*', Boca,

Boca you're my life, my heart's joy, and then as the volume increased into a roar they sang about Perón: '*Se siente, se siente, Perón está presente.*' We all feel it, Perón is here.

My blood ran cold. You could be killed for less.

During the Dictatorship, the television blared all evening and into the night at Mum and Dad's but there was no mention of death squads or disappearances, no jokes, no veiled references, no satire, no actual news, just a black hole into which whispers about the *Madres* and their disappearing children vanished into dust.

The 'Marxist unmentionables' never made an appearance, not even for a laugh.

The military fascists who ran the country always appeared nice and tidy, hair slicked back, speaking about national honour, pride and duty and how well everything was going.

El Pirata, a buffoon with an eyepatch, featured in all the comedy-sketch programmes that made Dad chuckle. Every Argentine knows that England stole the 1966 World Cup. The favourites, Argentina, Uruguay and Brazil, were allocated overgrown training grounds with no goal posts, trains were late, matches started late and hotel accommodation was poor. The ultimate stitch-up was when an English referee was appointed for the quarter-final between Germany and Uruguay and a German referee to the quarter-final between Argentina and England. The English referee promptly had the two best Uruguayan players escorted off the pitch by uniformed policemen. Uruguay lost. The German ref, now known as El Pirata, swiftly gave a red card to the Argentine Captain, Antonio Rattín, for dissent. Rattín refused to leave the pitch for nine minutes during which, according to Brian Glanville in the *Sunday Times,* the referee continued writing down the names of Argentine players like 'a schoolboy collecting railway engine numbers'. England won. Legendary manager Alf Ramsay called Argentine players 'animals' and forbade his players from swapping shirts at the end of the match. Five years later, El Pirata strutted about making Nazi salutes with a ludicrous German accent in sketch after sketch.

The murderous Nazis running the country were never mentioned.

Despite having unstable, overlapping identities, I have always supported Argentina playing football against England. I was deliriously happy when Argentina beat France in a penalty shoot-out and won the 2022 World Cup.

Argentine fans invented a racist chant about the French team, and the players bellowed it out again on the team bus after they beat Colombia in the South American Gold Cup in 2024. Chelsea's Enzo Fernandez posted it on his social media and players including the Scottish-heritage Argentine Alexis MacAllister insisted it wasn't racist.

Argentina is so deeply racist it doesn't even know what racism is.

> *Escuchen, corran la bola, juegan en Francia pero son todos de Angola, Que lindo es, van a correr, Son come travas como el puto de Mbappe, tu vieja es nigeriana, tu viejo camerunés, pero en el documento, nacionalidad francés.* Listen, spread the news, they might play in France but they're all from Angola, isn't it lovely, the way they run, like that trans eating faggot

> Mbappe, your old lady is Nigerian, your dad's from Cameroon but your passport says you're French.

In the current Argentina football squad, every surname is European: fourteen Spanish, eight Italian, one Polish, one Croatian, and a Scot, Alexis MacAllister. All with Argentine passports.

President Milei sacked his sports minister for suggesting the players should apologise and Vice-President Victoria Villarruel posted on X:

> No colonialist country is going to intimidate us for a song on the pitch or for telling a truth they don't want to admit. Argentina is a sovereign and free country. We never had colonies or second-class citizens. We have never imposed our way of life on anyone.

***

One Christmas, officers toured all three floors at the ESMA, *Capucha, Capuchita* and *Pecera*, unfastened all handcuffs, leg shackles and hoods and marched them downstairs. Prisoners assumed they were in for a thrashing or a massacre, but instead, The Tiger wished them a merry Christmas and invited them to feast at a table heaving with delicious food and drink while officers made speeches wishing them a happy festive season.

The next day the torture and beatings resumed as before.

The radio was always on at top volume to cover the screams. Although it drove people crazy, at least they always knew what date it was, and they were grateful for that.

After the dictatorship fell, some torturers went mad, others became religious fanatics, one or two felt remorse and the rest believed they had fought a crusade for Christianity and Western values and insisted they would do it all over again.

***

Late 1977, after some unusual storms, strange fish and naked corpses began washing up on the beaches in Colonia, a pretty coastal town in Uruguay.

The not knowing continued.

I have written about a few of those who survived the ESMA. But there are many who never got a chance to speak. There were 4,900 in the ESMA alone.

Tens of millions of invisible bodies have piled up since the conquest of America.

Geologists talk about *deep time*. A time scale that is unimaginably greater than the scale of human life on this planet. We live in an eternal present, apparently unable to imagine anything farther back than last week. The violence that enabled the settler colony did not happen in deep time. It's less than a blink of an eye in the life of this four-billion-year-old planet, but it could be a million years ago, a trillion years ago, ten trillion years ago, a time we can't even think about, deep time, time before we were, time before we became whatever we have become. We have forgotten it as if it never happened and yet it is soaked into every cell of our being.

***

In 1978, we were living in Oxford and my friend James, Dylan, and I watched the World Cup on a tiny, portable black-and-white television stuck on top of an upright piano in the kitchen, which we had fetched from Worthing after Grandpa Gordon died. None of us played the piano, Dylan flatly refused to continue with piano lessons and I couldn't face trying to force him. Anyway, forget the piano, that's where the television lived. We supported Argentina despite knowing that the dictatorship would see it as their victory if the tournament was a success. We couldn't help it. Neither could the prisoners in the ESMA who were sometimes invited to watch a match with their torturers whispering: '*Argentina campeón, militares hijos de puta al paredón*'. Argentina Champions, military motherfuckers up against the wall.

The ESMA was only two blocks from the World Cup stadium, where the world's press congregated.

In 1978, General Videla celebrated the centenary of the genocidal Conquest of the Desert and Argentina winning the World Cup. Before the Argentine players went on the pitch, aware that glory would be claimed by the junta, the chain-smoking left-wing manager, César Menotti, told his players to play for '*los carniceros y los maestros*', the teachers and butchers. Ossie Ardiles and Ricky Villa came to Tottenham Hotspur that year and Dylan and I have supported Spurs ever since. Menna, a young Palestinian who lives in my house, asks why I support a team that loses all the time. I reply that *it's my fate*.

Ardiles still lives in London and has always been adored by the Tottenham faithful.

***

The British stayed out of direct political involvement, but the bloodstained waves of the Dirty War lapped at the feet of some British community figures who had done nothing to annoy the military. Even the Anglican Bishop, David Leake, a friend of Dad's and no supporter of liberation theology, received an anonymous, threatening letter.

The Mothers of the Plaza de Mayo turned up at Robert Cox's office at the *Buenos Aires Herald*. 'Why are you coming to me? You know this is just a tiny circulation English language newspaper?'

'Because you're the only editor who will let us in the door!'

The Mothers travelled to Rome several times to petition John II, the popular anti-communist Polish Pope who enjoyed waving at fans from his popemobile. He always refused to meet them.

As evidence of state-sanctioned murder mounted, Robert Cox began publishing the names of some of the disappeared until one of those Ford Falcons drove up to his office and he was pushed into a cell with a big swastika on the wall. Cox was released a day later after a barrage of international condemnation organised by the *Herald*'s American owners, direct pressure from President Jimmy Carter, but not a peep from the British community. When Cox's ten-year-old son, Peter, received a crude, threatening letter, his Argentine wife, Maud, insisted they leave, and Cox moved his family to Charleston, South Carolina.

Cox was lucky.

Fifty Argentine journalists disappeared.

On May 24, 1979, the *Herald* headline was 'Mother, Father, 3 Little Girls Disappear'. The only daily newspaper that published news about the disappeared was the newspaper that was delivered to Mum and Dad's flat, and Dad read it cover to cover every day while Mum read her lesson.

But what were you reading, Dad?

Dad didn't want to know something that was very dangerous. It was easy for me, living in Oxford and dropping in for short visits every year or two, berating him for not knowing what he did not want to know.

***

Mariana, daughter of Police Commissioner Miguel Etchecolatz, was not surprised to learn about her father's crimes. Miguel had terrorised his wife and two children. He insisted on complete silence at home and she and her brother would hide in the wardrobe and pray he would die. When he beat them up, he'd complain, 'Look what you made me do!'

Analia Kalinex, daughter of another officer, had more complex feelings about her own loving father:

> At first, I needed to disassociate. I used to say, 'Well, on one side there's my dad and on the other side there's the torturer.' I needed that, or else my head would have

> exploded. But then I realised that it is in fact the same person. It is always the same person.

These daughters of torturers and murderers set up a group they called *Historias Desobedientes*, Disobedient Stories.

***

Michel-Rolph Trouillot reminds us that 'history is also produced outside of academia', it's the water we swim in. That thought is so obvious, so bloody obvious, that although I know it, I don't *really* know it. So much *stuff* has been spooned into me, clogging up my intestines, poisoning the air I breathe, not only in the classrooms of my childhood where slave traders were naughty but nice and the unspeakable remained unspoken and silence replaced shame.

Babar the elephant and his sweet, new wife, Celeste, sail away on their honeymoon in a hot-air balloon, which is swept up by a terrible storm and wrecked on a remote island. They hang their clothes out to dry, and Babar heads off to explore their surroundings, while Celeste takes a little nap. *As she slept the indigenes of the island, wild savages, found her.* These *cannibals* tie Celeste up with her own clothesline and dance around waving spears and whooping the way 'savages' do. Poor Celeste is convinced they are going to eat her up! Luckily, Babar comes to the rescue and he and Celeste hurl themselves on the nasty cannibals and leave dead black bodies scattered over a small hill.

When I was six, the entire British School gathered to watch *Tarzan the Ape Man* in the gymnasium. There were rows of chairs, but I was afraid, so I watched the film clinging onto the monkey bars like Cheetah. Beautiful Jane Parker's father and Harry Holt, the only white men in the film, hated Africa, 'this awful hole' obsessed with finding the elephant's burial grounds so they could make themselves rich by helping themselves to the ivory. When their porters, 'the boys', got spooked or tired, the white men and their foreman whipped them to 'give them something else to think about'. One the boys falls to his death. *Don't look back, Jane.* Crocodiles guzzle another two. And when more 'savages' turn up, they shoot them in their bellies for no reason. Tarzan kills another couple of Natives to avenge the killing of an ape by one of the white men, more 'savages' are mown down by a machine gun, and then a load of pygmies, 'African dwarves' appear screaming, dancing, waving spears and are trampled to death by a herd of elephants summoned by Tarzan with his special yodelling cry.

The 'African dwarves' were played by blacked-up, small white people and the elephants were Indian rather than African, fitted with big fake ears and tusks.

Tarzan the Ape Man currently has a 100 percent rating on Rotten Tomatoes.

Dear little Noddy drives his red and yellow car, *parp-parp*, pootling around carrying Mr and Mrs Tubby, Mr Straw, Buttercup, Daisy, Woolly, Long Ears and Mary Mouse and her six little children, until, oh dear, that awful Black Golliwog wants a lift to a party in the Dark Wood. That night, Noddy picks up Golliwog, who *was so black Noddy couldn't see him,* and he makes little chuckling noises, which Noddy doesn't like at all. As they drive into the dark, dark wood, the Golliwog says in a very nasty sort of voice, *There isn't a party. This is a trap, Noddy.* Three black faces appear and steal his car and his clothes. Poor little Noddy. *You bad, wicked golliwogs.*

I cherished Dad's copy of *Struwwelpeter* with its sadistic violence, but the story of the Inky Boys confused me, so I always turned those pages quickly. Some naughty boys tease *the harmless black-a-moor* when he goes for a stroll with his parasol. Agrippa punishes the jeering boys by dipping them in a huge pot of ink until *the silly little inky boys* are black all over like the *black-a-moor.*

I read *Gone with the Wind,* and Mum and Dad and I watched Hatty McDaniel playing Mammy and her husband Pork. Pork! Hatty was not invited to attend the whites-only premiere and her Mammy waddles around loyally, followed by that screaming Prissy with her squeaky voice, flinging her arms around like a crazy person. When the Civil War is over, jumped-up former slaves swagger about as if they owned the place and it's time for the Ku Klux Klan! 'Frankly, my dear, I don't give a damn.' *Gone with the Wind* currently has a rating of 90 percent on Rotten Tomatoes. I loved *To Kill a Mockingbird,* the book and film, where Atticus Finch thinks it is worth celebrating a jury, taking two hours rather than five minutes, to convict a clearly innocent black man of raping a white woman.

When Marlon Brandon sent Sacheen Littlefeather to announce that very regretfully he could not accept his Oscar for *The Godfather* in protest at the portrayal of American 'Indians' in Hollywood, John Wayne, who had played Breck Coleman in *The Big Trail,* led his group West and offered them land that was not his: 'The way is clear ahead . . . so drive down my friends and settle it!' John Wayne was so incensed that he waited in the wings to attack Sacheen as she came offstage and had to be physically restrained by six security men.

When bare-chested, long-haired 'Indians' whipped themselves into a frenzy and attacked the circled wagons, I was relieved when they toppled off their horses yelping like girls and dying like flies. I was in there, sitting tight in that circle until I choked, until I could no longer breathe and I ran out, in between the wagons and fled. I fled to what Fred Moten calls the *undercommons,* that wild place outside the fort where another history can be created.

***

In order for us to sit comfortably in our nice, clean houses, minding our p's and q's, with our nice, law-abiding Mummies and Daddies and our nice British schools and our nice cricket clubs, in order for us to chat around our *asados*, speaking Spanglish about who had married whom and who had a new baby and who, sotto voce, was *no better than they should be*, and when we turned off the lights and lay in our freshly ironed pyjamas, *night, night, don't let the fleas bite*, and *wakey, wakey, rise and shine*, and *you're treating this house like a hotel* – drinking our whiskey on ice and our Quilmes beer and baking our scones and Victoria sponges; in order for us to be *us* and not *them,* in order for rugger and tennis and hockey and please and thankyou and *will they ever learn*, and *where did we go wrong,* in order for our tiny sanitised hermetically sealed world to be so cosy, so safe, and, let's face it, mind-numbingly boring, there has been mass slaughter, sexual slavery, forced displacement, internment camps and the ransacking and obliteration of those who had lived here for thousands of years before we arrived. The past had been rubbed clean, replaced by a faded postcard of a prehistoric location outside time and space.

If bad things had happened, they had nothing to do with us.

And *they* must have done something to deserve it.

Anyway, we didn't pull the trigger.

Sven Lindqvist's *Exterminate All the Brutes* starts like this: 'You already know enough. So do I. It's not knowledge we lack. What is missing is the courage to understand what we know and to draw conclusions.'

***

The cheapest way to get Raúl to Europe, where we could be together, was on a cargo boat to Marseille. I sold all my possessions, my record player, my books, a moonstone brooch and a seed-pearl necklace left to me by my great aunts. I attempted to sell my long hair too, but they had the cheek to tell me I had too many split ends, a consequence of the nits episode. I worked for the English ball-bearing company, skipped lunch and saved all my wages for his ticket. I don't remember eating in the evenings when I met Raúl. Bobby the Buddhist wrote to ask why I was getting slimmer and slimmer, *are you suffering from poetry by any chance?*

Raúl made no attempt to contribute and graciously accepted me working like a dog on his behalf. I knew better than to mention it. Anything he perceived as criticism led to a punitive silence and me dancing around trying to wheedle him out of it. He'd snap, 'Why do you talk about things you know nothing about? It's embarrassing. People are laughing at you. Learn to keep your mouth shut.' I became even more silent and watchful. One night, at a house party, I was dancing by myself, absorbed in the music, when I noticed Pepe, the Montonero, whispering to Raúl sitting next to him on a couch. Raúl told me later that Pepe had asked him not to hurt me. I suspected he didn't even like me.

I had got what I wanted, but Raúl remained a stranger. One of the things I had found enchanting was that whenever there was a guitar lying around, he'd pick it up and strum the beginning of the *Concierto de Aranjuez* and lay it down again with a bashful smile. People would beg him to play more, but he always refused. It was a long time before I realised that was all he knew.

He wrote me one love letter that I still have, and even back then, when I was besotted, I didn't believe it was about me. I was pretty sure he was having an affair with Tamara, an older, more glamorous and sophisticated woman. Tamaaaara. She and Raúl spent afternoons together being creative while I was typing about ball bearings. I was insanely jealous. I think she must have dumped him because he suddenly stopped talking about her.

Penny my love. How to tell you things? I don't know how to do it. I only have eyes and hands to touch them.

> *I no longer know how to speak about things. Today is a strange day with flowers in the sky and stars and in the streets, I touch them (*here Raúl drew a little cluster of stars). *Touching words is beautiful. I love you Penny, I love you. I know I will love you more. A friend said, 'White is a sacred colour'. I give you the moon - Raúl*

This is the way people wrote back then. To be fair you can say things in Spanish that don't really work in English.

I am certain he wrote that for Tamara. Or maybe she wrote it for him.

***

The only Falkland Islander I ever met really did fuck sheep.

Raúl and I travelled separately, I could only afford to buy him a cheaper ticket to Marseilles on a cargo boat while I left Argentina for England on the Royal Mail *Arlanza* in May 1968. I resented being stuck in second class with boring middle-aged married couples instead of in third class, where all the fun was. We stopped off in Montevideo to pick up a group of pale Falkland Islanders who huddled together, and I befriended a rather handsome, slender man always in a dark grey suit and tie. I thought he was ancient but he was probably about thirty. He and I sat up late at night drinking whiskey and he confided that his wife, who had gone ahead to London, wanted to have children and he did not. She refused to use contraception and although they had been married several years, he would not have sex with her. When I asked how he felt about being celibate, he shrugged, 'It's no problem. I have sheep.' I took that in my stride although I worry now whether the sheep consented to his intrusions.

When I revealed to the Grey Man that I'd had sex with my boyfriend, he didn't believe me, and when I convinced him it was true, he never spoke to me again. When the Malvinas/Falklands war broke out some of the Spartacists unkindly called the islanders 'sheep shaggers' and I remembered that encounter.

On April 2, 1982, British Prime Minister Margaret Thatcher's popularity was at an all-time low; she had destroyed communities and created mass unemployment by smashing trade unions and deindustrialising the Midlands and the North of England. Her political career was rescued by the invasion of the Malvinas by the Argentine junta. It was the perfect pretext for a pointless war she could win by slaughtering hundreds of freezing young Argentine conscripts who hadn't been provided with weapons, training, or adequate clothing.

President General Galtieri, who had deposed Generals Videla and General Viola after a period of military infighting, was as deeply unpopular as Margaret Thatcher. Argentines were beginning to get restless. Everyone knew somebody who had disappeared, and inflation was at a staggering 210 percent with prices rising hourly. Dad loved to tell the tale about going out to buy a new plastic toilet seat that cost more than their apartment.

Losing the Malvinas War heralded the end of the dictatorship and the unstoppable rise of Margaret Thatcher.

After this war and every war, there were high suicide rates, post-traumatic stress disorder, depression, alcoholism and other mental illnesses among surviving soldiers on both sides.

We're not supposed to go around killing each other just because other people tell us to.

***

The war threw the British community into disarray. Mum told me that many of the old gents in the English Club died of shame when the *Belgrano* was sunk while retreating outside the exclusion zone, drowning 333 young men. Margaret Thatcher cried, 'Rejoice! Rejoice!' and *GOTCHA!* was the headline in the *Sun* newspaper. But this wasn't *fair play*, it wasn't *British.*

Not a single British community person was threatened or abused, but as a precaution, the plaque outside the English Club was replaced with a more modest inscription: E.C.

Dad was on the committee of the British Community Council and composed a telegram to Margaret Thatcher begging her to find a peaceful solution to the conflict:

> *On behalf of the British Community Council, which centralises the cultural, philanthropic and charitable activities of native-born Britons and people of British descent living in Argentina, who number in extent of 100,000 people, we respectfully wish to point out that we do not feel that our situation has been fully considered or taken into account in the difficult problem which has arisen between Argentina and Great Britain.*

> *Argentina has always shown every consideration towards the British community allowing it to run its own schools, churches, hospitals, old people's homes etc. In addition, members of the British community have integrated themselves into all aspects of Argentine life, playing a prominent role especially in business and agricultural circles.*
>
> The Association of British and British Descended Farmers sent their own telegram: *We have led our traditional, British way of life without any hindrance and our experience has led us to believe that the inhabitants of the Falkland Islands have nothing to lose and much to gain by coming under Argentine sovereignty.*

Some British community ladies appealed directly to Margaret Thatcher, woman to woman. All these missives stressed how politely Argentina had tolerated our refusal to assimilate with everyone else.

***

Isabelita Perón still lives in Madrid. In her old age, she forbids anybody to talk politics or mention the name López Rega. 'I remember him as a distant memory, and I wish I had never met him.'

Mario Rotundo, one of her domestic staff, was woken up by screams late one night. He found Isabelita standing on her bed, shrieking that a shaft of light was pouring out of the wardrobe where she kept Evita Perón's shroud.

Rotundo, a man in his sixties in his pyjamas, had to push the heavy wardrobe out of her room before she calmed down.

***

While Onganía was doing his best to wipe out the 'cancer of immorality', students in Paris were revolting. On May 2, 1968, De Gaulle's government closed the University of Paris and four days later, students and teachers marched on the Sorbonne, where hundreds of them were arrested and tear gas and batons dispersed the rest. On May 10, barricades were thrown up on the streets and there were mass confrontations with the C.R.S. - Compagnies Républicaines de Sécurité - the feared riot police. A million people marched through Paris and factory workers called a general strike in support of the students. Something new was happening and joyous slogans sprang up: 'Under the paving stones the beach . . . 'They buy your happiness, steal it!' . . . 'Barricades block the street but open the way.'

Raúl had docked in Marseilles two weeks before I was due to arrive in England and I had instructed him to hitch-hike to Calais, catch a ferry to Dover and pitch up at my Aunt Ethel and Uncle Peter's house and wait there for me, with Mum and Dad, until I arrived. Raúl couldn't speak French or English, and I wasn't sure how any of my relatives were going to react to this plan and thought it best not to mention it.

My ship pulled into Southampton after a month at sea from Buenos Aires. I was looking forward to seeing Raúl and rows of thatched cottages, Quality Street chocolate tins, Victoriana mixed with Carnaby Street cool, but all I saw were rows of small, dirty terraced houses caked in black dust on a dull grey day.

Mum and Auntie Ethel were there on the dock. There was no sign of Raúl, and I didn't dare ask whether they had seen him. Dad was in England on a business trip, and they had flown over. This was Mum's first time in England.

Mum, Auntie Ethel and I sat in a train carriage with two rows of narrow seats facing each other, like *Strangers on a Train*, and I munched a Dairy Milk chocolate bar, gazing out the window, missing the open spaces of Argentina and pining for Raúl.

Uncle Peter and Auntie Ethel lived in Purfleet, a Surrey suburb. Ethel was lovely and giggly, although I was baffled when she remarked, 'I don't know how we coped before the kitchen towel, do you?' I was surly and superior, above such banal preoccupations. For a start, I knew what real love was. It turned out that Ethel knew a lot more about that than I did.

Two weeks later, Auntie Ethel took pity on me moping and revealed that Raúl had been refused entry into England a week before I arrived. A customs officer telephoned the number he had given them and Mum explained that he was a bad lot who had seduced her daughter, and they were not to let him into the country. I pretended I was going shopping in London, hitchhiked to Calais and traipsed about for a day looking for him. Of course, this was decades before mobile phones.

A week later, Raúl rang the house again and this time Ethel answered. He begged her to give me an address in

Normandy and she did. I told more lies and hitched across Northern France, fighting off lusty lorry drivers, until I found Raúl in a small-town butcher shop. A young man I met on the boat, not the sheep shagger, had given me the address of his sister Monica in Paris and I told Raúl I would meet him there. I returned to Uncle Peter and Auntie Ethel's and informed Mum and Dad that I hated England and was moving to Paris with my new invisible friend, Melody.

Ethel cornered me in the kitchen and confided that although I seemed to think I had invented love, she and Peter were still madly in love after sixteen years of marriage. Peter worked at home, drawing cartoons for children's magazines, and she ran back to kiss him after every short trip to the shops because they hated being out of each other's sight. They had made love every other night since their wedding day. I was seriously impressed.

I wandered around the Latin Quarter in the middle of the night with £12 Grandpa Gordon had given me to buy a raincoat, clutching an address scribbled on a crumpled piece of paper. There was a febrile atmosphere, groups of young people roamed around cobbled streets climbing over the remains of burnt barricades and stray paving stones. I showed a young man my scrap of paper and explained in terrible school French, *je cherche mon amour*. A group gathered to help me track him down. We climbed all the way to the top of a tall building in the Latin Quarter and knocked on a door. A sleepy neighbour popped out and explained that Monica and Felipe had fled because the police were after them. Yes, there had been another Argentine man with curly black hair, but he was gone too.

A door opened and another neighbour scribbled a different address on my scrap of paper. It was a warm night, the moon was full, and I had to dismiss a treacherous thought that I was having fun dancing around the streets with people my own age instead of surly Raúl, who made me feel anxious all the time. The group led me down narrow streets to another tall building. One of the young men pushed open a huge wooden door leading to a dark stairwell and narrow marble steps. He followed me up the stairs while the others waited outside smoking Gauloises and wishing me, *Bon chance*! The young man and I climbed up and up and up and up eight flights to the very top. I knocked. There was silence, then footsteps. Raúl flung open the door, hair wild, completely naked.

'Penelope!'
The Young Man headed downstairs with a smile and a wave. I didn't want him to leave.
Who was this naked, needy man? Raúl looked frightened, lonely and desperate.
I thought, *What have I done?*

***

I believed I was on safe ground with the missionary Thomas Bridges and his third son, Lucas. They were the good guys in this movie, as Ana Testa said of the torturer who was kind to her. I thought they were proof that we were able to recognise the common humanity of *el otro,* the other. Apparently they had lived peacefully alongside the Selk'nam and

Yamana, learnt their languages, and Thomas had compiled his Yamana dictionary. As a young man, Lucas hunted and wrestled with Selk'nam young men and was initiated into Selk'nam secret ceremonies. He said he was proud to call them his friends.

Carlos Braun Menendez & Lucas Bridges in front of the exclusive La Cabaña restaurant, Buenos Aires, 1948.

After writing the first draft of this manuscript, I was tracking down a book about José Menendez, *King of the Pampas*, and discovered that it has its own Facebook page. On it was a small black-and-white photograph of Lucas Bridges standing next to Carlos Braun Menéndez outside the exclusive Cabaña restaurant in Buenos Aires. It was taken in 1948, Lucas was seventy-five, silver-haired, wearing a light suit with a striped tie and carrying a Panama hat. Carlos, son of the infamous Moritz Braun and grandson of José Menendez, two of the prominent landowners who had hired 'Indian hunters', stands next to him, cigarette in hand, legs apart in a slightly darker suit. By this time, the fabulously wealthy Braun and Menendez families had joined forces through marriage and owned three million sheep munching across four and a half million hectares. *What were these two doing together?*

My heart sank.

Excerpts from Lucas Bridges's memoir, *Uttermost Part of the Earth*, appeared in many academic papers I had read, and he remains a key source for detailed information about Selk'nam and Yamana culture.

When I read the entire book, it was profoundly troubling.

Lucas Bridges protects the identity of Alexander MacLennan, calling him McInch in order 'not to hurt the feelings of his descendants'. He recounts the slaughter of Selk'nam at low tide and MacLennan's view that 'the sooner they were exterminated, the better', going straight on to describe MacLennan as 'boyishly happy', adding, 'to be frank, I rather liked him'. He accepts that although MacLennan's methods were not always 'looked at with favour', his predecessor had honestly tried milder methods which had been unsuccessful. Lucas describes José Menendez as energetic and farsighted.

When Lucas is initiated into the Selk'nam Lodge he calls the ceremony 'this ludicrous show... whole days would be spent in futile talk, leading up to some seemingly childish performance'. When Ona friends explain their beliefs, he sneers, 'I thought what liars those young fellows must be'. 'Indians' were 'superstitious' while Lucas had a sensible religion with a punitive God, who condemned women to pain in childbirth because one of them ate an apple, ordered Abraham to kill his own son, a burning bush that could speak, a sea that parted and worshipped a man born from a virgin who could feed five thousand people with five loaves and two fishes, walk on water, was crucified and rose from the dead.

And in a private letter to Charles Wellington Furlong, Lucas Bridges says, 'only two hundred Selk'nam remain and the youth growing up now are completely Christian and usually die between 18 and 23 years of age which is no great loss.'

No great loss.

Lucas welcomed the arrival of the gold-panning miners who killed and raped Selk'nam and Yamana women and men because the Bridges had set up a general store selling meat and furs, so 'the advent of the miners was a godsend to us. By bringing us trade it helped my father to establish the Harberton settlement with something more than the savings from a missionary's meagre salary.' Lucas fails to mention that when business boomed, the Missionary Society issued Thomas Bridges an ultimatum: choose between commerce and the mission, upon which he and his close colleague John Lawrence immediately hung up their vestments.

In 1886, Thomas Bridges travelled to Buenos Aires to petition President Julio Argentino Roca for land, the very same Roca who had led the genocidal Conquest of the Desert. Lucas relates that President Roca received his father warmly, asking how his government could compensate him for all the fine humanitarian work he had accomplished.

> General Roca, an enlightened and progressive statesman had been a soldier as well as a politician. In his day he had led more than one punitive expedition against the turbulent pampa Indians, who lived in the grassy, woodless lands between the Andes and

> the Atlantic; and he had done more than any of his contemporaries to bring those fierce tribes to order.

The Bridges became one of the wealthy landowning families alongside Menendez and Braun and among the first to import sheep from the Falklands/Malvinas.

US journalist John Randolph Spears describes the grand house Bridges had built for his own family and the tiny, dirty shacks well out of view for the Yamana, saying that Bridges should 'hang his head in shame'. He observed that the Yamana disliked Bridges's authoritarian attitude, that each of the Bridges children had a Yamana servant and that Indigenous labourers were paid in food instead of wages and forced to wear clothes that made them sick. Thomas Bridges himself wrote in the *South American Missionary Magazine* that he had called a gathering of the natives and they had given him 'full permission' to own their land:

> I told them plainly that should they get tired of us they must not expect to drive us away and get the land back, that the land belonged not to this or that one, but to him or them who lived upon it, cared for it, fenced and made use of it and that if we should go to the trouble of fencing planting and building on the land, that the land became ours.

In 1898, Lucas Bridges personally selected two families for The National Exhibition in Buenos Aires for spectators to mock. He arranged for eugenicist anthropologists who were keen on racial classification to measure 'his Indians' until they got fed up with being prodded about.

When cephalic indexes indicated that Indigenous people had greater brain capacity than Europeans, these pseudo-scientists decided that actually the length of people's arms was crucial to determine inferiority, longer arms being closer to apes but revised this opinion because Fuegians had short arms. They never questioned this method of classifying people no matter how much evidence piled up to show how ridiculous it was.

Thomas Bridges did not return an inch of the land he had appropriated to the people who had lived there. Their name for themselves was Yamana but Bridges changed it to Yaghan because Yamana means person in their language, and he didn't believe they had the right to appropriate that word for themselves.

He did have huge respect for the Yamama language, admiring its nuances, but he wondered how such stupid, miserable people could have such a wonderful language and what they could possibly find to talk about. He told the French explorer Paul Hyades that although they were very good at talking to each other, they didn't understand what the words meant.

***

After the fall of the dictatorship, Manú bumped into The Tiger who offered to buy her a hot chocolate. Liliana sat next to the torturer Federico in 1985 on the subway. He attempted to have a normal conversation with her as if they were old friends. 'How are you doing?'

On December 19, 1986, President Alfonsín, fearing another military coup, passed *the punto final,* the full stop law, drawing a line under the arrest and trials of military personnel who had actively participated in the Dirty War.

It was a warm day. Sixty thousand people gathered in the capital in December 1986.

'No!'

Dylan and I were visiting Mum and Dad again and we joined the protest. By this time, I had become a filmmaker and Dylan a brilliant young photographer. We heard a roar.

Vienen las Madres! The Mothers are coming!

A row of furious women in white headscarves swept down the street holding a white banner the width of the road. Everyone scattered in front of them.

A murder of crows, a murmuration of starlings, a pride of lions, a rage of mothers.

Mariana, Analia, and other relatives of torturers marched under a banner *Familias de Genocidios,* Families of the Genocidal. They were very frightened about encountering the Mothers of the Plaza de Mayo.

The Madres embraced them.

***

At school I was taught to accept that things were the way they were because there was no other way they could ever be or could ever have been. Perhaps the Argentine colonialist genocide was less obvious precisely because our erasure of the *pueblos originarios* had been so efficient, despite the maids we ignored in our homes every day. President Sarmiento admired how the United States had corralled its 'Indians' in reservations, but reflected that the problem with this approach was that 'Indians' were able to preserve their culture and language and might one day become hostile again. He decided that dispersal was the way to go. After the Conquest of the Desert, ethnic groups and families were broken up and scattered to different parts of the country, into sugar plantations, the army, the navy and domestic labour, atomised and unable to communicate to anybody in their own languages:

> If any Indian remain they are isolated, wandering without any organisation worth considering and completely away from the authority of any known chief.

Settler colonialism is the most genocidal of all colonialisms. Settlers want empty land. They do not need or want to coerce Indigenous people into backbreaking work like plantation owners, who required intensive labour to grow and harvest crops like sugar, cotton and tea; or extraction capitalists who want a cheap labour force to extract rubber, wood and precious metals like copper, cobalt, zinc and minerals like coltan we use for technology. Sheep, cattle and grain just need grasslands. The people are in the way and must be got rid of by any means necessary.

Settler colonialism sets out to obliterate the culture and language of Indigenous people, physically wipe them out with murder, internment, alcoholism, suicide and despair.

It not only targets humans, as the European Holocaust did, it has also destroyed the balance between human and nonhuman life, all across the Americas and the Antipodes. Monoculture farming destroys diversity, drains the soil of nutrients and creates the deserts it claimed were there before.

At the time of writing this, murderous settlers continue their bloody work in Palestine, Israel bombards the residents of Gaza with leaflets telling them all to leave, that nobody cares whether they live or die. Donald Trump wants to build his hotels there and turn it into the 'Riviera of the Middle East'. This is not Tierra del Fuego in the nineteenth century, where methods of communication were slow. This time nobody can pretend they don't know what's happening.

***

I placed us at the centre of everything, but we were just a grubby part of it. It's hubris to think we were the worst of the worst. We weren't special. Our Hyslops, MacLennans and Radburnes killed as enthusiastically and callously as anybody else and our upper-class landowners, Camerons, Bridges and Lawrences, financed the violence along with the Spanish and German heritage Menendez Brauns, Anchorenas and Álzagas. The British bourgeoisie, well, we whined about Argentines being their own worst enemy, about how a rich country with so many natural resources keeps self-destructing, blah, blah, blah. Auto-flagellation is an Argentine addiction. We just did it in English and about *them* instead of *us*.

But we knew what we had done. And we also did not know.

I knew something had happened.

I just didn't think about it.

***

Argentina is a nation of migrants. Being a migrant entails a splitting of the self. We don't know who we are. We are strangers to ourselves. There's a rupture right at the centre of us. Argentina has one of the highest rates of anorexia in the world and the largest number of psychoanalysts per capita, one analyst per thirty people in a nation of disconnected peoples, all of us cut off from our roots, alienated and nostalgic in a nation built on colonialism and genocide, compounded by the traumas of national wars, dirty wars and violent dictatorships. The British community did not approve of navel-gazing, so we carried on chatting, chatting, chatting and bitching about everyone else.

We othered those we called Argentines and they othered us, but we were all European colonisers.

I think both my parents were depressed. My mother was fat and depressed, and my father was thin and depressed. He had contemplated suicide as a teenager and after I left home, he drank as much as he could. He confided in me one evening: 'When I wake up in the morning, it would kill me to think that was the best I was going to feel all day.' I hate to think how bleak he must have felt as he opened his eyes, and I could see that drinking made him feel better although it also made him very curt with Mum. When I grew up, Dad and I enjoyed drinking together, splitting a litre bottle of wine he would otherwise have drunk by himself.

In my twenties I informed Dad bluntly, 'The reason I broke away and did what I wanted was because you didn't have the courage to do it.' Dad would bring this remark up regularly over the years and I'd apologise for my careless cruelty, but he'd chuckle, 'You were quite right of course.'

***

Lucas Bridges wrote that when President Julio Argentino Roca was reelected, a *great, kind and wise leader,* he toured Fireland and popped in for a visit. 'Mother received him and was able to supply tea for all with strawberries and cream in real Devonshire style'.

Lucas and his siblings subscribed to *Boys Own Paper* and *Chums* comics from England, half a century later I received *Playhour,* illustrated by my Uncle Peter and then, in my teens, the much-treasured *Honey.*

There are moments where Lucas seems to step out of his racism. In his book he describes his friendship with Talimeoat, a 'most likeable' Selk'nam, and as they gaze across beautiful purple mountain ranges, beach forests and glistening lakes, he notices Talimeoat sighing and whispering, 'My country, my country'. Lucas writes, I wanted to help by every means at my command, the hereditary lords of the land, the people whom I was proud to call my friends.' This is the same man who, at the beginning of the next chapter, complains about 'the inclination of the Ona Indians towards murder and treachery.' But maybe there were two Lucas Bridges. He knows that the Selk'nam are noble and generous and he also knows they are treacherous and mean. He can find McLennan, the Red Pig both deplorable and necessary, he knows he has stolen ancestral lands, and he knows these lands are his because his father acquired the title deeds

Lucas juggled the world of *Chums* and *Boys Own Paper* and the life he shared with other rich landowners along with lives that could have been from another planet, but they were not from another planet, they were from this one, a planet with people who breathe as we all must, until our breath is taken away from us.

***

Everyone choked on silence for a long time after the coup of 1976. The habit of knowing and not knowing was deeply entrenched.

There were brave priests and nuns who worked with the poor, risked their lives and paid the ultimate price, but the hierarchy of the Catholic Church had no problem sanctioning torture and the 'humane' killing of naked unconscious dissidents, yet they remained firm about protecting the unborn child. If a female prisoner was pregnant, she was kept alive and relatively unharmed until she gave birth. Mothers were killed as soon as their babies were born and the babies were passed on to military families, some of whom had directly colluded in the murder of their parents. Many military couples knew exactly where their adopted children came from but there were adoptive parents who genuinely did not.

The daughter of one of the leading Plaza de Mayo Mothers, Patricia Roisinblit Perez, was pregnant when she was 'sucked up' and tied by one leg to a heavy desk in an Air Force detention centre until she came to term. Her husband was occasionally brought to visit her, badly tortured and in a terrible state. Her kidnappers reassured him that they would only hurt her after the baby was born. When she went into labour, she was driven to the ESMA, where she was attended by the resident military doctor and a couple of prisoners including Manú Gorretti, the artist. Three days after she gave birth, Patricia vanished from the ESMA and her body and that of her husband have never been found. The baby she named Rodolfo was presented to one of her torturers, Air Force Intelligence Officer Francisco Gomez, who nicknamed his adoptive son 'Jew,' and was violently abusive towards him and his long-suffering wife.

***

For many years the Mothers chanted, 'Aparición con vida o castigo a los culpables', bring them back alive or punish the guilty. They carried on for years, although none of the disappeared resurfaced. They had disappeared.

Then, around 1984, a North American geneticist, Dr Mary-Claire King, developed a mitochondrial DNA test that established a link between grandparents and their grandchildren. Advertisements were placed in national papers:

> If you were born between 1975 and 1980 and have doubts about your identity - if you think you might not be who they say you are, contact the Grandmothers of the Plaza de Mayo.

Twenty years later, Patricia Roisinblit's baby, now a grown man known as Guillermo, was tracked down by his older sister. The DNA test was definitive, and his world fell apart. He wasn't who he thought he was. When he visited Francisco Gomez in jail, the man he had called *Papá*, Gomez blamed him and threatened to put a bullet in his head. Guillermo now has a new family but remains in touch with his adoptive mother, who was also a victim. For him, this was a complicated truth.

Some young people had always felt they did not belong and fell gratefully into the arms of their biological families, but for those who loved and trusted their adoptive parents, it was a choice between a happy lie and a painful truth.

Some of those who were contacted refused to take the DNA test.

They didn't want to know.

***

When Christopher Columbus arrived in what he believed was India, he related at some length in his logbooks what he claimed 'Indians' told him about their lives and customs and the land they lived in. He just made things up.

Mutual incomprehension was followed by a holocaust on a scale never seen before or since.

There are eyewitness accounts of sickening cruelty. Bartolomé De Las Casas saw Spaniards sharpening their swords on whetstones and slicing up 'Indians' to check how sharp they were. There were reports of Christians stabbing children who could not walk fast enough or, if they were chained together by the neck, cutting off their heads so as not to have to stop to release them. De Las Casas writes:

> I testify that I saw with my own eyes Spaniards cutting off the hands, noses and ears of local people, both men and women simply for the fun of it . . . On several occasions I also saw them set dogs on the people, many being torn to pieces in this fashion, and they burnt down houses and even whole settlements too numerous to count. It is also the case that they tore babes and sucklings from their mother's breasts and played games with them, seeing who could throw them the furthest.

There are so many ways for us to live in this world and as Cabeza de Vaca discovered, many of them were found in the Americas before the invasion. There were egalitarian societies and deeply hierarchical ones, some that changed with the seasons, others that practised human sacrifice on a mind-blowing scale – the Aztec King Ahuitzotl sacrificed 80,400 people to inaugurate a single temple - and others that treated each other respectfully and tenderly. We can choose. It's not inevitable.

***

The Selk'nam woman who was shared by gold miners and raped until she was *set loose* as she was about to give birth, this Selk'nam woman rattles about in the wilderness of my mind, looking for a place to rest. I wish she'd go away. *Yesterday upon the stair, I met a man who wasn't there, she wasn't there again today, oh, how I wish she'd go away.* I abandoned her in a bleak place with rocks and thorns, with no food or water after a living hell. I left her in agony, giving birth alone. But what if this woman had a name and what if her name was Lola and what if an angel appeared to Lola when she was in despair like the angel who came to Hagar after Sarah, Abraham's wife banished her into the desert with her baby son, Ishmael? What if, like Hagar, when Lola's child cried of thirst and she had no water to give him, what if, Lola ran between two hills seven times until an angel appeared and struck the ground with his heel, causing a well to spring out of the ground? What if her baby grew into a great warrior *a wild ass of a man* like Ishmael? What if Lola became a magnificent warrior and chopped off the heads of the men who raped her? What if her people cared for her, soothed and welcomed her back to normal life and that time in the camp became a distant memory?

What if, what if, what if; what if, all my what ifs are there to console me for a past I cannot change and cannot bear to look at, inhabited by people whose thoughts and words are not recorded in the archive. The ESMA women, settlers caught by the boomerang effect Cesaire warned us about, bore witness to their own lives. They look into the camera, and they speak.

There is not a single testimony by a Yamana or Selk'nam woman from that time.

How to write about the impossible?

El Jimmy left me with another Selk'nam woman. He told his biographer that when he first sailed to Tierra del Fuego, he waved at a figure onshore thinking it was a man, until he realised she was a naked 'Indian' woman lassoed to a stake. An old sailor shrugged and reassured him,

> She ain't cold . . . She's lucky. She's getting' good grub from those miners and don't have to work, you'll be helping some of them poor squaws out yourself 'fore you leave the Island, eh?

Am I replicating the original violence by retelling these stories? Or am I forcing myself and the reader to look into the open casket as Emmett Till's mother demanded we do? Where can this woman, this naked, bound woman exist outside that sentence in Jimmy Radburn's book as his ship sails by? Is refusing to turn away, refusing to keep her story tucked away in my notebook, is this a way of jumping off the ship and swimming to cut her free?

Bullshit.

We are forced to keep sailing past her on a loop.

The rest is for her to know.

***

I was lost. I had run away from one world and I had no idea where I belonged. I was floating around rootless. I wasn't anybody from anywhere. I shed the Anglo-Argentine accent so quickly that nobody has ever asked me where I am from. The colour of my skin and the way I speak signals that I am English, but I'm not. And I'm not Argentine either. I am a bastard child.

I meet her in the archive. What the hell am I doing in there, this Anglo-Argentine settler? I am lost, lost and white, in a labyrinthine warren of dark corridors and there she is, even more beautiful in real life, and then she's gone. The men are there too. Thomas Bridges, Lucas, Jose Menendez and Alexander McLennan. There's the eugenicist Joseph Deniker. Deniker doesn't think much of me. I am letting the side down. The white side. I don't care, I want to find her again.

I first glimpsed this young Yamana woman online, desperate to put faces to the Indigenous people I was reading about, people dismissed as 'savages' by the enlightened evolutionists and the creationists. I typed *Yaghan* into the search engine and at first didn't even realise that different ethnic groups speaking different languages were bundled carelessly together in a digital bin. A search engine results page appeared with unidentified Yamana and Selk'nam females and males, canoe people and land people, all carelessly flung together, cut adrift on the internet, incorrectly captioned, long dead, poor images that have slipped their moorings, displaced, deracinated, condemned to drift randomly around the aether until they are lassoed onto a laptop by a keyword.

I was drawn to a photograph of a young woman standing with her friend, both looking boldly down the lens, self-possessed but wary, naked apart from a triangular piece of guanaco skin covering their pubic area, the *down there* Mum didn't like talking about, their bodies touching

Kamanakar Kipa & Chaoalouch Kipa, Tierra del Fuego, Argentina, (Photograph Paul Hyades), 1882-3.

easily all the way down to their thighs; the taller young woman appears both protective and hostile, her right breast lightly resting on her friend's left breast. I was intrigued by their powerful gaze, straight down the lens. I found the shorter one in four other photographs, in one, she sits at the centre of a group glaring and pugnacious, in three others she poses on her own, more vulnerable, holding a hand protectively between her legs. When I zoomed in to see her more clearly, she collapsed into pixels and dissolved. I became obsessed. Who was she?

I spent weeks trawling in the British Library until I found a reference by French American anthropologist Anne Chapman writing in 2010. She writes that a young Yamana woman was photographed multiple times by French medical doctor and explorer, Paul Hyades, who had led an expedition to Cape Horn in 1891. She claimed that Hyades reported that this young woman was intelligent and moved with a natural grace. I felt so hopeful after the horrors of the 'Indian' hunters.

The British Library holds a copy of Hyades's *Mission Scientifique du Cap Horn, 1882- 1883*; he prefaces his account by explaining that he has 'absolutely no preconceptions' while using the word *savages* about those he studies. At the end of the book, there are high-resolution captioned photographs naming Kamanakar Kipa and her friend Chaoualouch Kipa. But Chapman misquotes Hydes because what he writes is that Kamanakar was 'better looking' than other Fuegian women and that she was 'a good mimic'.

A good mimic. That word again. They just copy.

Along with the photographs, the book contains tables of measurements, forty-five measurements of eighty-seven people, infants, children, men and women, including Kamanakar and Chaoualouch. The tables consist of detailed measurements of every inch of their bodies, including the genitals. Hydes reports that Kamanakar had 'no trace of a clitoris' and that in all women 'the arrangement of the labia minora was like that of a gorilla'.

A gorilla.

I feel sick.

Now I am old. I never imagined I would get old. Seventy-five is old, there's no getting away from it. My body is OK, although I am only alive because the NHS stepped in a couple of times to put me back on my feet when my heart was racing or a kidney stopped working properly. I walk everywhere fast, but I am no longer the fastest. People say I look young for my age, but my hands have bulbous veins and brown spots like an old lady's, and I haven't had a period for twenty years. I wear trousers and T-shirts and dye my hair various shades of red, I have young friends and interesting projects and adventures and I have not lived the life of a British community lady, or any kind of lady really. And now this circling back to the beginning, looking closer at what I was running away from is bringing me up short.

***

Raúl had already left for Marseilles on a cheaper boat, so Mummy, Daddy, Pepe and Juan Carlos came to see me off on the Royal Mail Arlanza. It was very awkward, two warring sides of my life, neither speaking to the other. They trooped onboard and inspected my cabin, avoiding eye contact. Pepe and Juan Carlos regarded my parents as the enemy, and Mummy and Daddy viewed them as uncouth ruffians who had brainwashed me and ruined all our lives.

I was relieved when a steward walked down the corridor, ringing a bell, warning visitors to leave the ship.

Mummy, Daddy, Juan Carlos and Pepe stood on the quayside waving. I waved and waved until I got tired of waving and finally the ship started moving. They looked very small.

I ran to the bow and stood there by myself as the ship churned through the waves.

I didn't know where I was going.

I was off.

THE END

Acknowledgements

Colin Robinson suggested I write a book about growing up in the stifling Anglo-Argentine community. I didn't know it would turn into a horror story as soon as I started digging into my genocidal settler history. I didn't know, but now I do. It's always better to know, so thank you Colin.

To my editor Helen Armalas who polished my text. And thank you Ana Ratner, the desk editor who was endlessly patient with my struggles with the tech and Zahra Khan who proofread and encouraged me.

Special thank you to those friends who read early versions and encouraged me, James Dunkerley, Caroline Pick, Peter Symes, Bill Schwartz, Sarah Ainslie, Anna Valdez Hanks, Chloe Ruthven, Tim Hodgkinson, and Guy Holmes.

I'm deeply indebted to those authors, living and dead, who threw light into the void of my suburban upbringing.

And big love to all the great people I've met along my way, those who walked by my side, who loved me, who helped me think, who picked me up when I stumbled and even the few who kicked me down. To Dylan, Alice, Olivia and Juliet who bring me joy and finally, huge gratitude to my parents who did their best with their peculiar child.

Selected reading

Discourse on Colonialism - Aimee Cesaire
The Wretched of the Earth - Franz Fanon
Bartolomé de Las Casas - A short account of the destruction of the Indies
The Four voyages of Christopher Colombus - J.M Cohen
The Dawn of Everything - David Graeber and David Wengrow
Bartolomé de Las Casas - A short account of the destruction of the Indies
The Four voyages of Christopher Colombus - J.M Cohen
Cannibalism and the Colonial World - edited Peter Hulme, Francis Barker, Margaret Iverson
Necropolitics - Achille Mbembe
The Conquest of America - The question of the Other - Tzvetan Todorov
Silencing the Past - Michel-Rolph Trouilott
The Uttermost Part of the World - Lucas Bridges
Days and Nights of Love and War - Eduardo Galeano

Photo by Alice Dunhill

Penny Woolcock was born in Buenos Aires in the mid-20th century and raised in a conservative British expatriate community that few know exists. She grew up speaking English at home, attending British schools, and shopping at the only Harrods outside of Knightsbridge. Her great-grandparents were among the seven million Europeans who emigrated to Argentina in the 19th century.

Expected to conform to strict social norms, including marrying a suitable Anglo-Argentine boy, Woolcock felt stifled by her upbringing. After finishing school, she rebelled by joining a radical theater company, running off with a man considered entirely unsuitable, and becoming a single mother.

From these unconventional beginnings, she built a remarkable career as an award-winning filmmaker, opera director for the Metropolitan Opera in New York and the English National Opera in London, and a solo artist with exhibitions of her work.

www.ingramcontent.com/pod-product-compliance
Lightning Source LLC
Jackson TN
JSHW081240101225
95289JS00002BA/4
* 9 7 8 1 6 8 2 1 9 6 6 7 0 *